Wild Place

Wild Place

A History of Priest Lake, Idaho

KRIS RUNBERG SMITH
WITH TOM WEITZ

Tom Weitz

WSU PRESS

Washington State University
Pullman, Washington

Washington State University Press
PO Box 645910
Pullman, Washington 99164-5910
Phone: 800-354-7360
Fax: 509-335-8568
Email: wsupress@wsu.edu
Website: wsupress.wsu.edu

Library of Congress Cataloging-in-Publication Data

Smith, Kris Runberg.
  Wild place : a history of Priest Lake, Idaho / Kris Runberg Smith with Tom Weitz.
     pages cm
  Includes bibliographical references and index.
  ISBN 978-0-87422-329-3 (alk. paper)
1. Priest Lake Region (Idaho)--History. 2. Frontier and pioneer life--Idaho--Priest Lake Region. 3. Forests and forestry--Idaho--Priest Lake Region--History. 4. Priest Lake Region (Idaho)--Biography. I. Weitz, Tom, 1947-
II. Title.
  F752.B677S58 2015
  979.6—dc23
                                                                                    2014038131

Contents

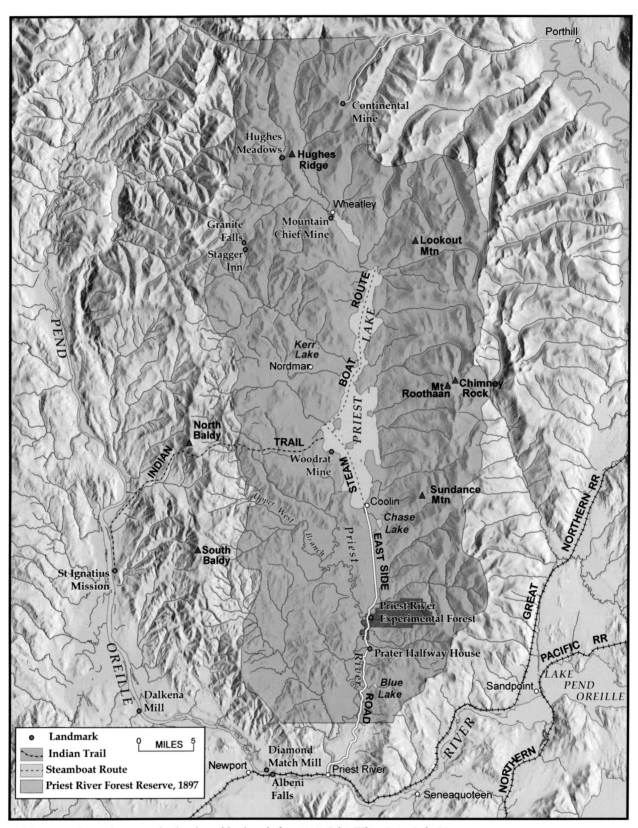

This regional map documents landmarks and land use before 1920. *Sylvie White, Priest Lake Museum*

Acknowledgments

In the summer of 2010 at the Priest Lake Museum Tom Weitz and I were lamenting the lack of trustworthy sources about the area's history. Together, we began to consider how the museum might solve this by creating a documented history of the region. After several years and a great outpouring of support, *Wild Place: A History of Priest Lake, Idaho,* is the result. Hundreds of people from around Priest Lake, around the Northwest, and around the country made this volume possible. We appreciate all their efforts, great and small, and want to acknowledge some key supporters who helped with fundraising, editorial work, research, and logistics.

The list of donors at the end of these acknowledgments speaks volumes about the commitment Priest Lake people share to see this history published. We are grateful to the friends around the lake who approached the museum about raising funds. Special thanks go to Joyce Miller, Candace Mumm, Heather Barbieri, and Brian Runberg. The Priest Lake Chamber of Commerce and People Helping People deserve recognition for providing the museum a strong foundation from which to manage this undertaking. Board member JoAnn Becker's successful grant-writing skills also contributed to the goal.

The project succeeded thanks to Priest Lake Museum editorial committee oversight. Pam Martin, Arley Sue Hagman, Tom Weitz, Mary Driscoll, and Jeanne Tomlin read, edited, encouraged, and advised through countless editions of the manuscript. We greatly appreciate other knowledgeable readers who edited and fact-checked chapters, including Charlotte and Hank Jones, Debbie Butler, Gary Weber, Jim Martin, Ann Ferguson, Marylyn Cork,

David Miros, Pancho Landa, and Carol Landa-McVicker. Idaho State Historical Society associate director Keith Petersen, always gracious and informed, shepherded this project to completion. Mary Read and Bob Clark at WSU Press patiently encouraged us. Editor Beth DeWeese and proofreader Kerry Darnall took great care with the manuscript and designer Nancy Grunewald transformed our vision into reality.

At the Priest Lake Museum invaluable logistical support came from Brooke Shelton Wagner, Martha King, Tess Becker, and Sarah Schoengold. Dave Becker ably handled technical issues and Tom Holman advised us about digital images. Ed Cushman edited our images. Cartographer Sylvie White created the maps and she worked determinedly to make sure they clearly conveyed the historical stories. Mary Karin Miller served as research assistant and navigator extraordinaire. In St. Louis, I appreciated the support of Lindenwood University Provost Jann Weitzel, humanities dean Mike Whaley, and colleagues in the history department. Nancy Durbin translated documents in French and reference librarian Carl Hubenschmidt tracked down obscure bits of information from institutions across the country. Student assistance came from Hannah Wickham, Julian Barr, Katharine McCabe, and especially the remarkable Lydia Hou.

I assumed the chapter on nineteenth century Priest Lake would be brief. Thanks to the expanding digital world and advice from former Bonner County Historical Society director Ann Ferguson I was proven wrong. Ann offered sources and directed me to critical events and collections. She made connections with the

Kalispel tribe and ensured I included women's stories. Diane Mercer and Marylyn Cork at the Priest River Museum provided much direction and encouragement. Carl Richie and Mick Schanilec at the Idaho Department of Lands helped to better understand the east side story. At the Priest Lake Ranger Station, Debbie Butler made available USFS resources, especially on recreation and the Recreation Residence program. Wayne Kopischke assisted us with historical documents and the location of sites around the lake. At the Idaho Panhandle Forest Service headquarters, Jamie Litzkow provided guidance with early Kalispel material.

Resource support from other institutions came from Dorothy Dahlgren at the Museum of Northern Idaho, Rose Krause at the Northwest Museum of Arts and Sciences, Faith McClenny at the Pend Oreille County Historical Society, Julie Monroe at the University of Idaho special collections, and Trevor Bond at the Washington State University archives. The staff at the Idaho State Historical Society provided direction, especially Peg Shroll and Carolyn Ruby. At the Boise State University archives, Alan Virta and Julia Stringfellow assisted in securing Priest Lake material. In St. Louis, David Miros at the Midwest Jesuit Archives graciously provided images and guidance. On the West Coast, Patty McNamee at the National Archives in Seattle provided direction, especially with Forest Service material. On the East Coast, Peter Brauer at the National Archives at College Park, Maryland, helped with the Northwest Boundary Survey material.

The Priest Lake Museum possesses an extensive collection because of the early energies of members like Marjorie Roberts, G. G. Fisher, Lois Hill, and Harriett Allen. Catherine and Claude Simpson, *Beautiful Bonner* editor Marylyn Cork, Gary Weber, and Forest Service archaeologist Cort Sims also provided me with a trove of primary sources. This project resulted in an additional outpouring of historical material thanks to the efforts of board members like Pam Martin. Just when we thought no other early images of the lake could exist, another family came to the museum to share their photo albums.

We appreciate those who advocated for the museum collections including Dick and Robert Hungate, Mary Rutherford, Heidi Rogers, and Sandra Olgard. Susan Monson helped me tell the story of her grandfather, Jim Ward; and sisters Ann Paden and Beth Nicholson organized and donated hundreds of images from the Forsythe and James families. Marilyn Lloyd and her sisters shared letters between their parents, William and Eleanor Lipscomb. Charlotte and Hank Jones began the museum's publishing efforts with an oral history transcription of grandfather Leonard Paul, and their continued donations and advice have been invaluable. Thanks to Roland and Linda Hall, we now have a much greater understanding of the relationship between the Continental Mine and Priest Lake.

Tom Weitz contributed his expertise on mining and geology for the text. He researched and outlined Chapter Three on mining. He appreciated the generosity of the Idaho Geological Survey who opened mining files for research. He worked closely with cartographer Sylvie White to create the original maps throughout the book. It was especially Tom's leadership as president of the museum that brought this book to reality. He tirelessly orchestrated fundraising, secured administrative support, coordinated efforts with other organizations, and made our partnership for this book work. Tom's wife Anne contributed in countless ways and we are indebted to her.

I grew up listening to my grandmother, Vivienne Beardmore McAlexander, tell Priest Lake stories and she was my inspiration to research a reliable history of lake. My family made invaluable contributions to the project, in particular, Jeanne Tomlin, who organized, sorted, indexed and—most important—edited so much of this book. Brian Runberg encouraged this project for years and helped it to materialize. Finally Jeff and Lucy Smith graciously and steadfastly supported and championed this project, and I dedicate this book to them.

Kris Runberg Smith
Spring 2015

PRIEST LAKE MUSEUM
Wild Place Contributors

Benefactor
Amy and Bob Adams
Heather Barbieri
Beardmore Company
Dave and JoAnn Becker
Marcella Cooper, in memory of Jim Cooper
David & Meridith Manlowe, in loving memory of Jinnie
  Manlowe
Betty and Ed McWilliams
Bishop's Marina
McGonigle Family
Papesh Family
Priest Lake People Helping People Inc.
Brian Runberg and Katie Gjording
Mary and Ron Taylor
Tom and Camilla Tilford
Tom and Anne Weitz

Sponsor
John and Terryl Black
Elin M. Furry
Ken and Allison Hagman, Copper Bay Construction, Inc.
The Hill Family
Kaniksu Lions
Pancho y Penny Landa
Daniel Lowe, in memory of Ethel Lowe
Joyce and Galen Miller
Mark and Barbara Ray
Old Northern Inn
Barbara Ann Wolf
John Young

Supporter
Family of Harriet K. Allen
Kathryn Barbieri
Paul and Jan Bastine
Anne Batey and Bruce Bayley
Beaver Creek Camp Association
David and Annie Bell
Nancy Billeter, in loving memory of T. Rodger Billeter
Larry and Jan Brown
Karen Johnson Carpenter
Rob and Sherri Carper
Wurth and Suzanne Coble

Kay and Russ Coykendall
Lee and Lou Daniel
Bob and Janet Davis
T.W. Dick and Cindy L. Dick
Entrée Gallery/Pam and Jim Martin
Vincent Erickson
The Fenwick Family
Terry and Marilyn Frost
Arley Sue Hagman
Leola Hagman, in memory of Karl Robert Hagman and
  Thomas Paynton Moar
John and Laura Hammarlund
John and Mary Hartman
Bob Harwood
Tom and Arlina Holman, Buena Vista Photos
Rich and Mary Jane Hungate
Connie and Dan Hungate
Bruce and Judy Klos
Niki and Darrell Kuelpman
Sam and Dorothy Latendresse
Albert and Pauline Leonard
Gehrig and Lu Loree
Stephen S. Luby Family
Daniel Lowe, in memory of Lee McClellan
Diane Maas
Ross and Candice McIvor
Mary T. Moss
Susan Munson, in memory of Ranger J. K. Ward and his
  wife Helen
Thomas and Wilma Page
Gregory Peterson
Jan Peterson and Mark Hammarlund
Sterling and Chris Polello
Priest Lake Ladies ATV Riders
Rex Theater Foundation
J. R. and Beth Riley
Heidi Rogers
Rutherford Family, in memory of Gordon and Thelma
  Rutherford
Carol and Jason Rutherford, in memory of Howard J.
  Rutherford
Mary Ann Rutherford
John and Roberta Sahr, in memory of Mildred and Lloyd
  Smith

Dick and Toby Schreiber

Polly Schreiber

Josephine Gumaer Sheffield

The James Short Family

Jack Simpson, in honor of Claude and Catherine Simpson

Julie Simpson, Dave Cummings and Katherine Grace
    Simpson Cummings, in honor of Claude and
    Catherine Simpson

Diane Sonnenberg

Jeanne Tomlin Family

Mary Toutonghi

Gary Weber

Don and Elaine Widman

Chuck and Judy Willits

Mary and John Ziegler, in memory of Ernest L. Ziegler

Contributor

Vince and Janice Aguirre

Linda Anderson

Don and Sharon Beckley

John and Lisa (Billeter) Bellefeuille Family

Barb Benscoter

Bruce and Shannon (Morissey) Billeter and Family

Stephen and Nancy Bonnington

Cheryl Bowers

Debbie Butler

Robert Connolly

The DiBello Family

Mary and Wally Driscoll

Bob and Cheryl Eckler

Craig and Bev Ehlinger

Bob and Renae Faulkner

Glenda Garcia

Jeff, Ariana, and Noah Hammarlund and Barbara Ruben

Nancy Hanford

Curtis and Erika Hennings

Pamelia Hilty

Wayne Hobson

Robert W. Hungate

Doug and Evelyn Jamieson

Mary Regina Jett

Michael and Eileen Kain

Jan and Jim McAvoy

Ellen Zimmerman Nelson

John Nunemaker

The Overby Family

Dan and Joan Peterson

Keith and Doris Pierce

Nancy Pool

Ruth Roberts

Cathe Rosenberg

Dean and Judie Showers

David and Janet Stephenson

Steven and Linda Swartley

Kathy Thiele

Mike and Mary White

Joyce and Jim Wills

Wesley Yasney

Anonymous

Introduction

Priest Lake, tucked way up in the Idaho panhandle, remains off the well-traveled routes of the Northwest. It lacks connections to navigable waterways, and mountains isolate it on three sides. This was true for the native people who first ventured over the mountains and it is true today for people driving up Idaho State Route 57. The paved road ends at the lake. The area's beauty and isolation led to the creation of myths about rugged, independent white men, needy natives, and valiant priests persevering in the region's harsh climate. *Wild Place: A History of Priest Lake, Idaho,* focuses on new stories about real people navigating the demanding physical, political, and economic challenges of Priest Lake. While perhaps not as romantic as earlier tales, this history offers a documented narrative to explain how Priest Lake negotiated Western development and why it today remains an alluring place for residents and visitors. It is organized primarily by topic, highlighting themes and issues that have resonated in the region throughout the decades.

Priest Lake's geography created a remote country ignored for most of the nineteenth century even as mining, railroads, agriculture, logging, and tourism expanded across the inter-mountain West. Early maps overlooked the lake and those that marked its existence disagreed on its location, its configuration, and its name. The difficulty of placing Priest Lake on the map speaks volumes about its relationship with the territory and how its development differed from other lakes in the West.

When President Grover Cleveland created the Priest River Forest Reserve in 1897, the federal government theoretically "reserved" all the land around the lake for a national forest. The modern map of Priest Lake still embraces hundreds of acres of national forest, but it also includes large tracts of Idaho State "endowment lands" along with a smattering of private properties. Today every acre and lot of Priest Lake land not under the control of the federal or state government tells a story about optimism, opportunity, hard work, greed, or politics. Much of the private land represents the efforts of homesteaders who chose to live in frontier conditions during the early twentieth century.

The establishment of the national forest set down restraints before exploitation and growth at Priest Lake could occur in ways that devastated other regions in the West. The government has always been entwined with the development of the region and, for better or worse, this defined the lake. Much of the responsibility fell to the United States Forest Service, which matured at the same time Priest Lake was settled. The region often served as a testing ground for the agency as it strove to balance the complicated tensions between private and public land use and access to natural resources. State ownership of the lake's east side starting in 1917 created another layer of challenges. Many current controversies at Priest Lake can be tied to the legacies of evolving land policies that resulted in uneven and at times detrimental decisions.

Opportunities for the development of the region's natural resources expanded after the turn of the twentieth century, especially in mining and timber. However, by this time many speculators and capitalists became more skeptical about the West's erratic extraction industries. For Priest Lake this meant outside influences were not as insidious as in many other parts of the West. Some of the region's most significant stories are about what did not happen, like a railroad to Coolin or the establishment of a town on the Upper Lake.

The peopling of Priest Lake began in the pre-contact era when the Kalispel and other tribes seasonally migrated—usually in the fall—to fish, hunt, and forage. By the turn of the century, sportsmen, tourists, and summer people made their way to the lake. Few stayed all year but many developed strong ties to the land. Permanent residents arrived in the 1890s as prospectors, speculators, and squatters drifted into the area. Homesteaders and loggers followed as they made their homes and livelihoods at the lake during the pleasant summers as well as the long, harsh winters. Population at Priest Lake accelerated after World War II, brought about by new logging technology, better roads, electricity, and retirees. Each generation wrestled with questions about who should have access to public lands and resources. Another constant for residents and summer people was frustration that decision making for these questions was often in the hands of officials in Boise or Washington, D.C.

For all that is included in this history of Priest Lake, it does not encompass every story or character. We tried to introduce new stories and voices but that meant less attention to often told or well-documented tales like moviemaker Nell Shipman's experiences or the intrepid river pigs on the Priest River. We chose to end this history in the early 1960s with the resolutions over the Upper Priest Lake Scenic Area. These resolutions represented acknowledgement of Priest Lake's fragile environment, the role of historical events, and the consequences of cooperation, or lack of it, between local, state, and federal agencies.

Priest Lake is often perceived as pristine, but the environment has been greatly altered since the 1897 forest reserve. Early advocates, often in the Forest Service, considered the impact of actions on the lake and their voices grew louder in the 1920s as they sought to balance economic and political forces with environmental ones. The massive white pine forest that dazzled the first timber cruisers was transformed. Shoreline development distorted the scenery, eliminated the cranberry bogs, and polluted the water. Species of fish in the lake and game in the mountains have been diminished and replaced. Priest Lake's history offers a cautionary tale for both inspired action and regrettable decisions. We offer *Wild Place* as a foundation for coming generations by providing a record of past dilemmas, solutions, and consequences.

CHAPTER I

Putting Priest Lake on the Map

VICTOR'S MAP

For generations, Kalispel families seasonally left their villages on the Pend Oreille River and crossed east over the mountains near North Baldy to Priest Lake, seeking food, furs, and spiritual nourishment. The Kalispel navigated the long lake and its tributaries using canoes crafted of cedar ribs covered with the inner bark of white pine, the seams sewn together with pine roots. The tribe's name for Two-Mouth Creek translated to "where they peel the bark for canoes." Four Mile Island served as a storage site for caches of camp materials. It was, according to tribe anthropologist Kevin J. Lyons, "the first and last site visited by the Kalispel families." They also hunted on the other islands that were "well-stocked with game such as moose, deer, [and] elk."[1]

In the early 1840s, Kalispel tribal leader Victor created one of the earliest maps of Priest Lake. On the bottom half of the page of ivory paper, he drew in pencil a round Priest Lake, where "waters are as clear as cristol" and dotted it with seven islands.[2]

It is likely Victor drew his map to introduce Jesuit Peter John De Smet to Priest Lake. The missionary first visited the tribe in 1841 and returned to spend the winter of 1845.[4] Victor stylized Priest Lake as round with the streams curved or straight, a characteristic of native mapmakers regardless of their region. He conveyed the size

Pictographs on rocks near Kalispell Bay stand as a reminder that generations of Kalispel people traveled to Priest Lake. The symbols were influenced by the Eastern Plateau Style, which indicates that they were created after the 1730s, when the introduction of horses allowed the tribe to make annual trips to the plains for buffalo hunts.[3] *Tom Holman, Priest Lake Museum*

The Kalispel crafted their canoes with distinctive snout-like ends, known as sturgeon noses, which allowed for better visibility and easier handling in the wind. *Spokane Public Library, Northwest Room*

of the lake to De Smet by telling him it took "4 days around the lake by canoe" and almost another day to navigate the Thorofare (a two-and-a-half-mile channel linking Priest Lake and Upper Priest Lake) and paddle around the upper lake.[5]

Victor rendered the twisting Priest River straight but indicated rapids that required portaging when the Kalispel brought provisions and furs downstream by canoe. A later map, based on Victor's, showed that the tribes established a trail along the east side of the river from the confluence with the Pend Oreille up to the south end of Priest Lake. This trail offered some of the first access to Euro-Americans who were stymied by the river with its "various windings" and "very strong & turbulent" current.[6] Victor placed Priest Lake between two mountain ranges, indicating that from the peaks to the east Lake Pend Oreille was visible, and the mountains to the west presented a view of the Pend Oreille River with the Columbia River beyond. He described how isolated the lake was; "the whole of this interesting basin is very mountainous, with here & there a beautiful prairie. The whole is densely timbered with all the varieties of pine & various turpentined cedars are abundant—cottonwood and birch are found in abundance along the rivers & lakes." He added that "the winters are very rigorous & snow falls very deep & remains ordinarily till late in the spring."[7]

De Smet's Map

Father De Smet met Victor in 1841 during his first year in the Oregon mission field as he traveled down the Pend Oreille and over to Fort Colvile. The Flemish Jesuit headed up efforts to establish a string of missions for the intermountain tribes. During the next several years he

Kalispel leader Victor created this map of Priest Lake in the early 1840s. While he drew a representational lake, he marked the mouths of the streams accurately. The tribe benefited from the wealth of these streams. According to Victor they "contained an abundance of fish, principally trout. Waterfowls abound." *Midwest Jesuit Archives*

crisscrossed the region, baptizing converts and locating mission sites. He returned to the Kalispel tribe during the harsh winter of 1844 and established St. Michael's Mission "placed near a beautiful waterfall [Albeni Falls]."[8]

De Smet traveled throughout the Northwest with only crude regional maps and recognized the importance of defining the region he envisioned for his mission field. During his forced winter occupation of St. Michael's from November to March, he set about mapmaking. He noted tribal villages, sites of successful baptisms, and the rugged country between that separated the tribes from each other and from white settlement. De Smet used his own knowledge from his extensive travels navigating throughout

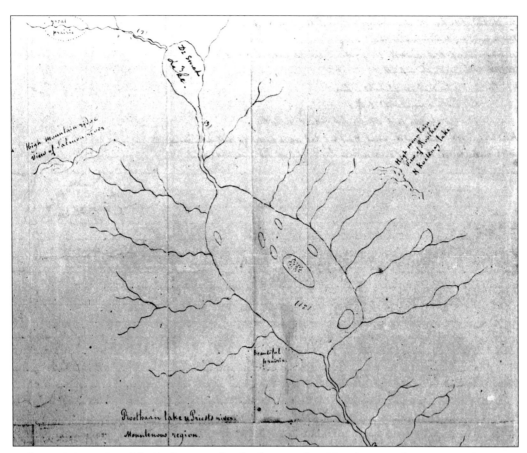

Jesuit missionary Peter John De Smet transferred information from Victor's Priest Lake map onto a thin blue paper, shown here, while inking in his own interpretations of the lake he probably never saw. *Midwest Jesuit Archives*

the region, but like other early explorers, he also relied on Indian informants like Victor who knew the lay of the land beyond the navigable waterways and established trails.[9]

When De Smet redrew Victor's map, he altered the scale of the islands, elongated the lake, and portrayed the streams with stylized wavy lines. He added an English narrative that expanded the brief French notations on Victor's map.[10] De Smet acknowledged his use of maps like the one Victor drew, explaining, "I availed myself of the best information I could obtain from trappers and intelligent Indians who were acquainted with the mountain passes and the course of the rivers."[11]

On other maps that included Priest Lake, De Smet labeled geographical features around the lake with no regard to the names used by the Kalispel or neighboring tribes. His nomencla-

ture for Priest Lake was "partly religious, partly personal in character, being borrowed either from the Catholic Church's calendar of saints or the names of living acquaintances."[12] He named Priest Lake in honor of his Superior General Johann Philip Roothaan. Other religious nods included labeling the river "Blackgown" and naming Kalispell Island "St. Ignatius," in honor of the Jesuit founder. De Smet created some of the earliest maps of the Pacific Northwest, linking together the waterways and marking the missions and forts throughout the region.

De Smet's series of maps agreed on one thing—they documented Priest Lake's isolated relationship to the navigable waterways that he and other explorers relied upon. When he laid out the region between the Columbia River and Flathead Lake, he described it as "a great cluster of mountains, connected immediately with the

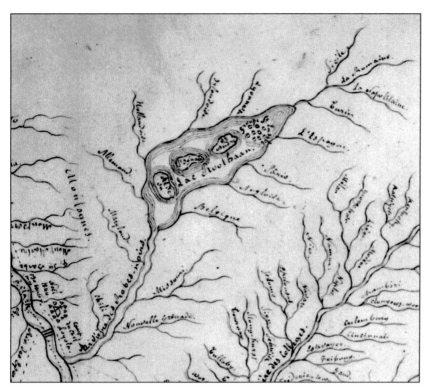

De Smet included Priest Lake in at least four versions of his regional maps. On each he depicted the lake differently, adding or subtracting streams and shrinking or expanding the islands. The lake's shape and bearing rotated from map to map and in one, seemed to migrate north into Canada. He eliminated the upper lake, while on another he drew two lakes above the Thorofare. *Midwest Jesuit Archives*

the lake to sustain the tribe, but he and other missionaries sought to end those seasonal movements and transform native peoples into farmers. He first traveled through what is now the Idaho panhandle in 1841, scouting sites for missions dedicated to the conversion of the native peoples scattered throughout the northern Rockies. Unlike the emphasis on acculturation preached by Protestant missionaries in the Northwest such as Marcus Whitman or Henry Spalding, De Smet envisioned a system of isolated "Reductions" based on a successful Jesuit South American Indian model. He believed that in this rugged mountainous region, tribes like the Kalispel could be cut off from encroaching white settlements and become self-sufficient

main chain in which a great number of lakes lie imbedded." He included Priest Lake, writing "Lake Roothaan is situated in the Pend-d'Oreille and Flat-Bow mountains, and discharges itself by the Blackgown [Priest] river into the Clark [Pend Oreille], twenty miles below the Kalispel [Pend Oreille] Lake." This was the only mention of Priest Lake in De Smet's known letters and journals.[13]

COMPAGNE DES KALISPELS

What remained consistent in De Smet's maps was the relationship of the Kalispel people to Priest Lake. On one map "Kalispel Country" was printed in French across Priest Lake.[14] De Smet understood the ways the Kalispel people cyclically used

Kalispel leader Victor first met De Smet in 1841 and the priest called him "Happy Man" because he was "remarkable for the generosity of rejoicing." The men met again in 1859 at Vancouver, Oregon, when this photograph was taken of Inland Northwest tribal leaders. Victor is sitting on the left in the front row.[15] *Jesuit Oregon Province Archives*

with farming only, thriving with the assistance of the Jesuits at mission villages.

De Smet's first mission attempt with the Kalispel at Albeni Falls failed when spring floodwaters quickly revealed the site unfeasible. He then selected another location twenty miles downstream and renamed the mission St. Ignatius in 1845. The mission grew around the church with over a dozen log houses surrounded by livestock and fields under the guidance of Dutch Jesuit Father Adrian Hoecken.[16]

The Jesuit strategy aimed to get the Kalispel to give up their "nomadic ways." Traditionally the people traveled from their annual camps at Priest Lake, going east in the summer to hunt buffalo and west to the Columbia River for salmon. In 1853 Dr. George Suckley reported that, "Although the tribe is emphatically a wandering tribe, yet the mission and its vicinity are looked upon as headquarters. To Lake Roothaan, long celebrated for the superior quality and the vast number of its beaver, they go to catch the latter animal and to hunt deer." De Smet republished a version of Suckley's account, but he left out the comment about Priest Lake.[17] This may have been just editing on the Jesuit's part or he might not have wished to draw attention to the fact that farming alone failed to support the Kalispel at St. Ignatius. He remained convinced of the Pend Oreille River valley's fertility, remarking, "I have no question that all the country…is adapted to grazing and culture." However Hoecken, who oversaw the Kalispel mission, admitted to the Jesuit Superior General Roothaan in 1849 that "the lands of these Indians are all sterile and little suited to farming; moreover the prairie is exposed to floods in May and June."[18]

The disparate views of De Smet and Hoecken reveal the disconnect between the optimistic reports of De Smet and the more realistic assessments from other Jesuits in the field. Roothaan became increasingly frustrated with De Smet. After several warnings the Superior General removed him from the mission field in 1846 and called him back to St. Louis.

Roothaan wrote, "It was impossible to keep the whites at a distance…and one cannot hope to wean the bulk of the savages from their nomadic life during the great part of the year when they are on the hunt and scattered and disbanded." While his travels remain feats of strength and navigation even today, the charismatic De Smet spread himself too thin across the mountains.[19]

Tired of struggling with flooding and food shortages, the Jesuits convinced many of the Kalispel to leave their Pend Oreille valley in 1845. They moved St. Ignatius Mission across the mountains to northwest Montana. Most Kalispel drifted back to their homeland within a year, including Victor who had become chief in 1853. Committed to his people and their country, including Priest Lake where the tribe resumed its annual encampments, Victor was described as "a man of intelligence but too much tender hearted."[20]

PLEASONTON INTERPRETS DE SMET

Back in St. Louis, De Smet continually revised the notes and maps from his Western experience. He generated a number of volumes concerning his mission work but most of his maps remained unpublished. Some of his observations, including his depiction of Priest Lake, eventually found their way into the works of other nineteenth-century mapmakers, among them Alfred Pleasonton. In the late 1850s when Indian uprisings broke out across Washington Territory, the Army sought De Smet's assistance to negotiate with the tribes he once proselytized. He traveled out West with General William Harney but arrived after Colonel George Wright had ruthlessly put down Indian resistance.[21] However during the trip the Jesuit grew close to Harney's adjutant, Captain Alfred Pleasonton, who wrote when De Smet resigned his post, "We all miss you so much."[22] Pleasonton published a series of maps where he acknowledged his sources were "from the Maps of the Reverend Father P. J. De Smet, S of J."[23] Pleasonton reproduced many of the features on De Smet's regional maps, especially the tribes, their missions, and their surrounding territories. He included many of the place names bestowed by De Smet, including "Roothaan" for Priest Lake.

DAVID THOMPSON'S MAP

One of the earliest depictions of Priest Lake appeared on the 1814 map of trapper, explorer, and North West Company partner David Thompson. He established a trading post, Kullyspel House, on Lake Pend Oreille in September 1809 while searching for rivers that could provide waterways across the mountainous interior. Thompson translated his explorations onto a map used for generations by the fur companies. His map, while noted for its remarkable accuracy, portrayed a misshapen and misplaced Priest Lake. Like De Smet, Thompson probably knew of the lake through Indian informants without having ever actually seen it.[24]

PUTTING PRIEST LAKE ON THE MAP

For the next fifty years Priest Lake remained elusive to the white explorers, missionaries, and trappers who produced maps of the region. They clung to navigable waterways like the Pend Oreille River so the lake, lacking easy connections to passable rivers or streams, remained uncharted.

It also escaped the federal government's gaze. In the 1850s the newly appointed Washington territorial governor Isaac Ingalls Stevens headed up one of five Pacific Railroad survey expeditions considering possible transcontinental railroad routes between the 47th and 49th parallels from the Mississippi River to Puget Sound. Stevens also received authority to serve as Superintendent of Indian Affairs. This prompted him to assign double duty to the survey party's surgeon and naturalist Dr. George Suckley. He instructed Suckley to canoe from Fort Owens in Montana to Fort Vancouver near the mouth of the Columbia to collect natural history specimens and to observe the tribes he passed.[25] Suckley came the closest of the government survey party to Priest Lake when he went down the

Pend Oreille River in November 1853. While staying at St. Ignatius Mission with the Kalispel he commented, "I learn that about thirty-five miles to the north there is a beautiful sheet of water called Lake Rootham [sic]. It is about the same size as Lake Kalispelm [Lake Pend Oreille] and, like it, beautifully clear, and surrounded by lofty mountains, but surpasses the latter in beauty by the great number of small islands it contains."[26] In spite of Suckley's mention, the map of the proposed Northern route depicted Priest Lake as a nameless oval floating just east of the St. Ignatius Mission.[27]

A MOST BEAUTIFUL SHEET OF TOPOGRAPHY

During the summer before the Civil War in 1860, Swiss-born topographer Henry Custer led his reconnaissance surveying party to Priest Lake because he believed it reached into Canada.[28] Custer worked for the United States Northwest Boundary Commission. They began in 1857 to survey the 49th parallel from the Straits of Juan de Fuca to the "summit of the Rocky Mountains."[29] Priest Lake, along with the rest of the Pacific Northwest, officially became part of the United States in 1846 when the long-running boundary dispute over Oregon Country with Great Britain was settled. Congress deferred ten years before providing monies to mark the newly established international boundary with Canada along the 49th parallel. The British created a mirror counterpart with the idea that the two survey teams would coordinate their efforts as they moved east along the parallel. Custer's American team at times numbered over two hundred men, including surveyors, astronomers, a geologist, a naturalist, and an artist. They were supported by crews of packers, axe men, cooks, messengers, Indian guides, and laborers. They began the land survey in the Cascade Mountains. Commission head Archibald Campbell quickly conceded, "It being impossible to follow the 49th parallel continuously, the line of the survey was carried over the nearest practicable route for the pack trail."[30] They agreed to mark points at intervals and just cut a narrow swath through the forests. As head of a Cascades reconnaissance party, Custer successfully located routes through land not yet charted in order to reach the parallel.[31]

As the survey party slowly moved east, they encountered the Idaho panhandle and the rugged Selkirk Mountains in 1860. Custer's boss, chief astronomer, and surveyor Lt. John Parke, warned "from careful inquiry, the entire distance is represented as mountainous and timbered excepting perhaps a short stretch in the valley of the Kootenay." Custer told Parke he thought that Priest Lake, which he called "Tekut," and its drainage might stretch far enough north to allow for a "practicable route" for him to survey the 49th parallel through the mountains.[32]

Custer first tried going down the Pend Oreille River, but when he got fifteen miles from the parallel "almost uninterrupted rapids and falls impassible for canoes" forced him back up stream. He camped at the abandoned St. Ignatius Mission and tried to get a Kalispel to guide him to Priest Lake over a route that could accommodate his crew and mules.[33] The Indians had taken him earlier on a trail near North Baldy Mountain to view the body of water. However in late July when Custer needed to get his reconnaissance party into the region, the Kalispel disappointed him. Custer lamented,

> They are not only unwilling to go but also unwilling to give you reliable information about it, one time there is no road at all, another time it is a very bad one, as when I proposed to one Indian to come only a day or so with me to show me the road, he told me I could find it myself & that it was fully practicable for animals. About 15 minutes before the same Indian had told me that it was utterly impractical for animals to go through.[34]

Others with the United States Northwest Boundary Commission echoed Custer's frustrations with Indian people. The survey crews considered the Indians as "pack animals," which provoked desertion and created hostilities that made the Boundary Commission nervous.[35]

Custer also had poor timing, approaching the Kalispel just as chaotic white encroachment was increasing the tribe's resentment. The government had earlier pushed tribal leader Victor to cede Kalispel lands, and the recent warfare that erupted across the Washington Territory left the tribe unsettled.[36]

Custer gave up on finding a Kalispel to lead him to Priest Lake, asserting "I have always found that I got along much better when being obliged to rely entirely on myself than to trust to guides." On leaving the mission site, Custer wrote to Parke, "I hope yet this expedition will make something creditable, although the beginning looks gloomy." He took his men and mules up the Pend Oreille River to the mouth of Priest River where he found the Indian trail north himself. Custer spent the next six weeks exploring the Priest Lake region, declaring, "It is altogether a delightful place" and deserving of "three hearty cheers."[37] Clearly his experiences banished any notions of the earlier gloominess as he systematically mapped the lake for the first time.

Custer's party followed the trail on the east side of Priest River and set up their first camp near McAbee Falls.[38] While his men led the mules, Custer wove back and forth across the river, making a trip up South Baldy Mountain, "where we had a fine view, gave a very favorable opportunity." Arriving at the lake, they set up camp on the southeastern shore of Coolin Bay. Custer climbed up Coolin and Outlet Mountains and paced along the shoreline during the three days it took for two of his men to construct a canoe. They paddled their way north through the Thorofare to the end of the upper lake.

Custer grew frustrated when he ran out of navigable water and still was not at the 49th parallel but by his calculations only at "48°46" & some seconds." He wrote to Parke, "I must confess I am almost ashamed to give you information of this result, knowing how much it disagrees with my former estimate."[39] Unable to get up the river at the head of the upper lake, Custer loaded one of his men, Hendshaw, with five days of provisions while he carried bedding

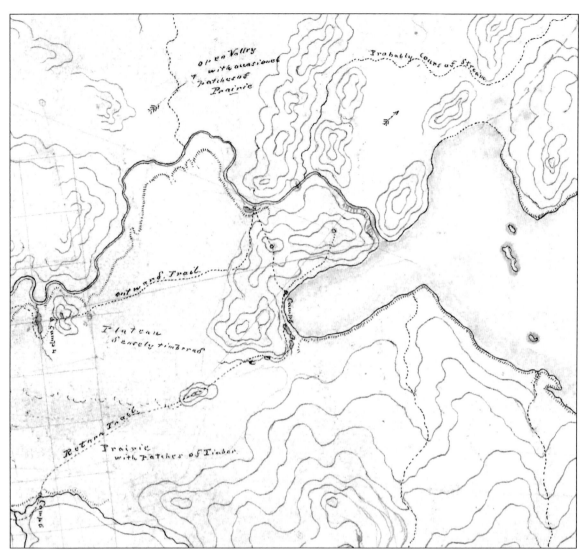

Henry Custer drew the first surveyed map of Priest Lake in 1860, shown here, as part of the Northwest Boundary Survey. He included his route up the Priest River and his campsites at Coolin Bay. He left his mules in "a splendid grazing place in a prairie" when the crew paddled to the upper lake. Like De Smet's earlier maps, Custer's survey of Priest Lake depended on the information of the Kalispel people and most of his efforts were never published. *National Archives at College Park*

and his notebooks. They headed straight north on foot toward the parallel. At the end of three days, they reached Snowy Top, "all together the highest mountain I ever ascended. Thanks to its height and more or less isolated position the view from its summit was splendid and unlimited almost to every point of the compass." From Snowy Top's elevation of 7,572 feet, Custer exclaimed, "You would be astonished of the extent of Country seen from there." Using his glass, he surveyed the 49th parallel and mapped the surrounding river valleys.

Heading back, Custer explored the east side of the upper lake while his men moved their camp to the Thorofare outlet. They climbed Lookout Mountain where they found "the view was more limited but the country which I desired to know better, namely that between the tales of Upper Tekwut Lake and the Cootnay, lay open before me."[40] Camping on the summit, Custer and his men were "witness of a terrific thunderstorm which swept over the mountain & completely drenched us." The morning brought fog so dense they needed a compass to find their way back to the lake.

For the next seven days, the survey party worked its way down the "meandering of the shoreline" of Priest Lake until "the whole was completed."[41] While on Snowy Top, Custer identified a pass across the mountains into the Kootenai Valley but "thinking it impracticable as well as unprofitable to cut across to the Cootny near the Parallel," the reconnaissance party returned to Coolin Bay.[42] They collected the mules and made their way toward the Pend Oreille River, this time cutting straight across Jack Pine Flats and ignoring the constant bends of the Priest River.

Custer estimated Priest Lake to be twenty miles long and eight to ten miles wide, at an elevation of 2,435 feet—only three feet off from today's reading. He proclaimed, "It is full of the most delightful nooks, corners and bays and has 4 large islands all of which I surveyed and meandered, it will altogether make a most beautiful sheet of topographic."[43] Thanks to his successful reconnaissance, Henry Custer now possessed the information to create an accurate map of Priest Lake based on survey readings and first-hand experience. As he finished his fieldwork in April 1861, word of the Civil War reach the party.[44]

Custer spent most of the war in Washington, D.C., refining the boundary maps, including Priest Lake. Before his work could be published, however, tensions between survey commissioner Archibald Campbell and his British counterpart John Hawkins grew as a result of their differences on how to accomplish their "Herculean tasks." The lack of cooperation resulted in separate reports, corrupt maps, and a frustrated Congress. In 1869, Congress questioned the expedition's expenses and refused to print the final report.[45] The survey's detailed maps, scientific reports, and scenic illustrations languished in various government offices and the final report disappeared. Unlike other western surveys, which received popular notice and ignited speculation in the Far West, the Northwest Boundary Commission remained obscure,

and the surveyed locations near the 49th parallel remained uncharted.

The General Land Office received copies of the commission's final maps that depicted a stylized Priest Lake between the Pend Oreille and the Clark Fork River labeled Lake Kaniksu. Parts of the commission's work were finally published in 1897 after Congress directed the Geological Survey to mark the boundary between Montana and Idaho thus prompting a search for the earlier maps of the 49th parallel. Cartographer Marcus Baker found much of the material in two blue chests in the library of the State Department and the rest scattered across Washington, D.C. He talked to survivors and pieced together many of the records but the final report never was found. The detailed maps prepared by Henry Custer and others remained inaccessible, like the land they recorded.[46]

Surveying Territories

In 1873, Henry Custer's boundary maps might have saved surveyor Rollin J. Reeves and his party from near starvation on Little Snowy Top north of Priest Lake. Reeves, under contract with the U.S. General Land Office (GLO), tried to mark the boundary between the territories of Idaho and Washington but an early winter in the mountains northwest of the lake overwhelmed his best efforts. Reeves began his survey at Lewiston where the natural divide of the Snake River ended and he needed to draw an imaginary line from "a point in the channel of the Snake River opposite the mouth of the Clearwater" up to the Canadian border. The survey party made quick work across the Palouse but once they crossed the Pend Oreille River on their hand-crafted log raft, "it was a race between the party and the approaching winter."[47]

As the men struggled up above Hughes Meadow close to the border, "numerous logs, stumps, and large bowlders [sic] are crossed every few chains thus, together with the abruptness of the grades, lose stones, thick underbrush, snow, cold and general exhaustions, have rendered the establishment of this mile one of the

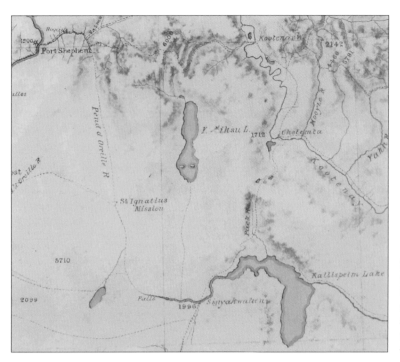

This 1869 map shows a more accurate depiction of Priest Lake. It was published by the British team surveying the boundary at the same time as the American Northwest Boundary Survey. It included the Indian trail across the mountains north of Priest Lake along the 49th parallel. *National Archives at College Park*

most difficult, tedious, and painful of the entire boundary."[48] Though the team was tantalizingly close to the Canadian boundary, the conditions of the next mile just west of Little Snowy Top Mountain spelled the abrupt end of the survey. Reeves lamented "last night the cook made

bread of the entire quantity of flour remaining, all other provisions having been exhausted. This morning the bread was rationed out to the men." With only scant portions for sustenance, the party frantically cut trees into the night to provide a clear view for one last observation but the sky proved too cloudy and cold. Almost starving, the survey team was forced to retreat just short of the international boundary. They floundered in the snow for three days before arriving back at their main camp. Reeves concluded, "By this time we were thoroughly convinced that to have remained only a day or two longer in endeavoring to push the work to its completion would have been fatal."[49] The survey boundary between Washington and Idaho remained incomplete until 1908. A crew finally surveyed the last mile to the Canadian border thirty-five years after Reeves' efforts failed.

The boundary survey between Washington and Idaho remained incomplete until 1908. Geographer C. L. Nelson brought wagons to Coolin, then put pack outfits and animals aboard a barge and steamer and took them toward the upper end of Priest Lake and unloaded at Reeder Creek Cabin. The party then took a trail up Granite Creek to the boundary. *Priest Lake Museum*

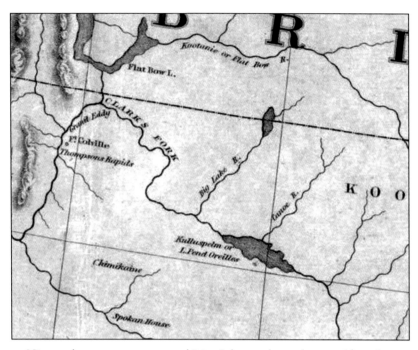

Nineteenth-century maps portrayed Priest Lake round or oval, some without the upper lake, others depicting the upper lake almost as large as the main lake. They situated the lake east and west rather than north and south, lying half in Canada or nearly touching Pend Oreille Lake. Maps in the 1870s alone labeled the lake as Kalish, Salikwa, E Sah Kwup, Kanusku, or E-Soc-Quet. This 1850 Department of War map labels it Big Lake and locates it Canada. It is not until the turn of the twentieth century that maps consistently label it Priest Lake and portray it in an accurate form. *David Rumsey Map Collection*

SCOURING PRIEST LAKE GEOGRAPHY

Priest Lake sits in a large basin dug out by glaciers. About 10,000 to 15,000 years ago the last of the continental ice sheets covered the Priest Lake basin and much of northern Idaho. The glaciers scoured out the valley floors and left striking U-shaped valleys, like the Upper Priest River valley. The granitic rocks—more resistant to glacial action—created Priest Lake Islands. The glaciers rounded and smoothed hilltops and ridges like Hughes Ridge, Horton Ridge, and Camels Prairie. Alpine glaciers formed on the higher mountains, carving out cirques, and jagged peaks such as Mount Roothaan, Chimney Rock, The Wigwams, and The Lions Head. As the glaciers retreated, they left beautiful alpine lakes (called tarns) in the Selkirk Mountains like Hunt Lake and Lookout Lake. They left the valley floors filled with glacial till—a mixture of mainly sands and gravels with rounded boulders and clay layers—creating Bismark Meadows, Squaw Valley, and Jack Pine Flats. Extensive deposits of glacial gravel filled the upper Priest River valley floor and other low-lying areas. More recent (geologically speaking) erosion of the glacial alluvium has left terraces and benches of glacial material around the lake and along Priest River. Both the Priest Lake Visitor Center along Highway 57 and the upper part of the Coolin townsite sit on benches of glacial gravels. The gravels around the south end of the lake may have dammed the water, causing Priest River to cut a new pathway through the outlet.

— *Tom Weitz*

The New York hunting party at Priest Lake in 1887. *Beinecke Rare Book and Manuscript Library, Yale University*

CHAPTER TWO

Intrepid Adventurers at Priest Lake
1885–1900

Exaggerated reports of Kalispel people shooting at prospectors brought Army Lieutenant William R. Abercrombie and his men up from Fort Coeur d'Alene to Priest Lake in the spring of 1886.[1] Miners and settlers had flocked to the region in 1885 with the arrival of the Northern Pacific Railroad and a lead mining boom at Metaline Falls. Whites began claiming tribal lands as their own and they hoped the presence of the military would intimidate the Kalispel into abandoning their territory. Abercrombie and other officers soon grew tired of the settlers' embellished tales of Indian threats and their manufactured demands for protection. One commander commented, "In the case of the Calispel [sic] Indians, they have a shadow of title to the lands in question but the settlers know they hold it by an uncertain tenure and the encroachments of the whites therefore continues."[2] Captain W. A. Thompson later wrote,

> I have just returned from a three weeks' trip through the Pend d'Oreille, Priest river, Priest lake and Calispel country. From the talk I had with the Calispel Indians…all these Indians, Kootenais as well as Calispels have had their property encroached upon and taken possession of by the white men in the most arbitrary manner. They have submitted quietly hoping that their rights would be respected and that they would have justice done them by the great fathers in Washington. In reference to the war scare in the Calispel country from my knowledge of these Indians I am very sure they are the last

people in the world to commit an overt act of killing anyone.[3]

PRIEST RIVER COUNTRY

Abercrombie first came west from New York with the army in 1877 to fight against Chief Joseph and the Nez Perce. For the next ten years he served at posts around the Northwest including Fort Coeur d'Alene. In 1886 he investigated rumors of a Kalispel uprising at Priest Lake. His earlier survey of Pend Oreille River and Lake in 1884 gave him a familiarity with the region, so he anticipated getting more use of his fishing gear than his rifle at the lake.[4]

As expected, Abercrombie faced no confrontation with the Kalispel. Instead he wrote a glowing report about the potential of "Priest River Country" and then left for New York City to get married to his general's daughter. Throughout the swirl of high society events, Abercrombie extolled the glories of Priest Lake, or E-Soc-Quet, as he labeled it. When he told of the exotic isolated Western landscape and the abundant fish and game, wealthy New York sportsmen took note.

A WILD SPOT IN IDAHO

In 1887, General Rodney C. Ward organized an expedition to "a wild spot in Idaho." For a price tag of a thousand dollars a person, the former Brooklyn police commissioner promised an adventure to "the remotest corner of the territory, represented as never having been trodden by the foot of man or at least more than one white man."[5] Isolated Priest Lake offered a rigorous but accessible wilderness experience complete with Indians and worthy of bragging rights back home in New York. Ward assembled ten colleagues to join him on his trek west, among them noted fly fisherman, nature artist, and early conservation activist Wakeman Holberton.[6]

In August, the men left from Grand Central Station, traveling on a private rail car they christened "The Wanderer." When the train pulled into Sandpoint, the nearest siding to Priest Lake, the men were outfitted for their Western adventure, "in the garb of woodsmen, and our costumes are wonderful to behold. What a sensation we would create on Broadway, Mr. Boocock creates much enthusiasm with his magnificent suit of fringed buckskin."[7]

Abercrombie engaged army colleague S. P. Sherwood as outfitter for the Priest Lake expe-

dition. Sherwood set up camp at the mouth of Soldier Creek where the army had stayed a year earlier. He hired guides and a cook and arranged with some of the Kalispel to assist. When Sherwood met the party in Sandpoint, his well-laid plans quickly unraveled. He discovered the intrepid New York adventurers brought so much extraneous gear he needed to hire "Siwash Mary," a Kootenai guide, to provide an additional pack train.

Sherwood led the group on a trail to Priest Lake over the Selkirk Mountains that, according to Holberton, was "over the worst ground possible up hills so steep we could hardly keep on our horses." A horse fell on George Masters, a party member, "but fortunately neither he nor his banjo were hurt."[8] Unable to reach the lake before dark, they spent a miserable, wet night without tents and ate soggy bread with bits of bacon. Holberton lamented the following morning, "How we missed our hot coffee!"

The 1887 hunting party christened this camp on the beach "Camp Boocock" after the young man in their party in charge of logistics. Each man had his own tent. A log and stone storehouse behind kept their provisions safe. The Kalispel who served as guides, packers, and boat men, set up the tepees at the far left. *Beinecke Rare Book and Manuscript Library, Yale University*

The camp cook tent, with cook Kiffy on the left, and waiter Julius on the right. *Beinecke Rare Book and Manuscript Library, Yale University*

Arriving at Coolin Bay, the bedraggled party exchanged their horses for boats in which they were rowed by Kalispel Indians to the camp. Cook Kiffy greeted them with boiled venison served by waiter Julius. For the next three weeks, the men hunted and fished with the help of Sherwood, and a team of guides and Kalispel Indians. Roughing it at Priest Lake included mail delivery from Sandpoint.[9]

On his first day at the lake Holberton directed his boat up Soldier Creek. He caught a two-pound black spotted (cutthroat) trout. For years afterward, he extolled this fish from Priest Lake, "which had practically never been fished before, excepting by a few stray Kootenai or Kalespell [sic] Indians, they were superb specimens, and we found none under a pound in weight, while the majority of them would run about two pounds each."[10]

Sherwood guided the men who preferred hunting to fishing to the upper lake in a futile search for caribou. Near the end of the expedition the men tried again, this time teaming up with Indian guides. After "many weary miles of steep hills," they had better luck, and killed a caribou cow with antlers still in the velvet.

"Pleasant are the evenings we pass around our big campfire. Messers Boocock and Masters generally bring out their banjos and give us some good music, this always attracts the Indians and guides who watch the scene very intently, making a picturesque and wild looking group." On the last night, the Kalispel invited the men to their lodge for dancing but Holberton found it "a very tame affair." During the festivities, the white guide Sutton stole liquor from the tents and shared it with the Kalispel. When the men stopped Sutton from breaking into the storehouse for more, he "got mad and opened fire on us with his Winchester" until Sherwood coaxed him to his tent to sleep it off.[11]

Holberton took special notice of the Indians, alternating between admirer, amateur anthropologist, and critic. He interchanged the term "Indian" with "siwash," a slang term in the nineteenth-century Northwest meaning savage. He noted where Indians served as guides. When a party member shot a buck on Outlet Mountain, the Kalispel cut up the meat and hauled it down to the boats. At the end of the expedition, the Kalispel, including "Jim the Chief" successfully canoed down the Priest River with the game heads slated for the taxidermist.[12]

However the party perceived the Indians, they dismissed them as a threat, and instead focused their disdain and frustration on white prospectors, who also had been drawn to Priest Lake by Abercrombie's earlier report. The first day at the lake, Holberton recorded, "We did not consider it necessary to place a guard over the camp although there were a number of hard looking prospectors around." These men invaded their pristine wilderness and even more audaciously, disturbed the wild game. The hunters blamed their poor showing on the prospectors, who according to Holberton, had with "their reckless blasting with giant powder… driven game back from the shores of the lake into the mountains where the hunting was very difficult."[13]

After three weeks in the region, Holberton lamented on September 23, "We must leave our delightful wild life and return to the land of boiled shirts and stovepipe hats. It was with great regret that we left our beautiful lake where we had spent so many happy days and which we shall never see again." It took the party two days to get back to Sandpoint, and from there they returned to New York by way of Yellowstone. The final count of their take included: "23 Blacktail Deer, 2 Virginia Deer, 1 Caribou, 1 Coyote, 2 Beaver, 1 Hare, 38 Grouse, including Ruffed, Spruce and Blue Grouse, 9 Wild Ducks, 285 Black Spotted Trout, 6 Dolly Varden Trout, besides Squawfish, Squirrels, Magpies, etc."[14]

In 1895, the Smithsonian asked Holberton to paint portraits of Priest Lake black-spotted trout for their collection.[15] Holberton enjoyed the notoriety of his recently published *The Art of Angling: How and Where to Catch Fish*, but he preferred creating more intimate books that he hand-illustrated and ornamented. He teamed up with amateur photographer Dr. C. W. Hoagland who hauled his bulky camera and glass plates to Priest Lake. To capture the spirit and images of their Western expedition they crafted fifteen copies of an illuminated diary that narrated their days.[16] Today these photographs represent the earliest known images of Priest Lake.

SALMO PURPURATUS. female.   SALMO PURPURATUS. male.
SALVELINUS MALMA. female.

According to artist and angler Wakeman Holberton, Priest Lake cutthroats "take a fly just as an Eastern salmon and it does not do to strike sharp at the rise but they must be allowed to turn, a simple taughtening of the line being sufficient to hook them."[17] *Beinecke Rare Book and Manuscript Library, Yale University*

Where No White Man Had Trod

The men who explored Priest Lake at the end of the nineteenth century often claimed it was a place where no white man had trod. This backhanded acknowledgement of the Indian people's claim to the land belied the frequent animosity found in the prospector's account. Stories of prospectors murdering Indians were fraught with disparaging dialogue railing against the Kalispel people. An 1891 newspaper account about Priest Lake warned, "The lovers of legend and story among the few trappers there at this time tell of many a bloody encounter between the redman and his foes."[18]

During this era, the Kalispel people increasingly felt threatened by white invasion. The United States government responded by pressuring the tribe to abandon their lands along the Pend Oreille River and Priest Lake and move to the Flathead Reservation in Montana. Victor, now chief, refused to relocate his people. His son Nicola was said to exclaim, "My country is my father and mother. I hate to leave my mother and father. Would you be willing to leave your father and your mother?" Diminished and abandoned by the federal government, the Kalispel still persisted with their annual fall trek to Priest Lake.[19]

For decades trappers also made their way through the region. Though the trading post systems died decades earlier, Priest Lake still offered a living by trapping. Men ran lines along the streams and gambled on portages down the Priest River as "it is about the only way for them to get out with their winter's catch of pelts and furs which makes it worthy of taking the risk."[20] In 1889, Harry Angstadt and Jack Hansen arrived to trap otter, beaver, and bear for eastern fur houses. The Lemley brothers joined them in 1895.[21] These men would expand their livelihoods to include other ventures over the next several decades, but continued to set their trap lines each season.

A Great Check on its Development

M. S. Lindsey, land speculator and manager of the Newport Transportation Company, planned a stage line from Albeni Falls to the foot of Priest Lake in 1894. Two years earlier the Great Northern Railroad had established a station near the falls and christened the nearby settlement Priest River. Lindsey envisioned developing a route to Priest Lake from the train station along the earlier Indian trail that ran east of the river to the foot of the lake. In spite of his efforts the route continued to vex travelers and even after it was widened to a wagon road, it still remained "miserable; but little more than trails filled with stumps."[22]

In spite of torturous roads, an increasing number of travelers found their way to Priest Lake by the turn of the century. "An enterprising prospector," Lorette Lejon, began pasturing horses and mules in the meadow at the end of the lake while providing boats and canoes for people going up lake.[23] Spokane machinist George Bartoo found enough business to begin offering regular trips around the lake in the steamboat he built. Prospector and speculator Andy Coolin opened a post office in 1893 that he named after himself, thereby naming the nascent community. The Brown Brothers joined Coolin and established a modest store. Prospector Al Pelky tried his hand at retail in the village after returning from the Klondike gold rush.[24] Walt Williams, an employee of the Great Northern Railroad, built a two-story log inn in 1900 to accommodate the growing number of travelers and prospectors. He christened it the Northern Inn. Many who made their way to Coolin before the turn of the twentieth century believed the burgeoning community's fate rested with the bonanza that was sure to come with the next eminent mineral discovery.

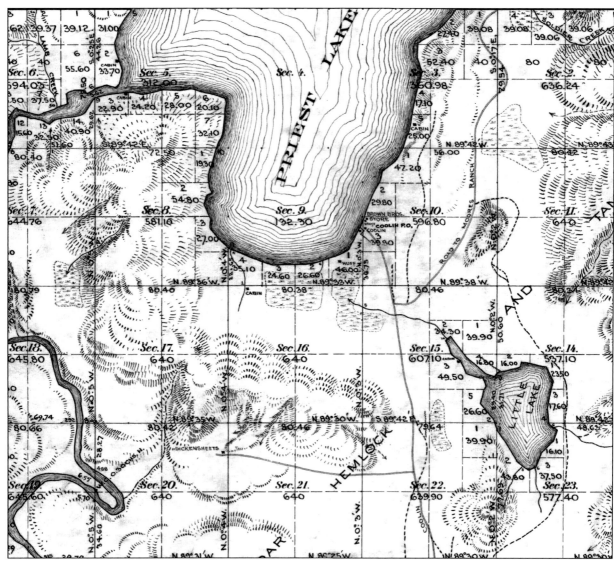

This 1896 map from the Government Land Office documented a handful of buildings in Coolin. A limited network of roads and trails connected the remote settler cabins like Dickensheet's located along the southern edge. Dickensheet left the area before 1903 but the road that connects Coolin to Highway 57 still bears his name. The Brown Brothers operated a short-lived store. Andy Coolin established a post office in 1893. *Bureau of Land Management*

CHAPTER THREE

Speculating on Priest Lake Mining

They came up here by the dozens. Each one convinced they were going to make a fortune from old mother earth. A few of them did, but it wasn't through the sale of ore. It was through the sale of stock to suckers who had more money than sense.[1]

—Leonard Paul

Wakeman Holberton and his New York party camped on Upper Priest Lake in 1887 and blamed their poor luck for hunting caribou on prospector Al Pelky. The miner blasted away with dynamite at the ledges of galena ore just above the waterline, driving game back into the mountains, according to the hunters. A year earlier Pelky and other prospectors came over the mountains into Priest Lake country after running out of luck with the Metaline Falls mining boom. Pelky built a crude sluice box and bragged about washing out five ounces of gold on his Eureka Placer Mine along the Upper Priest River near Hughes Meadow. However, a fellow miner reported, "what placer diggings there are in the creek…are of little value and no one but a Chinaman can make a living working them."[2]

The prospectors moved southwest to what they designated the "Priest Lake Mining District." In 1888 Pelky claimed the Pendleton Mine and next to him Jared Mitchell established the Tarcoo Mine on the west side of the upper lake. The district's development slowed following false rumors that Indians murdered Pelky and two other prospectors, but by 1891 the hills above Priest Lake again echoed with dynamite blasts. The prospectors set devastating fires, especially across Plowboy Mountain, to quickly burn away the forests that concealed the next big strike.[3]

Pelky gained a reputation as an experienced mountaineer and trapper as well as a prospector so he had little trouble convincing "city people" to grubstake him every year.[4] His mining efforts provided businessmen from Spokane and Sandpoint a kind of lottery as he exchanged 5 or 10 percent ownership of his next claim for enough provisions to last him the season. At Priest Lake he survived by hunting and trapping to augment his annual grubstake of sacks of flour, beans, and maybe rice, along with salt, rolled oats, and slabs of bacon.

In the summer of 1891 newspapers touted the Priest Lake mining district as the next Coeur d'Alene district, a region producing handsome profits since prospectors discovered gold there in 1882. The *Spokane Falls Weekly Review* featured an article by self-proclaimed mining expert Ed Tingle. He investigated Priest Lake mines by taking a steamer to the mouth of the Priest River and then following the trail up to the foot of the lake. He hired a rowboat to carry him to the upper lake and the promising ledges of galena ore. The *Spokane Chronicle* profiled pioneer prospector Captain W. P. Light who suggested would-be miners "take the train to Sand Point and take pack horses on the trail over to Camp Sherwood just past the Big Meadow… as recommended by Lt. Abercrombie." Both men agreed that it was difficult country. Tingle described it as "wild, rugged, and picturesque" while Light proclaimed it "the most inaccessible he has ever attempted to penetrate." Regardless of the difficulties, more than seventy-five prospectors joined Pelky in combing the mountains around Priest Lake, hoping to find a bonanza of lead, copper, silver, or even gold.[5]

THE ELDERS' STORIES

Sandpoint saloonkeeper A. K. Klockmann, a German immigrant, grubstaked Al Pelky during the season of 1891. Klockmann hoped the experienced prospector could locate the rumored lost Indian mine in the mountains north of Priest Lake. According to the saloonkeeper, an elderly Indian confided to him in broken English about a lead outcropping his people used to cast bullets for their guns secured from the Hudson's Bay Company. No Indian alive in the region had actually been to the site because bullets soon became readily available at Seneacquoteen and other trading posts, but several knew of the mine from their elders' stories. This tale inspired Klockmann, who had spent considerable time in Colorado and Nevada, "where the fever for mining got started in my system." He instructed Pelky as he left for Priest Lake to build a good cabin, a sturdy boat, and "never give up until they would find and locate this mine."[6]

That November, Klockmann encountered fellow German Henry Steidler filing a claim at the Rathdrum land office that sounded much like the one he had instructed Pelky to find. Klockmann bought him out in exchange for cash and a crude map to the rich outcropping of lead where

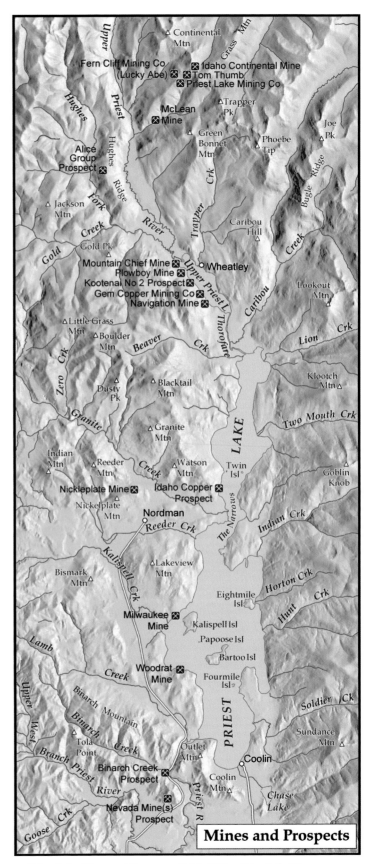

Priest Lake Mines and Prospects. *Sylvie White, Priest Lake Museum*

A. K. Klockmann, on the right, in the Continental Mine.
Boundary County Historical Society

Steidler's two other partners still labored at the mine.[7]

Steidler's partners Billy Houston and Fred Sutter heard the same Indian stories as Klockmann about the large exposed lead outcropping and obtained their grubstakes from several businessmen at the settlements along the Kootenai River valley. The men found the storied mine about ten miles north of the Upper Priest near the Canadian border and they claimed it as the Continental. Steidler left for the winter but in order to defend their claims, Houston and Sutter refused to leave the mountains. Winter proved too much for the seasoned prospectors, who, while trying to survive on caribou, became separated in the mountain snows.

Klockmann and Pelky eventually found an emaciated Fred Sutter holed up in a trapper's cabin at the head of the upper lake. They gave up on locating the mine that winter and snow-shoed out on the frozen lake with Sutter while assuming Billy Houston dead. The next spring Klockmann and Pelky returned to the site and as they neared the claim they saw a "walking object" slowly coming near. Klockmann wrote, "It was a man clad entirely in caribou hides, even his headpiece covering part of his face and stepping out to meet him it was no other than Bill Houston in pitiful physical condition from exposure in the deep snow all winter with nothing but caribou meat to live on." Houston survived but suffered from scurvy and exposure that "left its indelible mark." After his long recovery Houston supported Klockmann's efforts at the Continental for the rest of his life.

Klockmann later wrote a fascinating memoir about discovering the Continental Mine in 1892. Contemporary newspaper accounts and mining records contradicted much of Klockmann's heroic tall tale, but in spite of his romanticized accounts, his description of mining at Priest Lake illustrated the harsh realities of the "wild, weird and awesome" Priest Lake country.[8]

Billy Houston located the Continental Mine in 1891 and tried to remain at the site through the winter to keep claim jumpers away, nearly dying in the process. *Northwest Room, Spokane Public Library*

During the 1890s Klockmann struggled to develop the Continental Mine, fighting against claim jumpers, litigious speculating partners, and the challenges of geography.[9] The *Spokane Daily Chronicle* cautioned about mining at Priest Lake because "the hardships and difficulties of prospecting in this region are greatly increased on account of the character of the mountains which are very high and covered with a dense growth of timber and underbrush. This, connected with its inaccessibility from all outside points and the total lack of transportation facilities has been a great check upon its development."[10]

"Best Lead Ore Showings in the State"

It took Klockmann almost ten years to gain sole ownership and generate enough financial backing to begin mining the vein, a "brilliant exposure of untarnished and unoxidized galena ore" containing significant quantities of silver. The Idaho Inspector of Mines predicted the Continental "probably has one of the best lead ore showings in the State, outside of the Coeur d'Alene's."[11]

Klockmann found "the costs of getting provisions and supplies up to the mine were enormous." He first attempted to develop water transportation from Sandpoint to Upper Priest Lake. This approach failed when his first boatload of supplies overturned in the rapids in Priest River, not far below Priest Lake. Klockmann then cut trails from the lake to the Continental Mine for packhorses. In 1894 he realized a much shorter route to the mine by approaching it from the east in the Kootenai River valley. Klockmann and Houston cut a pack trail following Boundary Creek to the Kootenai River and abandoned the Priest Lake route. They built a cabin on the claims and began developing the mine first with open cuts and then with tunnels.

Albert Klockmann's work on the Continental Mine claim showed its merit, and by 1901 he obtained a patent for the claim, the first of fifteen he eventually received. The next year he acquired all interest in the property from his earlier partners and formed the Idaho Continental

Mining Company. Klockmann enticed timbermen from Minnesota to invest in the mine. Although they shipped very rich ore, investors soon realized the mine needed considerable capital to be fully developed so they withdrew from the project.[12] This cycle would be repeated numerous times at the Continental. The altitude, climate, and terrain made it a costly and ultimately unsuccessful venture, but not for lack of Klockmann's efforts.

"Why This Road Should be Built through a Rough and Undeveloped Country"

In 1905 the Idaho Inspector of Mines acknowledged that the Continental's "rather remote situation from railway transportation has been a drawback to its profitable operation."[13] Klockmann convinced Great Northern's Sam Hill and a company surveyor to visit the Continental Mine to see the potential.[14] Rumors soon circulated about the railroad building a cutoff from Marcus, Washington, north of Kettle Falls to Bonners Ferry and passing half a mile north of Upper Priest Lake. A Spokane newspaper admitted, "The questions may naturally be asked why this road should be built through a rough and undeveloped country?" Hill suggested such a cut-off could link the railway's mainline to Canadian lines. More importantly, if the railroad "passed Priest Lake there will be such a boom in that district as has been rarely known in recent years. The mineral wealth is there and capitalists are just awakening to the importance of the opportunities for investment." With the possibility of viable transportation and the successful patent of the Continental, Klockmann found himself surrounded by other mining companies also staking claims.

Andy Coolin helped to organize the Priest Lake Mining Company with financial backing from Detroit entrepreneur Charles McLean. Coolin supervised the work of twelve claims surrounding the Continental, including the Lucky Abe and the Mystery Mine. He asserted, "The Mystery is undoubtedly an extension of

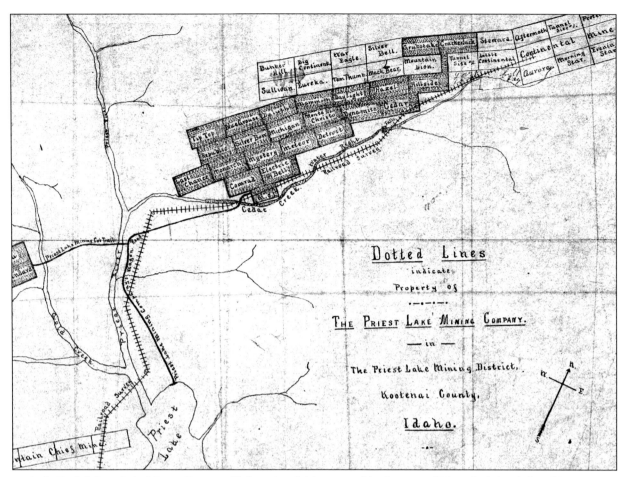

Andy Coolin's Priest Lake Mining Company filed a series of claims west of the Continental Mine, shaded with dotted lines. The Tom Thumb mine, worked by William Burke, appears north of the Priest Lake Mining Company claims. This map, circa 1905, marked the trail from Upper Priest Lake and showed a fanciful proposed railroad running along the west side of the lake, crossing the upper Priest River, and following the steep Cedar Creek drainage to the Continental Mine. *Priest Lake Museum*

the Continental." Other companies "dug gopher holes all over" the mountains surrounding the Continental and staked the Sullivan, Silver Bell, Cracker Jack, and Dark Horse Mines. The miners watched each other warily as they tunneled for ore as rich as the Continental. "They have got a big thing. I wish we could strike lead like that," lamented one manager.[15]

THE MICHIGAN MINING AND SMELTING COMPANY

Just because miners were making a fortune down around Coeur D'Alene and Kellogg, people from the east assumed the same thing for up here. That was a sad assumption for many.
—Leonard Paul

Priest Lake Mining Company manager Andy Coolin knew the country, the conditions, and the indispensable merchants needed to develop mining operations above the upper lake. Not so William Burke, who arrived from Eveleth, Minnesota, in 1904 to work for the Michigan Mining and Smelting Company. The company acquired several claims on the ridge southwest of the Continental Mine and sent Burke out to develop them. He quickly realized how difficult this would be as he tried to secure men and supplies in Priest River. He wrote to investors, "This is going to cost more money than you figured on. It cost lots to get [supplies] in here." The location of the claims meant Burke needed to expand the trail from Upper Priest

Lake. He moved five tons of supplies from Priest River through Coolin to the upper lake, and then on packhorses for the last nine miles. "It will take two weeks to get the stuff from the head of the lake."[16]

Burke fretted about the hundred-dollar expense of hauling an ore car and rails up the mountain and even briefly considered making tracks out of timber. He settled on ordering just the wheel truck for an ore car and added wooden sides at the mine site. Klockmann estimated transportation costs were "often as high as twenty-five cents per pound."[17] Burke told investors it "cost $350 per hundred [pounds] to get freight in from Spokane."[18] He discovered what others already knew: mines in remote Priest Lake cost more than eastern investors wanted to risk.

Burke and his seven-man crew built a camp and mill on a site so steep, "I had to hang on by my eyebrows to keep from falling." The men first worked their prospects with simple hand tools—picks, shovels and wheelbarrows. Burke carefully avoided other claims that surrounded him as he drove the Tom Thumb tunnel. When he first began, he could drive the tunnel about twenty feet in a week. As the rock got harder, the crew used hammers and chisels to drill holes in the tunnel face. They loaded the holes with explosives and blasted the rock to break it up. Burke hired a man just to sharpen the drill bits used to make the holes. His crew dulled two hundred bits on the day the Tom Thumb reached a hundred and sixty-five feet. Burke estimated he still had another seventy-five feet of tunneling to reach the lead vein but smoke from the dynamite and seeping water slowed them down.

"This is a Hell of a Place. It has been Snowing Eight Days and Eight Nights"

William Burke and the other mine managers struggled to support their crews, especially during the winter months. He ordered quarters of beef that failed to arrive so the men ate bacon three times a day. They could not rely on game since "the biggest thing I have seen is a chipmunk," Burke complained. Many days the wind blew up to fifty miles an hour and snow mounded over ten feet deep. He wrote to his investors, "This is a hell of a place. It has been snowing eight days and eight nights." He found it especially lonesome since he heard nothing from his wife in Minnesota. "I don't know what is the matter with her. It is an awful concern." Burke ceased shaving for six weeks and did not cut his hair for two months.[19]

Mail to the mine went through Coolin and up the lake to the mountain. Too often when the pack trains arrived, Burke's backers failed to include paychecks for the men. He stalled for weeks over the promised checks but finally four men quit, leaving only the cook, blacksmith, and one miner. A frustrated Burke wrote to Minnesota, "You folks are making a dam fool of me. We are black balled here, everybody knows that we have not paid." After the investors finally sent him funds he pointed out, "It is a hard matter to get men in here now. It takes twelve days to get men from Spokane."

Getting the Lead Out

Burke's transportation woes continued. "You can't make a move but they want pay and you have got to pay it."[20] By late fall, even after investors sent funds, the pack trains began to quit. Then neighboring mining efforts started to shut down, beginning with the Little Continental mine where "they didn't find anything." More companies pulled out. No one could locate an extension of the ore vein that made the Continental viable. It also became apparent that even if they found a promising vein, there was no feasible method to get the lead out.

Klockmann at the Continental tried hiring an "experienced and practical lumberman" to build a sleigh road like the ones used for logging. The distance and terrain made it useless for hauling ore.[21] Next he anticipated funds to build a railroad to the mine so he built a wagon road on a uniform grade from the mine to the Kootenai Valley.[22] The Inspector of Mines continued to report on the potential railroad annually for ten years, but it never materialized.

ANACONDA COPPER COMPANY

William Burke and the Michigan Mining and Smelting Company gave up, but A. K. Klockmann persisted in promoting his claims. He organized the Idaho-Continental Company in 1910 yet failed to sell enough stock to properly finance improvements needed to make the mine profitable. He turned to the vast Anaconda Copper Company, which loaned him $325,000 to be repaid by ore shipments to its International Smelter in Utah. Klockmann installed a compressor along with a concentrator that could process two hundred tons of ore per day. He built a hydroelectric plant and a fourteen-mile transmission line to power the machinery. By 1913 he expanded operations, employing more than one hundred men who mined a hundred thousand tons of ore containing 15 percent lead and an ounce or so of silver in every ton.[23]

The Continental began operating the concentrator in the spring of 1915 and it seemed the mine would finally turn a profit. Successful operations continued for two months until a fire completely destroyed the concentrator and all the equipment on July 30, 1915. Making matters worse, the Anaconda Company manager had underinsured the buildings and machinery. After reviewing operations, the company refused to put any more money into the Continental.

Undeterred, Klockmann formed another company, secured new loans and personal guarantees, and then immediately set about rebuilding the mill. He expanded the tunnels with the lower No. 4 reaching sixteen hundred feet into the mountain. Overall he boasted thirty-two hundred feet of underground workings including stalls for the horses used to haul the ore. Above-ground facilities included an aerial tramway from the mine to the mill, an assay office, a commissary, a bunkhouse, and barns.[24] A village of Klockmann grew at the mine, numbering 350 people and supporting its own school and post office. Klockmann operated the mine from 1916 until the fall of 1920 when he shut it down because it continued to lose money.

Klockmann next leased operations to the Bunker Hill & Sullivan Mining & Concentrating Company. The company financed improvements and in return the mine's concentrates were shipped to the Bunker Hill smelter in Kellogg. The company revamped the mill and began the No. 5 tunnel to find deeper ores. By 1928 the new tunnel produced disappointing results and engineers opined they had practically exhausted that ore body. Bunker Hill withdrew from the lease. Klockmann still maintained the "greatest confidence" in the mine. Unfortunately his minority stockholders did not.

Klockmann was forced to sell most of the valuable machinery in the mill and power plant to pay the company's outstanding debts in 1929. From that time on Klockmann extended leases to various miners to take out and ship crude ore. Trueman Higginbotham, "a practical miner as well as an expert mill man," proved to be the most successful of the lessees. He installed a small mill and added a flotation circuit that improved the quality of the ore concentrates they shipped from 1937 to 1942. Klockmann ruefully noted the only clear profit he ever made on the mine came from Higginbotham's $1,500 monthly lease.[25] Over forty years the mill produced close to sixty-three million pounds of lead, one hundred and twenty-five thousand

The biggest hurdle Klockmann faced developing the Continental Mine became getting the ore out to a smelter. The problem was solved in 1920 when he purchased two ten-ton Holt caterpillar tractors or "cats" that, with the help of trailing ore cars known as "kittens," hauled ore and concentrates out of the mine to the railroad in the Kootenai Valley twenty-six miles to the east. *Boundary County Historical Society*

During the 1920s the Bunker Hill Company leased the Continental Mine and financed numerous improvements including a tram, a mill, and accommodations for over three hundred people. The mine buildings stand in the foreground with timbers stacked to the left for shoring up the tunnel. A tramline ran down the mountain to the concentrating mill below. The long, low building to the left of the mill served as a bunk house. *Boundary County Historical Society*

pounds of copper, and one hundred thousand pounds of zinc. Also extracted were thirteen million ounces of silver and twelve thousand ounces of gold. It became the largest and most successful mine in the Priest Lake region and produced over five million dollars' worth of silver, lead, gold, copper, and zinc ore between 1914 and 1955.[26] The Idaho Continental Mine provided jobs and bolstered the economy of northern Idaho over a life-span of almost eighty years. Yet Priest Lake's most promising mine never became profitable because of its isolation and the diminutive ore vein.

THE PRIEST LAKE MINING DISTRICT

Mining was a mixture of a lot of things, especially up here. First of all I think you had to be a little crazy and you had to be a gambler at Heart; and I think most of all, you had to have faith in the land.

—Leonard Paul

Jared Mitchell, a Civil War veteran, left the world behind and found his way to Priest Lake to prospect. He claimed the Mountain Chief at the head of the upper lake in 1903, formed a company, issued stock, and, unlike many prospectors, put the money back into his mine. About every three months he rowed more than thirty miles down to Coolin for supplies but otherwise worked the mine until his death in 1919. After Mitchell passed away, Priest River boarding house owner Ellen Baker took over the mine until her death in 1922 at age eighty-three while hiking into her claim.[27]

Other prospectors, known collectively as sourdoughs, joined Mitchell on Upper Priest Lake, working claims with varying degrees of energy for decades. They formed mining companies and offered enough stock to cover their annual grubstake. The sourdoughs served as general managers and, during most seasons, as the entire workforce. Pete Chase organized

The General Mining Act of 1872 gave sourdoughs like Edward Moulton, shown here in the ore car, the right to locate mining claims on the Kaniksu National Forest. He needed to do at least a hundred dollars' worth of labor or improvements on his mine, the Kootenai No. 2, each year to maintain a valid claim. *Priest Lake Museum*

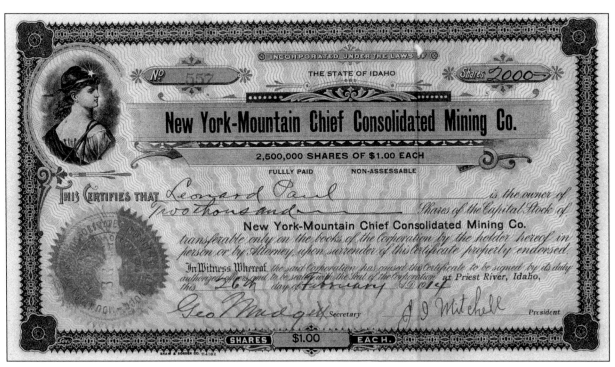

Jared Mitchell worked the Mountain Chief Mine on the Upper Priest Lake for sixteen years. In 1914 Coolin storeowner Leonard Paul paid for the sourdough to attend his Civil War reunion. In appreciation, Mitchell signed over to Paul dozens of stock certificates for his Mountain Chief Mine, shown here. The stock remained worthless but Paul appreciated the gesture. *Priest Lake Museum*

the Fern Cliff Mining Company that included sites on Trapper and Rock Creeks.[28] Edward "Dad" Moulton developed Kootenai No. 2 just above the head of the upper lake, and timber cruiser Howard Gumaer worked the Hawks Nest nearby. Moulton and other sourdoughs worked their claims enough to hold on to them but none received a patent and ownership of the land. For that they needed to prove an economically viable ore deposit existed, and in the Priest Lake area only A. K. Klockmann could do that with his Continental Mine.

The Woodrat Mine—"A Valid Mining Location"

Andy Coolin believed the Woodrat Mine just south of Luby Bay at the waterline would be his Continental Mine. Pete Chase and Charlie Carey first located the claim in 1905 and together with Coolin formed the Panhandle Mining and Smelting Company. Coolin's brother David along with Art Marston worked the mine as "the men on the ground." They followed the quartz veins, some up to four feet wide, which contained the lead mineral galena, as well as zinc, silver, and copper. The men found the best ore under the lake. Woodrat Mine maps indicated the main underground workings consisted of a fifty foot vertical shaft changing to an inclined shaft dipping forty-five degrees to the east, under the lake. Tunnels, called "drifts" were dug off the incline at each hundred-foot level. The mine shafts required pumps that ran constantly since most of the tunnels ran under the lake. By 1909 the inclined shaft reached a hundred and fifty feet and by 1913 the underground workings stretched more than three hundred feet. Since most of the mine ran under the lake, the tunnels needed to be pumped out day and night.[29]

The Woodrat sat on Forest Service land so expert miner Harry M. Booth examined the mine for the agency in November 1908. Unlike most of the claims on the Kaniksu, Booth reported favorably, "This is a valid mining location and a property of considerable merit."[30]

He also urged that a patent be granted when Coolin applied for it. Coolin never patented the Woodrat Mine but used it and other mines for speculation at the lake for almost thirty years.

A crew of men blasted out the ore in the tunnels and hauled it up to a stream-powered crusher on the lakeshore. They sacked up the high-grade ore to be shipped to a smelter but transportation expenses stymied the operation. During the long 1910 fire season, homesteader Harold Warren hauled supplies to the lake for the Forest Service. He hoped to make money on the return trips by moving the Woodrat ore. Warren rigged up a big wide sailboat with a small engine and brought the ore sacks from the mine to Coolin, then to Priest River and then by rail to the Silver Valley. The venture proved unprofitable.[31]

Andy Coolin leased the Woodrat Mine to Pullman, Washington, flour millwright Frank Gustafferson in 1915.[32] Gustafferson sold his mill to finance improvements at the mine including a flotation system. It separated out zinc from lead and silver so he could pack the ore into gunnysacks for shipping. He struggled to find a smelter willing to take such small quantities with steep transportation fees. Eventually shopkeeper Leonard Paul helped him locate a smelter in Utah who agreed to accept the bags, but would only buy the lead and not the zinc. Gustafferson responded, "Well, it's better than a peck on the head with a dull rock any way." He too abandoned mining at Priest Lake.[33]

The sourdoughs on Upper Priest Lake worked their own mines, but Andy Coolin often left hard labor to others and focused his energy on speculation. He raised money with a series of mining companies using fanciful newspaper stories and touting the magical possibility of striking it rich. Coolin enticed a string of "Detroit people" to invest in Priest Lake mining in the 1910s but most of his backers came from Priest River and Spokane. Beyond the Woodrat, he organized the Priest Lake Copper Mining and Milling Company that developed mines at Granite Creek, Binarch Creek, north of Lamb

The Woodrat Mine on Luby Bay held great promise for speculator Andy Coolin. Coolin, standing in front with the dark suit, is featured in this image published in the Idaho Mining Inspector of Mines 1905 report. *Priest Lake Museum*

Creek, and south of Luby Bay.[34] Coolin was masterful at getting newspaper press about the potential of his mines to attract capital. He also leveraged the potential of a railroad for years to encourage speculation on his mines, persuading investors to buy stock that provided enough money to keep his creditors quiet.

Coolin's luck ran out when he could not pay off the creditors of the Panhandle Copper Mining and Smelting Company in 1919. The sheriff sold off the Woodrat and three other claims, along with mining equipment, to settle his debts. The Woodrat's next owner, Spokane businessman J. W. Lloyd, formed the Kaniksu Mining Company in 1922. It consisted of four unpatented claims, a steam driven hoist, hand mining tools, and most of the directors from the defunct Panhandle including Andy Coolin and Charlie Beardmore.

Lloyd expanded the operation to eleven unpatented claims, a blacksmith shop, a bunkhouse, a cookhouse, and an icehouse by 1929. The tailing piles at the Woodrat grew through the 1920s but the cost of transporting the ore remained more than it was worth. Bureau of Mines records indicated the mine produced only thirty tons of ore, too modest to be financially viable with or without economical transportation.[35] When the depression hit Lloyd found himself "checkmated by numerous subsequent unfavorable events over which he had no personal control, and was finally forced into a continued shut down because of the ever recurring lack of finances."[36]

NICKEL PLATE MINE TESTS ARE PROMISING

Speculation ran high about the Nickel Plate Mine as it tried to rival the Woodrat in the 1910s. The mine, located four miles up Granite Creek from the lake, just north of Nordman, was claimed as early as 1898. Newspaper articles reported inspectors "were favorably impressed, especially with the showing of cobalt and nickel. No reasonable man after seeing these proofs and specimens can help but believe that the Nickel Plate mine will within a very few years be near the top of dividend paying mines of the northwest." The secretary of the company that owned the Nickel Plate told the *Priest River Times* "prospects were never brighter."[37]

The company transported machinery for a sawmill along with six tons of rails to Priest Lake in the winter of 1915. They brought in a steam-driven compressor to run the drills with air pressure and expected "to have a double shift working as soon as the machinery is installed." The company built a hotel near the site to accommodate miners and potential investors "for this promising property." Their efforts failed but Spokane stakeholders regrouped with the Nickel Plate Mining Company in 1917. The next year the company regretfully announced the Nickel Plate "has been affected by the high price of supplies, scarcity of labor and the difficulty in raising working capital." The property consisted of twenty-two unpatented claims with fifteen hundred feet of tunnels, shafts, and drifts. It changed hands again in 1923 but its prospects continued to dim and two years later

the inspector of mines found only assessment work on the claims.[38] The company forfeited its charter in 1925 when it sold the buildings and equipment to settle the debts.

The Nickel Plate Mine, like Andy Coolin's holdings and every other mine around Priest Lake except the Continental followed similar patterns. Speculation surrounded the mining claims with great promises to attract investors. Even the Idaho Inspector of Mines continued to write encouraging reports about the mineral potential of the Priest Lake area into the 1920s, claiming there were still "good opportunities that justify development. Mining in this county is in its infancy, and rapid growth that started during 1921 will soon place Bonner County in the ranks of principal mining counties. The county offers an excellent field for the investor and prospector."[39] Mining activity at Priest Lake continued until the depression, when investment capital for most companies dried up. Earlier dreams of striking it rich also dried up.

GEOLOGIC HISTORY

Priest Lake's topography, and the rocks and minerals that attracted prospectors, is the result of geologic processes that date back approximately 1.5 billion years ago.[40] During the late Precambrian era, sediments were deposited in a narrow ocean basin covering present-day southern British Columbia, northern Idaho, and western Montana. Over time these sediments accumulated to great thicknesses and consolidated, forming metasedimentary rocks called the Belt Supergroup formations. The Belt rocks around Priest Lake have been weakly metamorphosed to quartzite, siltite, and argillite. Large outcroppings of Belt rocks, members of the Prichard Formation, occur north of Upper Priest Lake, and between Lamb Creek and Binarch Creek on the west side of Priest Lake. Older, more highly metamorphosed, rocks (genesis, schist, and quartzite) of the lower Prichard Formation are present on the south east side of Priest Lake, from near Soldier Creek to a little south of Big Creek.

Molten igneous magma intruded into the upper parts of the earth's crust and the older Belt rocks. The granitic Kaniksu batholith, which surrounds much of Priest Lake and forms the crest of the Selkirk Mountains, formed about 70 million years ago. The magma cooled slowly, allowing individual minerals to grow, giving the rocks its granitic texture. Most of the granitic rocks around Priest Lake are classified as granodiorite and quartz monzonite, although many variations in composition and texture exist within the Kaniksu batholith and older granitic rocks.

As the magma cooled, cracks and fractures opened up in the rocks, and faulting occurred. More igneous activity formed coarse pegmatite dikes that intruded the granitic rocks and filled fractures. Other fractures were filled with veins of quartz and other minerals, some of which contained the metals (gold, silver, lead, zinc, and copper) that were sought by the prospectors. The ore deposits in the Priest Lake Mining District are hosted in both the granitic rocks and in the older Belt Supergroup rocks.[41] The mines and prospects were mainly lead-silver-zinc deposits, some of which contained copper and gold. Minor amounts of molybdenum and uranium have also been found in the granitic rocks.

Over time, and due to the shifting and warping of the earth's crust, the older rocks intruded by the magma were eroded away. Uplift formed the higher mountains now seen around Priest Lake. The Newport fault, a large regional fault, passes along the eastern edge of Priest Lake and Upper Priest Lake. Other large faults are present in the vicinity of Continental Mountain, between Upper Priest Lake and the Canadian border. Most of the mineralization in the Priest Lake area is associated with faults and fracture zones.

—*Tom Weitz*

Tensions ran high among Western politicians as the federal government sought to protect remote forests like the ones around Priest Lake from Great Lakes timber syndicates. Idaho Senator Weldon Heyburn ferociously attacked Forestry Bureau head Gifford Pinchot over the creation and expansion of forest reserves, including the land around Priest Lake. This William C. Morris cartoon from the *Spokesman-Review*, March 8, 1907, illustrated President Theodore Roosevelt's support for Pinchot and the forest reserve system that he expanded. *Spokesman-Review*

CHAPTER FOUR

Locking Up Priest Lake

Forester Gifford Pinchot proclaimed Priest Lake an "exceptionally beautiful place" when he camped with Andy Coolin on the upper lake in 1897. This was high praise from a man focused on "hard traveling and careful study" of the most remote forests in the American West. He ranked Priest Lake in the company of the rain forests on the Olympic Peninsula, the rugged Grand Tetons, and majestic Mount Rainer. However, when Pinchot arrived as special agent for President McKinley, he did not come to judge the region's scenery, but rather to recommend whether the forests should be set aside from private development.[1]

Miners, timbermen, and land speculators like Andy Coolin envisioned different uses for the land around Priest Lake but they all believed that it would be opened for commercial development. In spite of the rugged geography, they anticipated replicating the same patterns of exploitation and settlement that had pushed Americans across the West. Meanwhile, a growing number of easterners advocated a radically different vision of how this Western land should be used. They sounded an alarm over the end of the American frontier and proposed revolutionary ideas about managing the remaining remote public land. They argued that instead of repeating the devastating land use policies that crippled the Great Lakes states, these forests should remain protected and in the public domain so generations could benefit.

In response, President Grover Cleveland created twelve controversial forest reserves in the west in 1897 including one that encompassed Priest Lake. With the stroke of his pen the lake became caught in a perfect storm of national politics, Gilded Age economics, and environmental upheavals at the beginning of the twentieth century. These dynamics encapsulated the emotionally charged debate about America's remaining public land in the West.

"A GREAT BLESSING TO THE PRIEST LAKE COUNTRY"

Priest Lake sat in the middle of the controversial Priest River Forest Reserve that began six miles north of the Pend Oreille River and stretched fifty-five miles to Canada. Cleveland established the reserve on his way out of office in February 1897. His Secretary of the Interior David R. Francis promised that, "The deep and growing interest in the preservation of our forests will make the act of President Cleveland very popular." He then added, "With all except those who have selfish designs on the forests." Clearly, Francis lacked understanding of Western attitudes toward land. Whatever support the president once held in the Idaho panhandle vanished as local newspaper headlines screamed "Forests Tied Up."[2]

A few people like Civil War veteran and recluse Lucretius Horton, who lived eight miles north of Coolin, probably appreciated the imposed brake on development. However, Cleveland's pronouncement made most in the region angry. Many lake residents, as interior secretary Francis accused, had "selfish designs" on the surrounding forests. They believed in their right to the land as Westerners, held a distrust of Eastern influence, and expressed a shared vision that the lake held their future fortunes. A local editor proclaimed, "The tying up of this immense land has proven disastrous to these settlers, who are powerless with no prospects of the development of the surrounding country and with no opportunities for bettering their condition. Progress has been retarded."[3]

William McKinley inherited the political firestorm over the forest reserves and sent Gifford Pinchot out West to assess whether Priest Lake and the reserve lands should be set aside. Unlike interior secretary Francis, Pinchot recognized westerners' objections, so the president asked him to personally appraise the "economic relations to the regions in which they lie."[4] The wealthy, quirky Pinchot served on the National Forest Commission that recommended the forest reserve boundaries to Cleveland originally. As one of the first Americans to study the conservation practices of Europe, Pinchot became convinced that this country needed "a permanent tenure of forest land, continuity of management and the permanent employment of technically trained foresters."[5] He would became chief of the Division of Forestry in 1898 and organize the United States Forest Service in 1905. However in the summer of 1897, Pinchot knew that in order for the Priest River Forest Reserve to survive the immediate political assaults, there needed to be accommodations for mining, homesteading, and railroad interests.[6]

At Priest Lake, Pinchot might have crossed paths with Howard Gumaer, who was surveying the forests to assess the value of the dense timber stands for the Menasha Woodenware Company of Oshkosh, Wisconsin. Menasha, like other Upper Midwest timber product corporations, viewed the white pine forests of northern Idaho as their future since they had almost completely eliminated them in the Great Lakes states. As early as 1884, "old lumbermen from Michigan and Wisconsin say the timber [at Priest Lake] is as fine as any that can be found anywhere in America."[7] Regarding this point, Pinchot agreed with the timber barons. He asserted the region held the "most valuable body of timber in the interior of the Continent."[8]

Pinchot, however, disagreed with the timber interests about their forest practices. Companies like Menasha and the Weyerhaeuser conglomerate understood forests as something to be consumed, assets to use up before wild fires destroyed them. They clear-cut forests and then sold the cut-over land for agriculture. This two-tiered economic cycle worked its way west from the Atlantic Ocean for more than a hundred years. It destroyed forestland while ushering in agricultural economies. For timbermen like Gumaer, the process in the woods of northern Idaho would be no different. However, the establishment of the Priest River Forest Reserve challenged this long-held progression. The timber companies, along with Idaho settlers, called on politicians to open the region back up for land sales and homesteading. A local newspaper taunted, "The only way to take the conceit out of those effete Easterners who want to shoulder burdensome legislation onto the West is to show up in congress the vicious results of their humbug legislation."[9]

The "effete" Pinchot believed the Priest River Forest Reserve represented a new way of thinking about the remaining western forests. He argued that the Priest River Forest Reserve should be managed more like an agricultural crop, selling the old growth while preserving young timber and controlling forest fires. Rather than lock away the land from development, the proceeds of old growth timber sales could be used for local improvements like roads.

When Pinchot left Priest Lake he took the train to Spokane to enlist the support of his Yale classmate and *Spokesman-Review* publisher William Cowles. Pinchot remembered, "I went with my story that the Forest Reserves were made to be used, not just to look at; asked for his help; and got it."[10] He laid out arguments to Cowles about his innovative approach to the forests. He promised, "Miners, prospectors and settlers would be fully protected, that the reserve would not in any way interfere with the location and working of mineral claims nor with settlers locating on agricultural lands." Pinchot spoke with confidence because he knew that the politics behind the Priest River Forest Reserve had little to do with mining or farming. Rather, it had everything to do with large timber companies in the Great Lakes states poised to relocate their transformational operations into the far west. Cowles wrote a favorable editorial about Pinchot's scheme, promising, "If this plan is carried out the forestry reserve will prove a great blessing to the Priest Lake country."[11]

What Was in the Priest River Forest Reserve?

On Pinchot's last day at Priest Lake in 1897, he climbed Coolin Mountain, took many photographs, and caught a few fish for dinner. Later that night colleague John B. Leiberg dropped by his camp.[12] Like Pinchot, Leiberg came to the lake as part of President McKinley's efforts to tamp down the western indignation he inherited from Cleveland's forest reserves proclamation.[13] McKinley hoped to quash criticism by having the reserves systematically inventoried and mapped by experts like John Leiberg. Born and educated in Sweden, Leiberg settled near Coeur d'Alene, Idaho, and by 1893 served as a field agent for the Botanical Division of the Department of Agriculture. The U.S. Geological Survey hired him to survey the Priest River Forest Reserve.

Leiberg arrived at the lake earlier in May armed with crude maps showing that much of the area unsurveyed and dismissed as a "rugged mountainous region." He struggled his way through the reserve north and south with three different routes, frequently dodging east to west. Leiberg fought his way up Reeder Creek, littered with trees blown over by wind. He lamented the diminished navigation on the Priest River because of a series of rapids "mainly due to huge bowlders (sic) dropped into the bed of the river by its excavation through the moraine material." He contrasted the lower Priest River with the steep canyons of the upper forks and warned of the "tortuous channel" and sluggish current of the Thorofare.[14]

Leiberg made it clear in his final report that Priest Lake's economic future did not lay in farming. "The actual values of all agricultural improvements in the reserve to date are insignificant. There is not a single holding that produces nearly enough for the support of even a small family." He concluded the reserve "can never become an agricultural section, and all efforts to make it such should be discontinued." He urged, "it would be better to exclude agricultural operations altogether from the reserve."[15]

Leiberg dismissed homesteaders' providence, but he was not so quick to dampen the dreams of the prospectors hoping to discover

When President Grover Cleveland created the Priest Lake Forest Reserve in 1897, few people lived in the area. The land had not been surveyed or opened up to homesteading but squatters occupied some of the best acreage in hopes of obtaining it for farming or speculation. John Leiberg took this picture in 1897 to document the primitive conditions at Priest Lake. *National Archive at College Park*

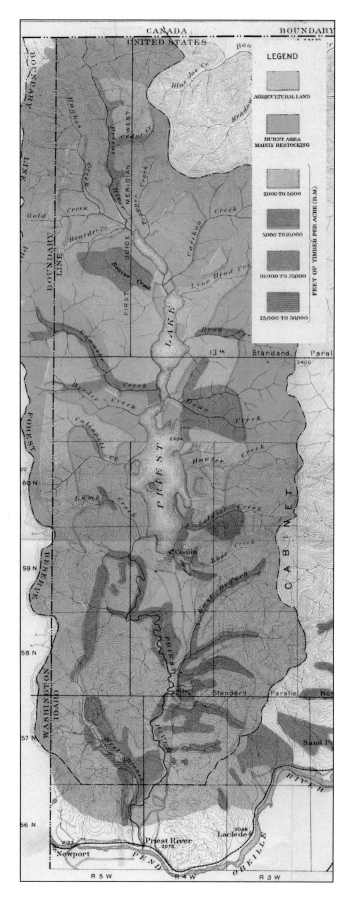

the mother lode. He listed three mineral belts around Priest Lake and acknowledged, "It is well within the range of possibility that profitable discoveries will eventually be made in this direction."[16] As for other economic opportunities, Leiberg saw little potential for hydroelectric energy, noting that there was only "one location for power on any of the streams." He gave no consideration for a recreation and tourist industry even though the lake already attracted adventuresome sportsmen.

Merchantable Forest

John Leiberg, like Gifford Pinchot, believed the tree-covered mountains represented the only real wealth of the region, a "merchantable forest." However, few residents could conceive of a world trade from the Priest Lake forests that would last for generations. Leiberg used his report to lay out the rudiments. He estimated trees covered all but three and a half percent of the Priest River Forest Reserve. He identified sixteen species but focused his attention on the valuable western white pine that made up almost half of the forest. The tree's grain ran straight, its wood was firm but still workable, and it proved satisfactory for almost every construction project. Builders demanded more and more white pine as American cities grew rapidly at the turn of the century and the forests of the Great Lakes states had all but been destroyed.[17]

Leiberg's insights and maps armed a generation of national policymakers with his portrait of the region's potential.[18] However, his findings appeased few western politicians. Idaho's Senator Weldon Heyburn charged

John Leiberg estimated that out of the 645,130 acres of the reserve only 9,990 acres were arable, mostly located near the Pend Oreille River. He argued against opening the area to homesteading, citing the harsh conditions. He conceded some land around Kalispell, Soldier, and Bear Creeks might be farmed along with acreage on Bismark Meadows, shown on this map in gold. However, Leiberg noted squatters had already claimed these natural meadows even though they required draining. *Spokane Public Library, Northwest Room*

that the forest reserves were "paralyzing the growth of the State of Idaho" and regardless of Leiberg's investigation, he stubbornly maintained that the Priest River Forest Reserve contained "a vast amount of land fit for home making and settlement."[19] Representative Louis Smith demanded the government vacate the reserve, alleging it "violated the implied contract existing between the people of the state of Idaho and the general government. People should have the full benefit of every natural resource with which nature had endowed the Territory." The reserve represented "a stagnation of enterprise, industry and growth within said region to the permanent injury of the state."[20]

In spite of such spirited protests levied by western officials, the Priest River Forest Reserve remained intact and was even expanded in 1900 under McKinley and again in 1907 by order of Theodore Roosevelt. The reserve, renamed the Kaniksu National Forest in 1907, withstood the political assaults. However, this struggle between public and private land would continue to rage for the next century and come to define much about Priest Lake.

Policing the Reserve

John Leiberg concluded his report warning, "Unless active measures are taken for policing the Reserve the present timber will soon share the fate of the other portions of the once magnificent forests." The often inept U.S. Government Land Office (GLO) was saddled with the protection of the reserves but lacked the resources or vision to administer them. The GLO relied upon political appointees like Robert Bragaw to manage them as best they could with scant funding. Bragaw became supervisor of the Priest River Forest

John Leiberg's map of the region's timber species emphasized the vast white pine forests. White pine brought twice the price of any other species, valuable enough to make the government's new approach to forestry economically viable. *Spokane Public Library, Northwest Room*

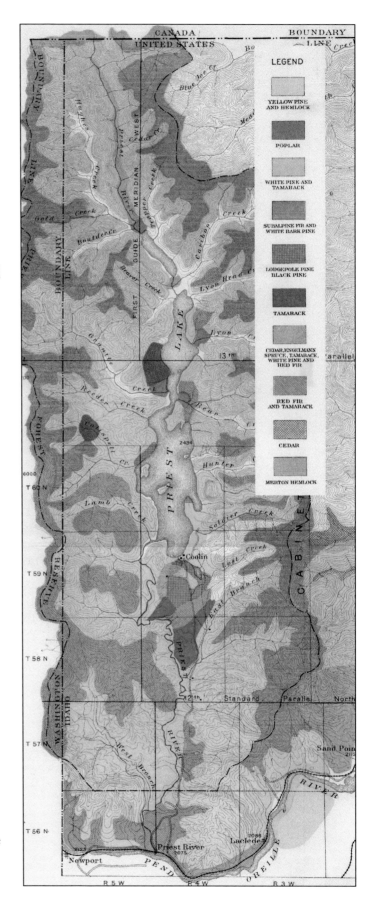

LEGEND

YELLOW PINE AND HEMLOCK

POPLAR

WHITE PINE AND TAMARACK

SUBALPINE FIR AND WHITE BARK PINE

LODGEPOLE PINE BLACK PINE

TAMARACK

CEDAR, ENGELMANN SPRUCE, TAMARACK, WHITE PINE AND RED FIR

RED FIR AND TAMARACK

CEDAR

MERTON HEMLOCK

The Government Land Office used political appointees like Robert Bragaw, far left, to protect the Priest Lake Forest Reserve. When Bragaw won the election for state auditor in 1904, Benjamin McConnell replaced him as forest supervisor. The lack of professionalism in the reserve system contributed to President Roosevelt's decision to create the Forest Service under the Department of Agriculture. *U.S. Forest Service, Northern Region*

Reserve after his 1899 defeat for Idaho Secretary of State. He never bothered to move his family from Rathdrum to the reserve headquarters. He just lodged at the Alberts Hotel in Priest River when he chose to attend to his duties.[21]

In 1904, Bragaw won election as state auditor and Benjamin McConnell, a ranger on the Bitterroot Forest Reserve, replaced him as forest supervisor. McConnell studied law at the University of Michigan and "was a good-fellow-well-met, everybody liked him."[22] He also was as well connected in Idaho as a person could be, with a father who served two terms as governor and a sister married to Senator William Borah.

Neither Bragaw or McConnell, nor the GLO, put much energy into protecting the reserve, let alone developing it. This all changed in 1905 when Gifford Pinchot, with the support of President Roosevelt, wrestled control of the forest reserves from the Department of Interior and helped to establish the United States Forest Service under the

Department of Agriculture. Gifford took the title of Forester. The following year, Leiberg's policing recommendation finally took effect on the Priest River Forest Reserve.

FROM FOREST RESERVE TO NATIONAL FOREST

In 1906, a dapper Rudy Fromme stepped off the train at the Great Northern Station in Priest River, Idaho, ready to take up his duties as ranger in the Priest River Forest Reserve. A native of Indiana, he had recently attended the Yale University program in forestry and this was his introduction to the West. The station agent pointed him to the reserve office in a small frame building just up the road. He suggested, though, that if he wanted to find his new boss, Ben McConnell, to look in Harvey Wright's saloon across the street. "Ben may be there as it's purty early yet for him to be in his office." As warned, Fromme did not find McConnell in the unimpressive, three-room office but instead discovered "liquor-stained tin cups, torn paper-backed blood and gore novels on the floor, along with half-smoked cigars and empty whiskey bottles that really built the atmosphere."[23] Fromme spent his first day on the job cleaning as he considered the condition a disgrace for the forest supervisor's office. He eventually found McConnell at the supervisor's office cabin in Coolin where he was greeted with mulligan stew, a mess of trout, and generous pours of whiskey.

Fromme represented the new army of college educated young men, known as the Old Guard, that Pinchot ordered into the field to professionalize forestry work. He hoped men like Fromme could overcome the "tide of crookedness and incompetence" on the reserves where congressmen found jobs "for their deadhead friends."[24] Idaho forest superintendent, Major F. A. Fenn, agreed with Pinchot, arguing that the state's reserves were "a political catchall into which was cast whatever discarded baggage the dominant party could not deposit elsewhere. The Forest Reserve was purely political."[25] Priest Lake bore out Fenn's opinion as political appointees rotated through the position of forest supervisor, all described as "incompetent inebriates."[26]

Ben McConnell, sober or inebriated, "was always shooting" his .38 Colt automatic. He kept a shattered alarm clock as proof of his aim even when roused from a drunken stupor. His bedroom shared a wall with his landlady's kitchen that soon became riddled with gunshots, much to her dismay. As the forest supervisor, McConnell kept no records and placed the paperwork of his predecessors in the outhouse at the Coolin ranger station for use in place of the customary mail order catalog. He expected the five seasonal rangers under him to track forest fires they could reasonably reach, but only in areas with "good timber." He neglected to build trails and refused to develop sales for "timber pirates." He resented the growing number of campers around the lake, especially those from the Palouse whom he referred to as "barnyard savages." When McConnell ordered the con-

Midwesterner Rudo Fromme, known as Rudy, represented the first generation of professional trained forest rangers sent out to transform the reserves. He arrived at Priest Lake in 1906. Fromme's enthusiasm for the new rigid federal guidelines prompted Coolin residents to start a petition for his removal. *National Archive at Seattle*

struction of a two-room ranger station at Priest Lake, he mistakenly erected it on Andy Coolin's homestead land instead of on the government strip to the south.[27]

Rudy Fromme cut quite a contrast from supervisor Ben McConnell with his Yale degree and "funny looking eastern clothes." Their divergent attitudes and lifestyles pointedly illustrated Gifford Pinchot's challenge as he sought to remold the Forest Service into a professional and respected institution. When Fromme first arrived at Priest Lake, storekeeper Leonard Paul recalled, he "wasn't very popular with the home guards here. When they sent out a young man from college from the East they couldn't understand him.

All in all they got up a petition to have Fromme fired."[28] However, it would be McConnell, not Fromme, who found himself dismissed from the Forest Service a year later. Fromme and the other Old Guard ultimately prevailed.

Forest Reserve Supervisor

Rudy Fromme's first assignment at Priest Lake involved a fifteen-mile rowboat ride with "the dead and dread monotony…of aching shoulders mile after mile. Stealing side glances at the distant shore it seemed like we were practically standing still." Fromme spent his first summer organizing fire crews and learning how to use the newly installed typewriter. Each month, he dutifully sent his report to "The Forester" Gifford Pinchot. His missives contrasted his own professional, effective activities with veiled references to McConnell's inappropriate behavior.[29]

The next summer McConnell attended the supervisor's meeting in Missoula where he bragged that he drank the "government highhats" under the table. Three days later, Chief Inspector E. A. Sherman arrived at the Priest River Forest Reserve to assess the situation himself. Three days after that he sent Inspector Paul G. Redington to document McConnell's tenure. After interviewing Fromme and others, including the landlady with bullet holes in her kitchen wall, Redington wrote such a scorching report on McConnell that not even his brother-in-law Senator Borah could "straighten things out."[30]

With McConnell removed, Fromme became supervisor of the Priest River Forest Reserve. Redington advised that the headquarters be moved because "no dignity attaches to the office of Supervisor at present." He felt Priest River residents spent too much time on "the affairs of the National Forest…conducted over the bar. The residents, as a whole, have no sympathy in what the local officers are trying to do. This is not surprising in view of McConnell's friendly relations with the shiftless and drinking element of the community."[31] By the next month, Fromme relocated to an office above the Reid

Hardware Store in Newport, Washington. With a new supervisor and headquarters, the Forest Reserve was rechristened the Kaniksu National Forest, a name Fromme claimed he suggested.

Before Redington could file his final report, two of the forest's most experienced rangers, Sam Davis and David Coolin, spent three days drinking at the Northern Inn after giving Fromme grief over the dismissal of McConnell. Their binge began when Redington warned the men about the agency's policy toward heavy drinking. They "immediately proceeded to disgrace themselves and the service," including tipping over a rowboat loaded with Forest Service equipment. Their behavior required action "sufficiently severe to show the members of the force, as well as the settlers, that this drinking to the neglect of work will not be tolerated." Because of his checkered record, Davis was dismissed. David Coolin, however, presented a conundrum to the agency.[32]

David Coolin represented the type of man the Forest Service relied upon and the plans for Priest Lake depended upon his knowledge and skills. Pinchot recognized he could not create an effective organization with only eastern-educated graduate students. He also needed the experience and talents that local men like Coolin possessed. The 1905 act that created the Forest Service mandated that "supervisors and rangers be hired when practicable, from qualified citizens of the states in which the reserves are situated."[33] Redington was mindful of this as he refrained from recommending a whole new crew at Priest Lake. He advised "Fromme can do much better work with their help than with a new and inexperienced force." Coolin received a six-month suspension.

Establishment of the Kaniksu National Forest

At supervisor Rudy Fromme's first meeting, he made the men take turns reading out loud from Pinchot's *Use Book*, a guide with regulations and instructions. Under him, the Kaniksu National Forest literally "went by the book."[34]

Rudy Fromme spent his evenings next door to the Coolin Ranger Station at the Northern Inn with the other rangers. He enjoyed the company of tourists from Spokane and serenaded them with a repertoire of Yale songs on his mandolin. The Coolin Ranger Station is shown here on the left with the Northern Inn on the right. *Priest Lake Museum*

He ordered the headquarters in Coolin torn down and had rebuilt on government land a two-story board-and-batten office building. Every summer, his Newport office essentials were loaded into a wagon and hauled up to Priest Lake.[35] The men connected the office with phone lines from Priest River to Priest Lake and then began to string them up around the lake. Fromme oversaw a number of sites around the lake that were "withdrawn," claiming key locations for future ranger stations such as the mouth of Beaver Creek and Bismarck Meadows. He dealt with homesteaders and tried to encourage forest sales to timbermen. However, for all of Fromme's efforts, local timbermen became increasingly frustrated as Priest Lake forests became embroiled in a national debate over "school lands."

HOW THE STATE OF IDAHO CAME TO OWN PRIEST LAKE'S EAST SIDE

After sharing a campfire at Coolin in 1897, John Leiberg met Gifford Pinchot again some months later in Washington, D.C. This time they conferred over the best approach to Priest Lake and the problems with school lands. Pinchot felt pressure from Idaho senators to compensate the state for land lost to the national forests. Leiberg assured Pinchot that they could create a working plan for the lands and the senators "heartily agreed."[36]

At statehood, the federal government transferred three million acres to Idaho for support of the "common school." Thomas Jefferson originally created this scheme to encourage education for the young country by dedicating section sixteen of each new township to generate school

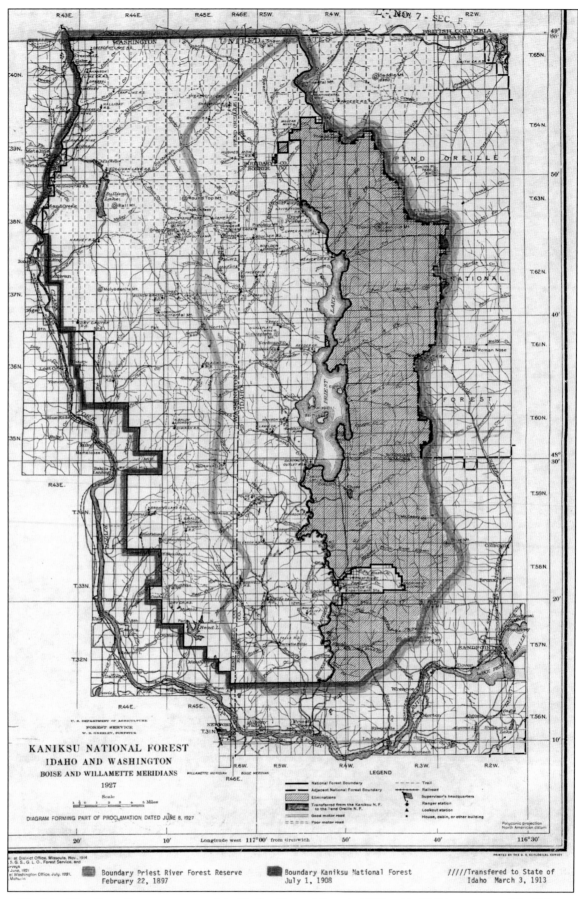

KANIKSU NATIONAL FOREST
IDAHO AND WASHINGTON
BOISE AND WILLAMETTE MERIDIANS
1927

Scale

DIAGRAM FORMING PART OF PROCLAMATION DATED JUNE 8, 1927

The Priest River Forest Reserve was renamed the Kaniksu National Forest in 1907 and in 1973 became part of the Idaho Panhandle National Forest. *U.S. Forest Service* revenue. By the time the large western states, including Idaho, joined the union they received an additional section. The forest reserves contained scores of these unsurveyed state school sections that proved difficult for the Forest Service to administer. This was especially problematic at Priest Lake where the land itself was not valuable, but the timber on it was.

School, or endowment, lands needed to be in large compact bodies to manage timber sales effectively.[37] Leiberg's working plan involved trading all the single school land sections from around Idaho and exchanging them for one large swath of reserve acreage on the east side of Priest Lake. He argued Priest River, the Upper Priest River, the lake, and the crest of the Selkirk Mountains created a natural boundary between federal and state land.[38] This way the federal government compensated the state for the school land, which was virtually lost by the creation of the national forests. Idaho could then take control of all its endowment lands.[39]

It took ten years of talks before the Secretary of Agriculture made an agreement with the governor of Idaho that federal land could be exchanged with state land. In October 1911 Idaho became the second state behind South Dakota to work out such an arrangement.[40] However, bringing this plan to fruition stretched on for five more years. It involved endless negotiations between the state and the Forest Service, a proclamation from President William Howard Taft, a multitude of court cases, much lobbying by the timber industry, issues with the Priest River Experiment Station, an exception for pasture land around the Coolin ranger station, and lastly, an act of the U.S. Congress. The state finally received title to the eastside land that was once a part of the Kaniksu National Forest in 1917.[41]

The process began in 1911 when each side appointed surveyors to determine the value of the land to be exchanged. The Forest Service tapped professionally trained Carl Krueger. The state of Idaho appointed "a charming chap named Ben McConnell, [who] was looked at very much askance by the Forest Service selec-

tion board, for reasons of suspected instability of character."[42] McConnell, the politically connected former Priest River Forest Reserve supervisor, boasted one sister married to Senator Borah and another sister married to the Idaho Land Agent Ben Bush. Bush led the state's negotiations for the school land swap. His brother-in-law plagiarized Forest Service records instead of actually surveying the land and then "worked his reports up from that in the backroom of a saloon."[43]

McConnell's derisory services contributed to the federal government's concern about the State of Idaho's track record for handling school lands. Assistant District Forester R. H. Rutledge grew frustrated as negotiations stalled. Idaho maintained incomplete records on prior land actions and Ben Bush struggled to document the exact status of many of the school sections.[44] District Forester F. A. Silcox heard an earful about the "dangers of the state not being able to handle lands turned over to them by the Federal Government."[45] The U.S. Department of Agriculture solicitor Francis G. Caffey tried to be more encouraging, trusting that Idaho "could in time redeem its responsibility of the handling of its school lands, and that although indications of loose methods in the past, it should have the opportunity, if given practical organization units, of redeeming its past mistakes."[46] Silcox expressed little support for the state's abilities, but declared that the federal government had already granted the lands to Idaho and that the Forest Service now needed to make it "practicable for the State to administer these lands."[47]

Solicitor Caffey observed, "Turning over a large area of land to the State has excited considerable interest and talk among the lumbermen."[48] Local timbermen agreed in principle about the exchange, but feared Idaho politicians planned to hand over the consolidated forestland to the mammoth Weyerhaeuser conglomerate.[49] The corporation's aggressive interest in Northwest timber in part prompted the original creation of the Forest Reserves but it still managed to acquire sizable holdings, thanks to influential relationships with state officials. The independent timbermen's "fears are well founded," concurred district forester Silcox. "If the records of the past sales of State timber can be taken as any criterion, there is certainly danger and a grave one that the State would allow the exchange area on the Kaniksu to pass out of their control under such terms and methods as virtually means turning it over to the Weyerhaeuser interests."[50]

The timbermen pushed for a series of more modest swathes throughout Idaho so the Priest River region "will not have to bear the greatest burden of State mismanagement."[51] In the final agreement, Priest Lake's east side made up the largest tract of the school lands for the state but was balanced by smaller ones in the Pend Oreille and Payette National Forests.[52] The tract also became less attractive to large timber interests when the Forest Service Experiment Station's land south of the lake remained under federal control.

By the time the Forest Service and the State of Idaho reached a tolerable agreement, other western states, especially California, had become embroiled in court cases over school lands. The U.S. Congress, the final step in ratifying the exchanged land titles, refused to act on Idaho's land swap until the other states resolved their issues. This meant that Priest Lake forests remained in limbo. The Forest Service was reluctant to open the lands for timber sales even as loggers and the town of Priest River protested about the economic blow.[53] Timbermen insisted on the right to log on the disputed land, but the state land commissioners insisted on obtaining the profits even though they still lacked the title. *Priest River Times* editor John Schermhorn repeatedly demanded action by the Forest Service, but Supervisor Mallory N. Stickney pointed out that while the state had already selected the land, it required an act of Congress to ratify the agreement.[54]

In the spring of 1916, a desperate Idaho Attorney General J. H. Peterson appeared before a U.S. House Committee on Public Lands. He pleaded, "I would pray to the committee on bended knees…that you assist the state of Idaho in obtaining this title to this school land."[55] Congress obliged. The transfer of title to the state of Idaho now divided the lake politically as well as physically. For the next hundred years, timber practices, recreational management, cabin leasing, and fire protection on the east and west side of Priest Lake would no longer mirror each other.

CHAPTER FIVE

Homesteading in the Twentieth Century

"GOBBLE UP TIMBER LAND AT THE EXPENSE OF THE INDIVIDUAL SETTLER"

Bachelor Lewis R. Chase squatted on unsurveyed land a mile south of Coolin in the spring of 1896, near a small lake that soon bore his name. Chase, known to his friends as Pete, built a modest log cabin, barn, smokehouse, and a large woodshed. He planted a few fruit trees, cut hay from the nearby meadow, and harvested six hundred pounds of potatoes. The potatoes might have contributed toward his reputation as one of the best moonshiners at Priest Lake.

Priest River Forest Reserve officials labeled Chase "Intruder Number 60" in 1902. He found himself caught in shifting land issues that began in June 1897 when political maneuverings in Washington, D.C., suspended the establishment of the newly designated forest reserves for nine months. This "allowed sufficient time for speculators and adventurers to go upon the land and establish claims against the government," according to economist John Ise.[1] Chase's land, along with other sections at Priest Lake, were swiftly surveyed and platted by the end of the year. A month later the Northern Pacific Railway Company selected Chase's acreage to fulfill its land grant from the federal government. The General Land Office (GLO) hastily approved the railroad's request and issued patents by summer 1898. Unbeknownst to Chase, he was now considered a trespasser on railroad land. Other men in the area like George Bartoo found themselves caught up in the same land grant issues. Bartoo tried to homestead on the lake's largest island but lost the land when the railroad claimed it.[2]

Next, under the 1897 Forest Lieu Act, Northern Pacific calculatingly exchanged Chase's marginal isolated acreage for more accessible, valuable land. A cynical local editor explained that under the act the Northern Pacific could trade forested land for valuable property elsewhere. "In other words, giving the land-granters a chance to realize several hundred thousand dollars on worthless land and giving lumber barons an easy chance to gobble up timber land at the expense of the individual settler."[3]

Chase's land then reverted back to the Priest River Forest Reserve. Government officials ordered Chase, Intruder Number 60, to cease trespassing and to remove his buildings. Chase neglected to file for a homestead in 1897 so they added unsympathetically, "If Chase ever acquired any rights therein by virtue of settlement thereon, such rights were lost through his laches in failing to assert them at the proper time."[4] Priest Lake rangers were to report him to the U.S. District Attorney if he failed to move. Instead, ranger Sam Davis, who enjoyed Chase's moonshine, took advantage of the ineffective GLO management on the reserve. He inspected Chase's claim and declared him a "bona fide settler in every respect." Now Chase could apply for the right to file a homestead on land he had been living on for seven years. Nothing happened with this application. Two years later deputy forest ranger, and fellow drinking buddy, David Coolin again recommended Chase be allowed to make an entry on his claim. Forest supervisor and frequent moonshine customer Ben McConnell supported the application, swearing he too had inspected Chase's farm a

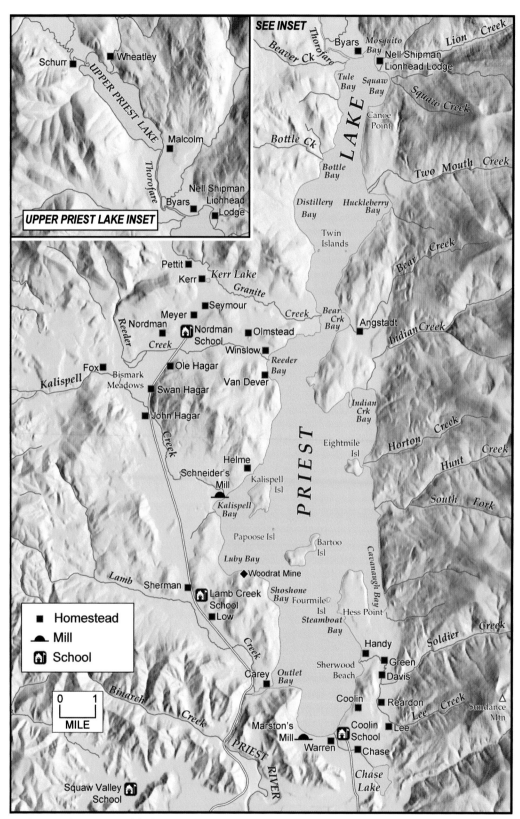

This map shows many of the homesteaders who "proved up" their claims and were granted patents signifying they owned the land. Homesteaders needed to stay on the land five years (later, three years), build structures, and improve the land for farming or ranching. Many families who tried to homestead at Priest Lake failed before they could get a patent. *Sylvie White, Priest Lake Museum*

number of times. He agreed, "It is one of the few bona fide claims on the reserve."[5] With McConnell's testimony, Chase finally received a patent on his land in September of 1906.

Unlike Pete Chase, several other early Priest Lake residents took advantage of the 1897 political window of opportunity. The number of area homesteaders jumped from two in 1896 to twenty-four in 1898, including Andy Coolin, Fred Schneider, Harry Angstadt, and Richard Handy, who all claimed lakefront property.[6] They raised no crops, cleared little land, and made only modest improvements in the form of their log cabins. However, these homesteaders more or less lived on the land for the required five years, got each other to serve as witness to that fact, and received title to their waterfront property.

Later, Andy Coolin laid out a village on his homestead where the stage road ended at the south end of Priest Lake. North from Coolin at Camp Sherwood along Soldier Creek, Richard Handy divided his lakefront homestead for tourist accommodations and vacation home sites to attract Spokane businessmen. Up the lake past the Narrows, Harry Angstadt patented a hundred and sixty acres along the lakeshore at Bear Creek in 1904. On the west side of Priest Lake, Fred Schneider built tourist cabins and divided shoreline lots for sale on his hundred and seventy two acres along Kalispell Bay. While the government controlled most of Priest Lake's shoreline, these first homesteaders created pockets of "deed land" that over time became developed as private cabins and businesses.

June 11th Claims

These homesteaders were the exceptions on the Priest River Forest Reserve, where between 1898 and 1906 only forty-seven entries were filed. This reflected the efforts of Gifford Pinchot who tried to prevent timber companies from exploiting the homestead process by essentially stopping it on the reserves.[7] This added fuel to the political fires already stirred up over these lands especially by Idaho Senator Weldon Heyburn.[8]

Early homesteader Fred Schneider eventually built tourist cabins on his land along Kalispell Bay. *Priest Lake Museum*

It pushed Pinchot to agree to a compromise of sorts in the form of the 1906 Forest Homestead Act, passed by Congress on June 11th. The act allowed homesteaders to request agricultural land on the reserves. Pinchot accepted homesteading in the national forests in return for gaining control of the reserves from the General Land Office.

The western tradition of homesteading, land speculation, and the lofty goals of the national forests soon collided at Priest Lake, and Forest Supervisor Rudy Fromme found himself caught in the middle of a political battle that reached from Coolin to Washington, D.C. Pinchot tried to restrain timber speculators from using the Forest Homestead Act to support conglomerates like Weyerhaeuser. Speculators for the companies paid individuals to file homestead claims but not to improve the land. Instead the companies cut the timber and returned the abandoned, now worthless, land back to the government.[9] Pinchot admonished his protégés like Fromme to be vigilant about releasing only farmland and no marketable timber that would encourage speculators.

Opening day at the land office for the June 11th Act homesteads on the Priest River Forest

Reserve saw "twenty-five people lined up, waiting for the doors to open. Most were young or middle aged men but two were women." All told, the reserve received 250 applications.[10] Charged with inspecting all these new homesteads, Rudy Fromme's by-the-book approach differed sharply from his predecessors. He challenged any application that did not appear to be agricultural land and rejected those that contained substantial timber stands. A Spokane schoolteacher reported she faithfully cleared and cultivated several acres and kept two horses on her homestead west of Priest Lake. When a suspicious Fromme inspected her claim, he found an excellent body of white pine but "no clearing, no cultivation and no evidence of livestock present or past."[11] When pressed by the land office judge, the teacher admitted she visited the place only once with a friend who happened to be a professional locator. She also clarified her application to indicate the two horses mentioned were actually two sawhorses.

Charles W. Carey, Andy Coolin's nephew, chose an eighty-six acre tract at the Outlet, where the Priest River drains from Priest Lake. Fromme inspected it to make sure that it was more "valuable for agriculture than timber." Buckbrush covered much of Carey's tract, and on the whole site "there was only one tree, down by the creek, a white fir." Convinced the land lacked valuable timber, Fromme sent out the surveyor. "If there was a clump of good trees on this quarter section," the surveyors at Priest Lake measured off around them, according to Leonard Paul. Because of the Forest Service's obsession over timber, Paul quipped, "all these plats in the early homesteads up here are so cut up they are like a jigsaw puzzle." Carey's survey proved fairly straightforward and Fromme agreed to open it for entry as a homestead. This meant Carey needed to file on the land he selected within sixty days, after which anyone else could claim it.[12]

Carey moved from Coolin over to the Outlet in 1907 to begin meeting the homesteading requirements. He built a cabin out of cedar logs and brought out his new wife in the spring of 1908.[13] He met Katherine Heberling when she came to Priest River as a schoolteacher. She waited until after the birth of their daughter, Nell, to move to Priest Lake. Carey warned Kate, "if you go outside the cabin while I'm gone today, be sure to latch the door. There's a cougar around that could come in and get the baby otherwise."[14]

The isolation of the lake intensified the hardships of the homesteading experience. Not even a pack trail, let alone a road, connected the Careys to the outside world. They rowed across to Coolin or relied on the seasonal steamboat. They cultivated little from their garden because of "too much acid in the soil" and they nearly starved those first seasons. Kate fished and foraged in the woods and quickly learned "you could get a lot of living out of the lake and off the land then too."[15] The economic realities of homesteading at Priest Lake soon caught up with the young couple and they were forced to borrow money to hold on to their land. The Careys survived their required five years in 1915 and claimed title to their land at the Outlet.

Creating Community

John Nordman tried for years to get permission to homestead Bismark Meadow a couple of miles west of Priest Lake. Under the June 11th Act he could finally file. Only two weeks after the act went into effect, Priest Lake rangers rowed ten miles up the lake to Reeder Creek to once again inspect the quiet Swede's claim. The Forest Service earlier prevented him from claiming the big meadow but the changing political landscape worked in his favor this time and he received his patent in 1913.[16]

Nordman originally came to the lake in 1892 to try his hand at mining, but later took over a cattle ranch on the meadow. Earlier squatters abandoned the ranch because its remoteness made farming economically unfeasible. Undaunted, Nordman cut a trail down the west side of the Priest River to the Great Northern Railroad and soon began driving his livestock to market. June 11th homesteaders like

Olaf "Ole" Hager and his family joined Nordman along the natural meadows and over the next decade settlers began developing the west side land with "more or less of success."[17]

The challenges of Priest Lake's physical geography became a tender subject with homesteaders. Surveyor John Leiberg made it clear in 1899 that the region could not support farming. "There are many squatter's claims but only a minimum of cultivation has been done on any of them." He pointed out that, unlike the cutover areas of the Great Lakes states, the soil could not support agriculture even after they cleared the forests. He questioned the feasibility of planting even modest crops of oats, potatoes, and a few other vegetables found along Priest River because they were "subject to frost at any time during the growing season."[18]

Leiberg completed his economic analysis of farming at Priest Lake by arguing that even if the soil, weather, and farmer's efforts could assure successful crops, the area lacked a local market and cheap transportation to the railroad station. He concluded that the "natural peculiarities are such that it can never become an agricultural section, and all efforts to make it such should be discontinued." For all of his rational arguments, Leiberg's assessment represented blasphemy for most westerners who held unwavering faith in the myth of an America occupied by yeomen farmers. At Priest Lake several generations of homesteaders would try to support themselves by farming but Leiberg's observations would ultimately prove nearly irrefutable.[19]

FOREST HOMESTEAD ACT OF 1912

Newcomers who filed under the June 11th Act often arrived at Priest Lake with great enthusiasm but unreasonable expectations. Charles and Kate Carey's nearest neighbors, a family named Tonnet, "commenced homesteading and gave up quite early and abandoned it" like the majority of June 11th homesteaders.[20] Some became "victims of unscrupulous locators," men who for an upfront fee pledged to find promising, available land potential homesteaders could claim. According to the forest inspector, "A great many of the applicants had never set eyes on the tracts applied for, but had evidently taken the locator's word regarding the character of the land, and had simply been bilked out of their money." Priest River land locator M. S. Lindsay acquired a reputation as early as 1904 for collecting money, but failing to secure land. Others like seasonal ranger Sam Byars would "locate these fellows for $100."[21]

Senator Heyburn blamed the June 11th failure rate on a mulish Forest Service, so he and Senator Borah launched one more effort to shake agricultural land from Idaho national forests. In 1912, they pushed Congress to amend the Forest Homestead Act to mandate the agency to select and segregate "as soon as practicable

The Tonnet family, shown here in 1911, filed for a homestead at Kaniksu Point, half way between the Outlet and Luby Bay. Like many homesteaders at Priest Lake, they failed to survive on their land for the required five years. *Priest Lake Museum*

all lands that could be considered appropriate for settlement."[22] At the same time, they dropped the required occupation time on a homestead from five years to three.

The Community of Nordman

Walter Seymour, an ailing bookkeeper from Indiana, came to Priest Lake with his wife Barbara in 1910 to take advantage of "some golden opportunities—free land, growing settlement, the stuff that makes fortunes." About the same time Thomas Kerr quit his mason business in Spokane to homestead west of Reeder Creek on a small lake. His relatives, Earl Olmstead and Marshall Pettit, followed him to establish homesteads on Granite Creek. That same year Walter and Ethel Harris sold their hardware store in Tacoma, left the city, and filed for a homestead near Reeder Creek. They built a small house and began clearing land. In 1915 Jess Johnson sold his farm in Wisconsin, married "his best girl" Lillian Peterson, and got on the train to Priest River following the advice of his cousin. They homesteaded on Granite Creek, built a log cabin and a barn. Johnson started a freighting business with two teams of horses and bought his first truck two years later. Lillian Johnson felt her homestead at the lake "was the loneliest place on the face of the earth." They left their home-

stead as soon as they proved up and moved from Priest Lake.[23]

Some of these families symbolized a national back-to-the-land movement that drew urban dwellers in the rapidly modernizing twentieth century back to homesteading. They left behind much of the technology and many of the conveniences most Americans had come to expect. Others felt the lure of acquiring land in exchange for their labor. Up and down Priest Lake's west side homesteaders arrived, encouraged by high agricultural prices during World War I and the shortened time required for proving up their claims.[24] Forest Service Supervisor Fred Forsythe acknowledged that with much hard work at Priest Lake "agricultural pursuits have been carried on successfully in the Reeder Creek basin for the past ten years. The fact that over fifteen bona fide residents occupy the township at the present time makes it self-evident that some of the land is suitable for agricultural purposes." He cited ten more homesteaders in the surrounding area and another twenty families south along Lamb Creek who had been able to make a living that "is sufficient to warrant the statement that the land has agricultural possibilities."[25] It would seem that the earlier agricultural assessment by surveyor Leiberg ignored the economic and social pressures that influenced people to homestead marginal land.[26]

In 1915 Walter Seymour, buoyed by the growing number of families, opened a store. He built a large frame building north of the Big Meadow near Reeder Creek. The *Priest River Times* praised Seymour's efforts: "There are a good many homesteaders in that region now and others are coming and this will be the first store in that section." As settlement snowballed Fred Schneider opened a sawmill on Kalispell Bay to support all the building activity. The Forest Service added to the area's growth when it made extensive improvements on the Bismark Ranger Station.

As the number of Nordman homesteaders grew, Sam Hawley extended his stage line from one day a week to "a regular passenger and

Jess and Lillian Johnson, seen here at Nordman in 1917, moved from Wisconsin to homestead on Priest Lake. *Bonner County Historical Society*

This fall 1915 *Priest River Times* ad for Priest Lake stage lines testifies to the development of community on the west side of the lake. *Priest River Times*

freight line up the West Side." Arie Meyer's Kaniksu Ranch served as Hawley's headquarters and provided accommodations for visitors. Rival Walter Seymour, not to be outdone, developed his own Nordman Stage Line that ran on opposite days from Hawley. By fall their success prompted Mrs. S. Sherman to open up a halfway house near Lamb Creek to lodge travelers.[27]

In all a critical mass of homesteaders on Priest Lake's west side had fashioned their own economy and appeared to be thriving. It was the kind of progress Senator Heyburn envisioned in Idaho national forests.

In the wake of economic development, community symbols multiplied quickly. Seymour initiated efforts for a post office, requesting the name Hager after a homesteader who filed on the Big Meadow in 1910. The Postal Service reported Idaho already listed a Hager, so Seymour changed the name to Nordman in honor of its earliest resident. The steady income for the position of postmaster went to his wife Barbara. The first mail arrived safely in a locked bag in October 1915, but a chagrined Seymour learned that their supplies and mail came through the post office at rival Coolin across the lake. "Nordman should be supplied from Priest River," an indignant customer remarked. But for the next two years, the mail arrived by boat in the summer and in the winter it "was a skating or snowshoeing trip down the lake."[28]

Homesteaders came together for dances and box socials. The self-proclaimed "Pioneer Settlers of Lamb Creek" held a picnic on the beach by the Outlet. "Nearly all the homesteaders of this beautiful and fertile valley assembled to visit and feast in a shady grove by Idaho's inland sea." After remarks by Thomas Byers, who had filed his homestead only five months earlier, neighbors enjoyed a "bounteous feast." For July Fourth festivities Nordman families gathered at Vandever's landing on the lake at the south end of Reeder Bay.[29] After everyone sang the national anthem, the ladies debated on women's suffrage even though Idaho gave them the right to vote in 1896. Ice cream followed and dancing lasted until late into the evening. At Christmas time, the Barnes family opened up their new home near Reeder Creek.

Nordman families organized a new school district, numbered 54, in August 1915. They held a house-raising bee, quickly built a schoolhouse, and hired schoolteacher Miss Monica Burke. The new building also hosted the Nordman Sunday School and served as the voting polls where citizens could also enjoy free coffee. With the onset of World War I, the Red Cross Society met at the school.[30]

Pictured here at the Nordman School in 1923 are Grayce Marquette, George Mack, Robert Marquette, and Clara Elsesser along with teacher Mrs. Hawkins. *Priest Lake Museum*

Community organizations and events brought isolated Nordman homesteaders together during the 1910s. The Barnes family hosted a sewing club that brought the women together for socializing. Pictured here are women and children from the Kerr, Pettit, Hunt, and Barnes families. *Bonner County Historical Society*

On Reeder Bay, homesteader Bert Winslow challenged the Forest Service in 1918 when he found that a corner of his Lake View Ranch was on federal land. The *Priest River Times* reported on February 7, "Bert says he built and cleared according to a map that was given him by one of Uncle Sam's college boys. And so Bert feels peeved, worked, and upset." Winslow's homestead, seen here, later became part of Elkins Resort. *Priest Lake Museum*

"Peeved, Worked, and Upset"

The relaxed requirements brought by the Forest Homestead Act of 1906 meant for most claimants "very little trouble will be had in making final proof." There were distressing exceptions. Johnny Malcolm filed along the Thorofare, made improvements, and managed to survive for five years. In May 1915, he went to the Coeur d'Alene land office and filed his final proof. Waiting at the train station to return to Priest River, "a government clerk rushed up to him and thrust a letter into his hand from [Washington] D.C. stating that the land Johnny had spent five years of his life working to obtain belonged to the railroad company and the government had nothing whatever to do with it." Down on Big Meadow, John Eastlund homesteaded near neighbor John Nordman. However, Eastlund failed to secure naturalization papers that threatened his ability to patent the claim. "This and other troubles over land which had been working on his mind for some time" provoked him to commit suicide in 1916. John Nordman later made final proof on Eastlund's homestead for his heirs back in Scandinavia.[31]

"Very Eager to Sell Out"

Walter Seymour opened Nordman's first store, secured the post office, established a stage line, and became a bellwether for Priest Lake growth. He proved up his homestead in May 1918. Then he left. Seymour sold his store to D. C. Barnes and his stage line to William Boer and took a job in the State Auditor's office in Boise. Jess Johnson relocated into Priest River because his wife Lillian found their homestead too isolated. Ellen Fox received her land patent in September and moved before the end of the month to Pullman for a lucrative nine-to-five job. A year earlier, Marshall Pettit packed up his family and moved back to Minnesota. Walter and Ethel Harris headed back to western Washington as soon as they proved up in June 1920.[32]

By 1922 according to Kaniksu National Forest ranger Harry G. Ade, "many of the homesteads have been abandoned and are lying idle. In the vicinity of Nordman this condition seems to be worse than anywhere else where the homesteads taken under the Act of June 11, 1906 are not being developed." Homesteaders abandoned 75 percent of the land after becoming discouraged over "the cost of clearing the land, distances to outside markets, lack of local markets and the rather severe climatic conditions retard the agricultural development."[33] More than half of the "pioneer settlers" at the 1915 Lamb Creek picnic failed to prove up and many who did immediately sold their patented land. As quickly as the west side of Priest Lake developed in the 1910s, families melted away after acquiring title to their land. A homesteader who left reflected, "The simple life and near-to-nature's heart stuff was just fine when taken in small doses, and a season apart."[34]

For all of Nordman's boosterism, the rapid decline came as no surprise to forester Fred Forsythe. During the peak year of homestead applications in 1914 he predicted, "It is very doubtful if the first settlers in the area will be the permanent residents in this community… Claimants are very eager to sell out and buy smaller tracts of improved agricultural land elsewhere immediately after securing patent." The majority of Priest Lake homesteaders sold out to timber companies.[35]

"Mail Day Twice a Week and the White Sandy Beaches"

Not all June 11th homesteaders abandoned the lake. The Kerr, Hager, and Winslow families remained and others such as the Kenyons and Gregorys joined them in the 1920s. However, few depended on their land for their livelihoods and instead turned to logging, tourism, mining, or the Forest Service.[36] But the legacies of the hopeful 1910s remained. The West Branch road eventually became a paved road, allowing for closer connections to Priest River, the railroad, and the markets beyond. A store and the post office remained. The Nordman and Lamb Creek schools continued to educate generations of students while providing community centers for celebrations.

John Nordman ranched until his death in 1938. His obituary read, "What a privilege was his to see the development of the Kaniksu Forest. Old trails have vanished. Broad highways cut thru gigantic cedars and towering white pine have taken their place. A Forest Service highly organized. Mail day twice a week and the white sandy beaches around Priest Lake, the playground of America."[37] A hundred years after Nordman patented his homestead, his acreage and that of his neighbors created private land in the middle of the national forest where development still continues along Highway 57.

CHAPTER SIX

Andy Coolin's Schemes

When Andy Coolin filed a homestead at the foot of Priest Lake, the Canadian native never envisioned himself as a small farmer eking out a living on 158 acres. Coolin found his way to Priest Lake after facing charges of assault with a deadly weapon in 1892. An acquaintance pulled a gun on him during a quarrel on the street in Chattaroy, a village outside of Spokane. Coolin emptied his revolver, missed, and started to run. After being aquitted, Coolin retreated to the lake and patented a homestead on the bay near the south end. For Coolin, a government homestead represented the first step to becoming a capitalist. When he received his patent in 1903, he planned to leverage his marginal land twenty-eight miles from the nearest railroad into a financial empire. Coolin embodied the Western spirit at the turn of the twentieth century when men schemed of making it rich at the expense of the government by exploiting public land. He almost succeeded.

Coolin formed the Priest Lake Town Site and Improvement Company with his brother and other local investors in 1907. He boasted

Andy Coolin established and named a post office for himself at Priest Lake in 1893 and devoted the next forty-eight years as a "prospector and mining man" with big dreams. *Priest Lake Museum*

that his homestead was "the only available piece of patented ground on the lake and it is the key to the rich Priest Lake country."[1] He sought to replicate the fashionable, genteel resort communities popular in the East for generations. Spokane's growing population of middle- and upper-class families enjoyed more income and vacation time for such pleasures, so resorts began to flourish at nearby lakes. Coeur d'Alene, Hayden, and Liberty Lakes already boasted stylish hotels, excursion boats, golf courses, and regular railway connections.

Coolin promised to establish "hotels, club-houses and other buildings for amusement purposes" at the foot of Priest Lake. He leased the Northern Inn across from his cabin and put his sister, Martha Carey, in charge of creating a respectable establishment. She "had considerable experience in this line." Above the inn, construction began on a saloon. Down the hill, Coolin's brother Dave started a two-story frame hotel near Joseph Slee's docks.[2] A Spokane businessman, Slee operated a steamboat connecting the lake with supplies, mail, and transportation. Slee and his son Walter considered replacing their modest *Kaniksu* with a larger steamboat as the prospect of more vacationers grew.

Two miles up the lake from Coolin near Soldier Creek Richard Handy developed his homestead at the old Camp Sherwood into a resort with well-appointed cabins for prosperous clients. He bought a team of horses to push through a road, constructing "a picturesque driveway, following the shoreline wherever possible."[3]

Progress stalled when Handy died unexpectedly on July 4, 1907, and Dave Coolin died six months later.[4] Handy's son Harry took up the development of Camp Sherwood but managed it as a long-distance project from India, where he also operated a circus. Handy's widow, Ida, took over Dave Coolin's nearly finished hotel and opened it as the Idaho Inn in the spring of 1908.

An Unsuccessful Venture

Englishman Cecil Wheatley imagined transforming his homestead into a resort community but his claim was on the Upper Priest Lake, more than twenty miles north of Coolin at the mouth of Trapper Creek. He built a sixty-five-foot, double-decked Mississippi River-type paddle steam-

Cecil Wheatley's paddle steamboat, the *Banshee*. *Priest Lake Museum*

Wheatley's plat of his planned Upper Priest Lake resort. *Priest Lake Museum*

boat to transport investors and potential homeowners to his wilderness town site. The *Banshee* could navigate the shallow, unpredictable Thoroughfare and even boasted a separate ladies cabin. A newspaper predicted when Wheatley launched it in June 1908, "It is expected this steamer will be a big factor this year in popularizing Priest Lake as a summer resort."

Wheatley offered lots "placed on such terms and prices that they are within the reach of everyone." The creek offered "plenty of power to furnish all the electricity that can be used and will allow every lot being thoroughly supplied with water." Wheatley even planned for a post office.

The *Banshee's* steam engine required a prohibitive amount of wood and even with a shallow draft Wheatley hit the rocks at Kalispell Bay. After he damaged the boat, Wheatley declared, "the hell with it" for his upper lake development.[5]

After Leonard Paul opened his Coolin store, he acquired the post office. In this 1910 Frank Palmer photograph, Paul leans on the porch post in the center and Andy Coolin sits at the far right. *Frank Palmer, Northwest Museum of Arts and Culture*

Andy Coolin's ventures attracted the attention of Priest River merchant Charles Mears. With the promise of growth, Mears recruited his nineteen-year-old nephew, Leonard Paul, to open a general merchandise store next door to Coolin's cabin. They hired homesteader Tom Benton to build the twenty-by-thirty-foot log store in fall 1906. At Thanksgiving, Paul delivered milled windows and doors. He spent the holiday sleeping on Coolin's kitchen floor and eating at the Northern Inn so he could supervise the installation of counters and shelves. After New Year's, Mears helped select the stock in Spokane. In spite of heavy snows, Paul opened his doors on February 15 with "the first fully equipped store on Priest Lake [to] fill a long felt want." Coolin's vision of a vital resort community began to take shape as "never before has Priest Lake been the scene of such activity."[6]

THE PANHANDLE ELECTRIC RAILWAY AND POWER CO.

The entrepreneurs who strove to expand the lake's infrastructure for a viable resort economy all faced the same considerable obstacle. Priest Lake, unlike Hayden or Liberty, lacked daily excursion trains from Spokane delivering tourists to its shores. Vacationers endured two days just to get to Coolin. They rode the Great Northern Railway to Priest River and spent the night at the modest St. Elmo Hotel. Early the next morning, passengers boarded a horse-drawn stage for the arduous ten-hour trip to Coolin. The only road to the lake followed the east side of the Priest River which required fewer bridges to cross its many branches. This also meant steep hills that often required passengers to disembark and walk. Travelers reported, "The roads to the lake are miserable; but little more than trails filled with stumps." Weary guests welcomed a lunch stop at Prater's Halfway House while drivers changed horses for the rest of the trip to the lake. A passenger remembered, "Quite often as we came to the crest at the top of the hill, getting the first glimpse of the lake and the Northern Inn, someone shot off a gun to announce us."[7]

Thirty miles of poor roads stood between Andy Coolin and his vision. Whatever scheme he or anyone else dreamed about at Priest Lake, whether a fashionable resort community, a mining industry, a robust real estate market, fertile ranches, or expansive logging operations, they all hinged on transportation. In the West in 1907, that meant a railroad. So Coolin conceived of the Panhandle Electric Railway and Power Company and offered his newly platted homestead for its northern terminus. When he announced the company's incorporation, he promised, "The almost unlimited forest areas, the mountains filled with precious metals, and the openings for transportation schemes make it a very rich field for the capitalist."

Coolin's optimism was not entirely misplaced. Across the Northwest, the Great Northern and Northern Pacific railways served as trunk lines to a growing latticework of spurs and short lines. They opened to commerce remote mining districts, timber operations, and even

The ten-hour stage ride crossed Jack Pine Flats and came into Coolin, as shown here in 1911. *Priest Lake Museum*

tourist attractions like Yellowstone. Big corporations developed some of the short lines, but regional interests like those belonging to Coolin and his board of directors orchestrated others.

Andy Coolin believed Priest Lake resources merited such a line. He was "indefatigable in his efforts to bring the country to the attention of capitalists." Coolin's boosterism was hyperbolic but his enthusiasm held merit. The Northern Pacific railroad contemplated a route involving Priest Lake in 1904. Great Northern engineers considered a line that would sweep within a mile of the lake as it ran from the town of Marcus, north of Kettle Falls, to Laclede, just west of Sandpoint.[8]

Coolin recruited for the Panhandle Electric Railway a board of directors guaranteed to impress investors. Detroit lawyer Thomas W. Payne served as president and lynchpin for the project. The "eastern capitalist" contributed funding but more importantly instilled confidence in Spokane backers, who may otherwise have believed this was just a local, harebrained ploy. Payne held investments in the Cabinet Range mines near Priest Lake and his reputation back home seemed solid. Reporting on his efforts with the railway, the Detroit press testified, "For a young lawyer to have undertaken and carried the enterprise through with such success is proof of his keen vision for opportunity and his resourcefulness in making the visions become realities." General Manager Amasa Smith, depot agent of the Great Northern in Spokane, lent an air of authority as did a number of prominent Spokane businessmen who served on the board. By the spring of 1907, Coolin announced the scheme had attracted enough financial backing to make the railway possible.[9]

Payne made Coolin's scheme more marketable by adding waterpower to the project. Increasingly, Western railroad builders believed electric lines to be more profitable. The Panhandle Electric Railroad Company proposed to "construct, equip, and operate electric and other kinds of railroads, to construct and operate power houses and sell electricity, to own and use water rights; to build canals and ditches and to own and sell stocks and bonds." Coolin managed to secure the water rights from the Forest Service to construct a dam and build powerhouses on the Priest River.[10] They planned to generate electricity on the dammed Priest River to operate the railroad along with the industrial infrastructure it attracted.

The Forest Service often found Andy Coolin's schemes exasperating, if not illegal, but eagerly joined forces with him for a railroad. The agency controlled the water rights and much of the land needed for the right of way. Inspector Paul G. Redington wrote "the construction of this railroad will mean much to the country and will largely benefit the National Forest, since timber, now inaccessible, will be rendered available to market."[11] Coolin's railway provided the necessary infrastructure to make extensive logging in Kaniksu National Forest possible.

Coolin negotiated with the Forest Service for a right-of-way exception. He argued that he needed three hundred instead of two hundred feet "to make sure that none of the unusually tall pines and tamaracks will fall and obstruct the road."[12] He provided a detailed engineering study of the route, lying out the grades, trestles, and costs for each of the twenty-eight miles in the branch from the Great Northern tracks from Priest River. District forester William Greeley agreed to request the withdrawal of the land in 1909. The Idaho State Senate supported his application by petitioning Congress for the right of way.[13] Gaining approval, Coolin announced that the Spokane firm of Grant Smith and Company would spend one million dollars on construction of the Panhandle Electric Railroad in the next year. "Dirt will begin to fly within two weeks," promised the *Northern Idaho News*.[14]

The economic potential of the railway increased as Coolin lined up other key elements. Anticipation of a major mining discovery fueled much of the investment excitement. "The

Priest Lake
TO HAVE A
Railroad
— AT LAST —

Smelter and sawmill now under construction.

We have the only patented ground at the gateway for a town platted. Fine water front lots at a bargain for a few days. Resident lots and summer home tracts $200 and up.

There are gold, silver, copper, lead and zinc and other mineral on and near the lake, and lots of it; millions of feet of timber, principally white pine, to be manufactured into lumber, shingles, etc., and other resources that go to make a good live town. The lake is 27 miles long and the prettiest thing on the map. Fish and game of all kinds.

Make arrangements to go Sunday.

For further information see

VAN DEVER & WOODWORTH, 110 Wall St.

This October 1909 newspaper ad announced a railroad to Priest Lake. When Coolin's Panhandle Electric Railway failed to begin construction, Forest Service officials used his engineering report to entice Great Northern Railway officials. They estimated a railroad could be built for $23,000 per mile along with the roundhouse, water tanks, and rolling stock. Two steam-driven Baldwin locomotives would cost only sixty-one dollars a day to operate. *Spokane Daily Chronicle*

Continental and other mines in that country already beyond the prospect stage [are] only awaiting the advent of the railroad to prove that the mineral deposits in this country will be a close second to the Coeur d'Alene's."[15] Promises of logging, agriculture, and even tourism lured shareholders. The line would tap "a country rich in timber and mineral resources and ring into easy communication with the outside world one of the most picturesque lakes." Coolin was said to be considering offers for his approved right of way. "The Great Northern, the Spokane International, and the Chicago, Milwaukee railway companies are all attempting to secure control for the project line from Priest River."[16]

"Preparing to Put on Metropolitan Clothes"

As the project advanced, Andy Coolin replaced his earlier vision of a resort community with an industrial, metropolitan hub. The Panhandle Electric Railway promised to transform the village of Coolin into the distribution and transportation center for the economic growth that would consume the Priest Lake area. His former homestead "would be the most active place in the Northwest" when he built the railroad, a sawmill, and a smelter.[17]

Coolin announced the construction of a shingle mill, followed by the installation of a lumber mill. He sought to rival the Dalkena and Humbird mills, regional giants that dominated the Pend Oreille River valley. He publicized, "The Idaho Copper Company was clearing for a smelter in anticipation of the railroad."[18] The Forest Service promised new wharves so Coolin talked about a fleet of steamboats to support the mills and smelter, moving ore and timber down lake.

"Coolin is preparing to put on metropolitan clothes," declared the *Spokane Chronicle* in 1910. The sleepy stagecoach stop seemed headed in such a direction.[19] Andy Coolin cleared much of the town site and encouraged land sales, promising "lots will double in value before the end of this season." Former prospector Al Pelky refurbished the Northern Inn, added a café and planned grounds dotted with small bungalows. William Jascott bought

a lot to build a barber shop and cigar store but in the meantime set up business at the Northern Inn. Down the hill at the Idaho Inn, Ida Handy doubled her capacity with an addition that was "first class in every particular." Near the steamboat dock, homesteader Harold Warren and his partner Clarence Burch opened a store to rival Leonard Paul's. The school moved from Camp Sherwood to just north of Coolin to accommodate new families. Coolin even announced a bank for the village.[20]

Coolin's proposed developments began to transform the bay, though not at the scale he intimated. The government-backed wharves turned out to be a narrow dock for the Forest Service boats. A sawmill began operations at the foot of the bay but under the direction of Art Marston its modest machinery only seasonally produced rough-cut boards. Coolin assured

Spokane businessman Joseph Slee organized the Priest Lake Navigation Company by 1896. He brought the steamboat *Kaniksu*, shown here, to the lake on a lumber wagon and began operating a boat livery in Coolin from April to October each year. After his son Walter contracted polio during the Spanish American War, the boat was outfitted so he could pilot it with the assistance of a fireman. As business on the lake grew, they built a larger steamer, the *W. W. Slee*. Priest Lake Museum

backers that "large passenger and freight steamers, which are now under construction, will ply the lake in all directions."[21] The reality was more modest. Joseph Slee expanded his fleet with the thirty-five-foot *W. W. Slee*, named for his son, Walter, captain of the ship.

Coolin envisioned "a large number of the best people of Idaho and Washington and several Eastern cities" enjoying the lake's resorts but accommodations remained small and primitive even by Northwest standards. His Priest Lake ads, full of potential, were juxtaposed in the newspapers with articles about the flourishing resorts near Spokane. One ad promised, the "links at Hayden Lake are in fine shape. The resorts never prettier and the trains leave from Spokane four times a day."[22]

Forest Service to the Rescue

No dirt flew for the Panhandle Electric Railway Company in 1910 or 1911 in spite of Andy Coolin's frenetic efforts. His prospects brightened in 1912 when he gained a powerful ally in William B. Greeley, the Forest Service's assistant forester. While Northern District forester, Greeley had secured the project's right of way and now, as second in command in Washington, D.C., he renewed his energies to see the Priest Lake railroad built. His boss, forester Henry Graves, aggressively supported building logging railroads in order to open up timber sales in remote national forests.[23] Greeley believed the railroad crucial for opening the vast Kaniksu National Forest to logging and hoped to entice the Great Northern Railway to build the Priest Lake spur. Under the Forest Service plan, the Panhandle Electric Railway Company would lose its right of way and the Outlet would now serve as the northern terminus. Coolin still stood to gain as the largest landholder on the bay and he confidentially provided Greeley with his detailed engineering report.[24]

Greeley traveled to St. Paul, Minnesota, to discuss the Priest Lake line with Great Northern's president Carl Gray and board chairman Louis D. Hill.[25] Meanwhile, district forester Ferdinand A. Silcox attempted to coax the railway's assistant to the president, Luthene Gilman, in Seattle. The men discussed government plans to soon open huge blocks of timber for sale near the lake. They suggested an excellent mill site at the southern end of Priest Lake, promising forests that could supply "better than seventy million [feet] a year for at least twenty years. After that period of growth the younger timber could be counted on for a continuous and perpetual supply."[26] The agency extolled the agricultural value of the region, especially after opening the logged off land.

Greeley and Silcox presented the district engineer's revamped version of Coolin's plan. Greeley reported he "had a very satisfactory conference in St. Paul. The construction of the spur was something which the Great Northern has had in mind and that the matter would be carefully reconsidered in light of the proposed development of the valley in connection with timber sales and the opening of agricultural land by the Forest Service."[27]

In Seattle, Silcox's discussions with Gilman proved less satisfactory. Gilman served as company representative to a number of subsidiary short lines. He understood the balance between remote pockets of ore or timber and the cost of transportation. Silcox admitted mining at Priest Lake remained fruitless. The Continental Mine, the one productive mine, "at the present time considerable [road] work has already been done on an outlet to Port Hill," a route that bypassed the lake.

Silcox also revealed the recent success of log drives further and further up the Priest River. It now seemed plausible timbermen could soon float logs all the way from the lake to the Pend Oreille River. He reported, "Mr. Gilman was not inclined to be enthusiastic about the proposition, feeling that the water competition would make it exceedingly questionable whether or not the railroad in there would pay." Gilman informed Silcox "the matter had been up for consideration a number of times" but the ability to drive the logs "made him hesitate to put up any great amount of money for the construction of a road at Priest Lake." After the meetings, weeks went by with no word from the Great Northern. When pressed for a response in February 1913, President Gray stalled Silcox, "We are still considering the matter…no definite determination has been reached."[28]

Meanwhile, Andy Coolin leveraged his Priest Lake homestead land to keep the railway project viable. He traveled to California and Arizona in attempts to raise quick money while dodging rumors that suggested he was no more than a swindler. He assured Priest River backer C. W. Beardmore, "I have the right men this time." When it turned out that his statements lacked truth, Coolin promised Beardmore: "My pile will be spent at Priest Lake where I will never leave again if I get back safe." Eventually, he returned to the lake, though unable to cover his debts. Andy Coolin's dreams of a metropolitan hub ended when the sheriff sold his remaining homestead land on the steps of the Bonner County Courthouse in Sandpoint in 1914.[29]

The next month the remaining directors of the Panhandle Electric Railway and Power Company held their annual meeting in Spokane. Their assets now consisted only of the power plant site on the Priest River. Their plans to build a dam, construct a canal, and then charge for every log sent down the river dragged on for years. Finally, in 1928, an older and wiser Thomas Payne took legal action, alleging fraud in the failure to develop a power project on the Priest River. Even as late as 1931, disgruntled Panhandle Electric Railway stockholders sued, claiming the contractor violated his agreement by failing to construct the dam.[30] The Washington State Supreme Court dismissed the suit.

The village of Coolin, with no railroad, fell back into slow growth, dependent on summer vacationers and servicing activities around the lake. Art Marston's modest sawmill was all that remained of Andy Coolin's industrial vision. Without the promise of the railroad, Warren and Burch ceded the store business to Leonard Paul. Reeder Bay homesteader Bert Winslow bought out Slee's Marina. The Northern Inn exhausted a number of owners before Ida Handy took over.

Andy Coolin moved across the lake to the Outlet after losing all his property in his namesake town site. He lived in a log cabin with his young son Stewart. He spent much of his next fifteen years unsuccessfully pursing one scheme after another at Priest Lake, most involving mining. He often vexed his old allies at the Forest Service. They suspected him of salting mines or trying to make mineral claims on summer home sites. Andrew Coolin died broke in a Spokane hotel for workmen in 1936.[31] His dreams of an industrial town at the south end of Priest Lake never came to fruition.

Spokane photographer Frank Palmer captured the village of Coolin in 1910. On the waterfront from the left are the Idaho Inn, the *Kaniksu* at Slee's dock, the false front of the Warren and Burch store, the rounded roof of Clarence Burch's boathouse, the swamped steamer the *Banshee*, and the Forest Service dock including the boathouse for the *Firefly*. *Frank Palmer, Northwest Museum of Arts and Culture*

Detail: The Warren and Burch Store.

Detail: The Northern Inn, the Coolin ranger Station, and the swamped *Banshee*.

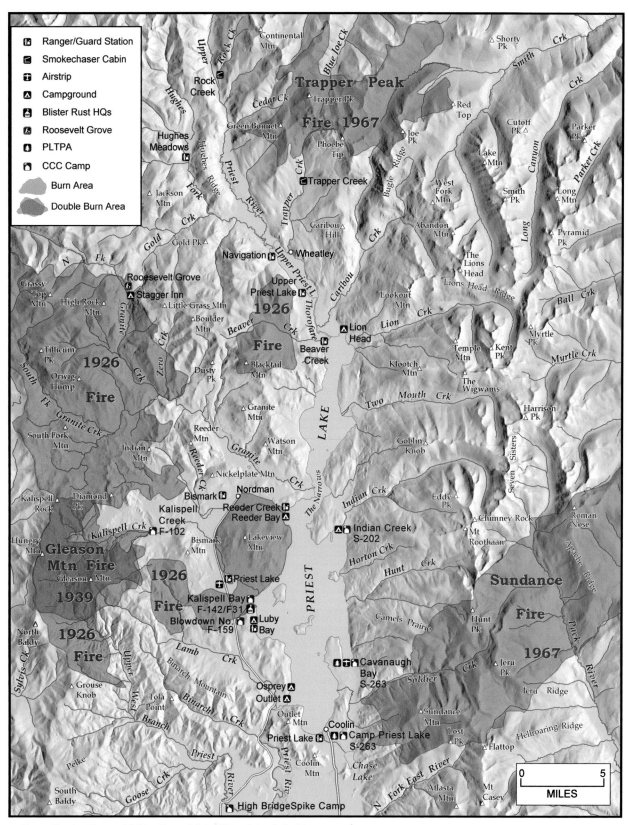

Legend:
- Ranger/Guard Station
- Smokechaser Cabin
- Airstrip
- Campground
- Blister Rust HQs
- Roosevelt Grove
- PLTPA
- CCC Camp
- Burn Area
- Double Burn Area

Continental Mtn

Upper Rock Ck

Blue Joe Ck

Shorty Pk

Smith Crk

Rock Creek

Cedar Ck

Trapper Peak

Trapper Pk

Fire 1967

Red Top

Hughes

Green Bonnet Mtn

Phoebe Tip

Joe Pk

Cutoff Pk

Parker Pk

Hughes Meadows

Priest River

Hughes Ridge

Trapper Creek

Bugle Ridge

Lake Mtn

Parker Crk

Long Canyon

Jackson Mtn

Trapper Crk

West Fork Mtn

Smith Pk

Long Mtn

Gold Crk

Caribou Hill

Abandon Mtn

Pyramid Pk

Gold Pk

Navigation

Wheatley

Upper Priest L

Caribou Crk

The Lions Head

Ball Crk

Roosevelt Grove

Stagger Inn

Upper Priest Lake

1926

Lookout Mtn

Lions Head Ridge

Grassy Top Mtn

Little Grass Mtn

Boulder Mtn

Beaver

Crk

Thorofare

Lion Head

Lion Crk

Myrtle Pk

High Rock Mtn

Fire

Beaver Creek

Klootch Mtn

Temple Mtn

Kent Pk

Myrtle Crk

Tillicum Pk

1926

Zero Crk

Dusty Pk

Blacktail Mtn

The Wigwams

Orwig Hump

Fire

Granite Crk

Granite Mtn

LAKE

Harrison Pk

South Fork Mtn

Reeder Mtn

Watson Mtn

Goblin Knob

Seven Sisters

South Fk

Indian Mtn

Granite Crk

Kalispell Rock

Diamond Pk

Nickelplate Mtn

Nordman

Indian Crk

Eddy Pk

Chimney Rock

Roman Nose

Bismark

Reeder Ck

Reeder Creek

Reeder Bay

The Narrows

Mt Roothaan

Kalispell Creek

F-102

Bismark Mtn

Lakeview Mtn

Indian Creek S-202

Hungry Mtn

Kalispell Crk

Gleason Mtn Fire

Horton Crk

Hunt Crk

Sundance

Gleason Mtn

1926

PRIEST

Camels Prairie

Hunt Pk

Fire 1967

1939

Fire

Priest Lake

Apache Ridge

North Baldy

1926

Kalispell Bay F-142/F31

Jeru Pk

Fire

Blowdown No. F-159

Luby Bay

Soldier Crk

Jeru Ridge

Sylvis Ck

Grouse Knob

Lamb Crk

Binarch Mountain

Cavanaugh Bay S-263

Pack River

Upper West Branch

Tola Point

Binarch

Osprey

Outlet

Hellroaring Ridge

Priest River

Outlet Mtn

Coolin

Sundance Mtn

Lost Pk

Pelke

Priest Riv

Priest Lake

Camp Priest Lake S-263

Flattop

South Baldy

Goose Crk

Coolin Mtn

Chase Lake

Atlasta Mtn

Mt Casey

High Bridge Spike Camp

N. Fork East River

0   5
MILES

Forest Service Sites and Major Fires. *Sylvie White, Priest Lake Museum*

Fred Williamson, shown here with Claire Luby, manned the Luby Bay Guard Station during the summers. *Priest Lake Museum*

At first, lookouts consisted of crude platforms on medium-sized peaks like the one at Kaniksu Mountain shown here. A nearby cabin provided shelter for the seasonal spotter who often had to hike between several sites every day. *Weber Album, Priest Lake Museum*

Cougar Gus Johnson, shown here at the right, was one of the local smokechasers with knowledge of the North Idaho woods. *Weber Album, Priest Lake Museum*

Love Letters from a Lookout

William A. Lipscomb wrote letters to his future wife Eleanor M. Husbands during the summer of 1932 while manning lookout towers northwest of Upper Priest Lake. The often lonely Lipscomb shared the challenges he faced working for the Forest Service.

Hughes Meadows, July 13, 1932

I am writing from Hughes Meadows, that beautiful little spot set in the heart of Northern Idaho mountains, one thousand acres of meadowland, ladies and gentlemen, all untouched by plow, disc, or spade. One thousand acres of the finest, richest, blackest, most fertile soil that ever man set eyes on, and now going to the highest bidder. I am staying at the Meadows because this is an intermediary point. I can run three and one half miles up hill to the west and reach Jackson, trot down and run one and seven tenths miles up hill to the east and I am on Hughes Ridge. Since the last period I have killed about seven hundred mosquitoes and have made a good start on another hundred.

Jackson Peak, July 18, 1932

Having nothing else to do, I re-read your letters the other night. And being alone I read them aloud. Either you are a very clever humorist or else the high altitude and loneliness have combined to unbalance my mental equilibrium because I was able to get a great kick and many laughs from re-reading them.

I ordered some grub about ten days ago which was to be delivered the middle of last week, but the pack string never showed up. Now the packer is engaged in packing building materials up to one of the peaks on which they plan to build a new cookout house so it is doubtful if he will be here this month. I have plenty of food to do me for another month but it is getting to be too much like hash every day. All I have left is carrots, spinach, stringbeans, corn, roast beef and ham. Oh, and about a dozen cans of mixed fruit.

Jackson Peak, August 12, 1932

I reported three fires and then was ordered to go to one of them (of course the one farthest

William A. Lipscomb is shown here in a lookout tower northwest of Upper Priest Lake. His telephone is behind him and to the left is the Osborne Fire Finder that allowed him to pinpoint the location of the fire. *Priest Lake Museum*

away). I grabbed my pack and away I went; two miles by trail and one mile through the thickest snowbrush I ever saw. We worked on the fire all night and had it out by 10:30 the next morning. Since I have had a recent experience at firefighting, I begin to doubt that I would have made a good smoke chaser. Really, it is the hardest work I have ever done.

I had to take a cut [in pay] at the beginning of the season, and now I am one of the two lowest paid men in the district. Furthermore, I have worked in this district longer than anyone (including the ranger); my area is the most hazardous fire district of the Kaniksu; I have been first to report fires, more than all the other lookouts together; three-fourths of the fires this season have been in my area. Next year I suppose they'll have us working for our board too. Just to make matters worse, the fellows at Beaver Creek called us and told us they were going to Coolin to the dance.

August 30, 1932

Imagine my astonishment to wake up yesterday morning and find that it was snowing! "And that ain't all," it continued to snow until 2 p.m. Then the snow turned to rain and kept up most of the night. Talk about cold! Burrr! I nearly froze night before last.

—William A. Lipscomb letters, 1932, Priest Lake Museum

Lookouts conveyed the locations of fires to smokechasers stationed in log cabins on key watersheds between the lake and the mountain peaks. Assistant regional forester Elers Koch reported, "The men I saw in the Coolin district area are examples that Kaniksu has a strong smokechaser personnel. These men were all woodsmen. The three I saw trap in the winter and work for the service in the summer."[14] The smokechasers roamed their sections equipped with detachable handle shovels, axes, and three days of rations. They carried topographic maps that showed telephone lines and tool caches, but the men mostly relied on their own knowledge of the area.

Smokechasers like Cougar Gus Johnson worked out of cabins between the lookouts and the lake. These were often local men familiar with the woods who could quickly locate the fires. A ranger remarked, "Cougar Gus Johnson can find his way…however, for the man not thoroughly familiar with the country this is impossible."[15]

Guard stations around the lake served as part of a network to support fire prevention and called the Coolin Ranger Station at any sign of fire. At the Luby Bay Guard station, each Tuesday Fred Williamson "made the twenty-mile fire patrol through the southern part of his district,

and Thursdays he made a twenty-mile forest patrol through the northern part. On the other days of the week he would walk up Lookout Trail each morning to two rocky promontories on a ridge at the south end of the bay and if it were hot day, again in the afternoon."[16]

By the first of October, men packed out from the lookouts, leaving only blankets and canned goods.[17] They shut down Beaver Creek Ranger Station for the season and neighbor Elmer Berg kept the snow off the roofs. The seasonal personnel went back to their winter jobs. Jim Ward was once again by himself, left to manage the district until the next summer.

IDAHO IDEA: PRIEST LAKE TIMBER PROTECTIVE ASSOCIATION

Protecting the forests on the east side of Priest Lake became problematic after the state of Idaho finally received title to their "endowment lands" in 1917. Most states harvested timber from their school lands and then sold the "cutover" land for farming.[18] But in Idaho the forests themselves generated funds for the educational coffers so it was financially beneficial to retain the land. Along with the state land, a number of timber companies also owned east side tracts.

A decade earlier, Idaho lumbermen pioneered the timber protective associations. These

The *Kaniksu* serviced the roadless Beaver Creek Ranger station, towing barges of supplies, men, and pack strings. Rum runners originally operated the sleek launch on Puget Sound until the Coast Guard confiscated it. The Forest Service acquired the boat and shipped it to Priest Lake where it served until 1948. Every fall, it took two days to winch up the *Kaniksu* out of the water for the winter. *Ryder Chronic, Weber Album, Priest Lake Museum*

volunteer organizations cooperatively managed lands owned by the state and private businesses. The approach was "so novel, it became known as the 'Idaho idea.'" Chief forester William Greeley asserted the associations probably "exerted more influence on forestry in this country than any other except the establishment of the national forest administration."[19] He argued that fires did not respect boundaries so it was wise for the federal and state governments to collaborate with timber companies. Initially, Priest Lake land fell under the Pend Oreille Timber Protective Association. However, when the Diamond Match Company bought more than twenty-five thousands acres from the state in 1920, they orchestrated the creation of the Priest Lake Timber Protective Association (PLTPA) the following year.[20]

Members financed the PLTPA with annual assessments based on acreage and the expenses incurred during each season. The state held 90 percent of the Priest Lake land, about two hundred thousand acres. Next largest was Diamond Match with twenty-five thousand acres. Over

The Priest Lake Timber Protective Association was established in 1921 to cooperatively manage state school lands and private forests on the lake's east side. The organization acquired the launch, *Honeymoon*, from bankrupt movie star Nell Shipman in 1924 and built a boathouse for it in Coolin. *Priest Lake Museum*

the years others—including Dalkena, Humbird, Schaefer-Hitchcock, and the Clearwater timber companies—owned several thousand acres each. The Northern Pacific Railway held its three thousand acres for most of the PLTPA existence.[21]

Traditionally, timber companies preferred to "cut and run" rather than pay taxes on land that would not produce another crop for decades. The government tried to encourage companies to hold on to the land and harvest the trees methodically by offering money. Congress allocated funds through the Forest Service under the Weeks Act of 1911 and expanded it with the Clarke-McNary Act of 1924. The agency in turn granted the money to the state of Idaho to support fire control with a state match of funds. The year the PLTPA formed, Congress substantially increased the Weeks Act allotments. The association received $2,308 from the Weeks Law in 1923. During the same period Diamond Match contributed $997.[22]

Ben Bush headed up the newly formed PLTPA in 1921 and promptly contracted with the Forest Service to provide fire protection. It fell to district ranger Jim Ward to develop a workable relationship with the association. For him it proved to be "one of the most difficult and vexing problems on the Priest Lake district since two sets of accounts and records are necessary and confusion is almost inevitable with equipment and supplies handled by two sets of temporary men."[23]

The ranks of seasonal workers formed a porous relationship between the Forest Service and the PLTPA. Local residents Elmer Berg and Pete Chase worked for both agencies, providing "spring protection" and in the fall laying telephone lines.[24] During their first year, the association focused on stringing telephone lines, manned two lookouts and cleared old trails, but did not expand the network it inherited from the Forest Service.

The PLTPA experienced few fires in their first several years of operation. However in 1924, fires on Caribou, Bear, Lion, and Two

Jim Ward was the face of the Forest Service at Priest Lake from 1916 until 1938. He spent much of his career at the Coolin Ranger Station where Hank Peterson remembered him as "the most sincere, conscientious and honest man I have ever known." *Priest Lake Museum*

Mouth Creeks illustrated their critical lack of resources, especially north of the Priest Lake narrows. In response the next year they built lookouts on Hunt and Lookout Mountains along with a guard station at Two Mouth Creek.[25]

"I CAN STILL RECAPTURE THE TERROR"

Early in the summer of 1926 the Priest River Experiment Station cautioned "unusual conditions at this season of the year warrant unusual attention to the fire problem." By the end of April, twenty-three fires already burned on the Kaniksu because of sparse snowfall, light spring rains, and low humidity. A dry thunderstorm swept through on July 5 sparking sixty-five fires around the lake. Crews managed to hold the blazes. Clarence Strong, after fighting fires near Lionhead for four days, lamented, "We were all so exhausted by the time we had that fire under control that we could barely muster enough strength to drag ourselves back to camp."[26]

A week later another storm broke all records. Strong recalled, "At almost any time during the entire night I could have read by the light from the lightning flashes. When daylight came there were smokes curling upward in every direction one looked. I guessed there were forty fires on the Lamb Creek drainage alone."[27] The Kaniksu National Forest's previous record from a single storm stood at a hundred and one fires, but on July 12 one hundred and fifty blazes lit up the mountains around the lake.

The Forest Service summoned all the logging crews and brought in emergency firefighters from Spokane. By the end of the week, more than twenty-five hundred men fought on the lines. They had to construct their own trails to reach the fires at Big Creek, Continental Mountain, and Kent Peak. Bismark ranger Hank Peterson recalled, "All of the camps were crying for more men, but few came. The atmosphere was so thick with smoke that lookouts were useless. Fire scouts made trips, but when they returned they did not know where they had been since visibility was almost zero."[28] Men deserted the ranks almost as quickly as the agency could recruit them.

Despite valiant efforts, fires jumped out of control and for six desperate weeks, crews fought to control the blazes. On July 18 a fire wiped out most of Nordman. It burned the post office, the Pleasant Inn, and several ranches. The *Priest River Times* reported, "Mrs. Kenyon says they have lost everything. Ole Hager's ranch is gone, and the Meyers ranch, near the Nordman school, is burned, but the schoolhouse is still safe."[29]

When the fire on Lakeview Mountain jumped the lines, vacationing families on Kalispell Bay awoke to a "great honking of horns" as an urgent warning went out. They quickly organized themselves as women filled pots and pans with heirlooms to bury in the sand. One man coordinated launching boats and getting children into lifejackets while others loaded on bags of groceries. Betty James remembered, "We kids were wildly excited. We were all going to the island." As the wind rose and the water got rough James watched. "It was very frightening to see the fire approaching, catching the wood piles and porch furniture. Some seventy years later I can still recapture the terror I felt as I watched our beloved cabin begin to burn."[30]

Jim Ward made his way south to Luby Bay to apprise families of the firefighters' efforts. He warned, "There is no certainty we can stop it. So take what you can in your boats and bury

the rest in the sand." The Lacy family dragged their mattresses, cooking utensils, canned food, and furniture in to several piles on the beach, covered it all with blankets, and piled sand on top. They headed to the Outlet and eventually escaped to Spokane. The morning after fire swept down Kalispell Bay in 1926, the sun shone, but a heavy white smoke hung in the air. Betty James recalled, "It was a devastating sight. The tall, proud chimneys and beautiful fireplaces stood ghostlike in the fog and smoke, deep in ashes." It took the ashes a week to cool enough for families to dig up their cooking pots of possessions from the sand.[31]

Ward set a backfire and managed to keep Luby Bay unscathed. Exhausted crews lost track of how many fires they put out during those chaotic days. Clarence Strong found that "the smoke pall was so heavy we never saw the sun again till rains came around the 20th of August." By that time, more than one hundred thousand acres at Priest Lake had burned.[32]

THE LUCKY STRIKE FOREST

If Priest Lake forests escaped devastation during the 1910 fire season, the summer of 1926 made up for it. Rangers with gallows humor took to calling the Kaniksu "the Lucky Strike Forest"

Fires in 1926 destroyed cabins in Kalispell Bay, much of the village of Nordman, and thousands of acres of timber. This picture was taken the year after as seasonal men camped on Kalispell Bay while planting seedlings. *Bonner County Historical Society*

after a popular cigarette brand that advertised it was toasted.[33] District ranger Fred Mottell said, "There were many bitter disappointments that came to us out of the 1926 fire season. The large acreage of land burned over will for a long time be a matter of disappointment and possibly discouragement to all of us."[34] However, the devastation failed to shake the Forest Service's belief that fires could be eliminated. They responded with plans to expand the network of trails, lookouts, phone lines, and roads to better control the fires at Priest Lake. The fires provided the Forest Service with an opportunity to transform hundreds of burnt acres into more marketable timber.

In a case of bad timing, the Diamond Match Company bought Northern Pacific Railway land in the Kalispell Creek drainage earlier in the summer of 1926. The fire damaged their newly acquired white pine stands. The Forest Service, fearful that Diamond would abandon the acreages, offered the burnt timber from adjacent public land to make it financially feasible for the company to salvage the timber.[35] That fall Diamond Match constructed a logging railroad from Kalispell Bay up to Deer Horn Creek—almost seventeen miles—to access the timber. Meanwhile Dalkena Lumber Company logged the fire-killed timber further north and dumped the logs into Granite Creek to float them down to the lake.

On the east side, the 1926 fires overwhelmed the Priest Lake Timber Protection Association. They still struggled to recover from the thirty-one fires the year before and had begun to use smokechasers along Lookout and Navigation trails. The fires doubled in 1926 and their costs jumped from $20,651 to $35,820. The Forest Service inspector monitored the association's accounts with concern. "While our cooperative work activities in the past have been handled in a most flexible manner and a very lenient interpretation given these [Weeks and McNary] Acts, there was 'borrowing.'" After the 1926 fire season, the Forest Service established limits for using federal money by the association.[36]

CREATING A VALUABLE FOREST

The following spring Carl Krueger worked for the Forest Service and found himself on a number of crews that supported the fire reclamation. First he worked with surveyors to map the burns around Priest Lake and recommend marketable species to replant. They started on Granite Creek, then moved to Zero and Gold Creeks, and ended up at Hughes Meadows. Krueger explained, "At that time the only three species of trees being produced and planted were western white pine, western yellow pine and Engelmann spruce. So on the maps we designated western yellow pine for the warm, dry sites; spruce for the wetter areas and white pine for north and east slopes and deeper spoiled areas on all exposures."[37]

After a summer of mapping, Krueger found himself on a different crew replanting the areas he just surveyed. His crew consisted of "transients recruited off Spokane's skid row and were a real bunch of characters." Snow closed the planting camp by the middle of October so Krueger moved on to seed extraction.

The Forest Service built a seed extraction plant at the Falls Ranger Station and bought white pine cones for seventy-five cents a sack. After the 1926 fires, the plant was expanded to two-and-a-half stories where, "the cones would go in one end and seeds would come out the other."[38] The seeds went to Forest Service nurseries and came back to Priest Lake as seedlings ready to plant across the burnt acres.

The Forest Service next assigned Carl Krueger to a timber stand improvement crew just south of Priest Lake. By the 1920s, the Forest Service gave up trying to get timber companies to clean up the forest floor after logging but, believing it was a crucial step toward making the forests more marketable, the agency hired men like Krueger to manage their own crews. He followed Dalkena Lumber Company loggers to "pile the brush of burning, cut small grand fir and hemlock, girdle the big ones and generally open the stand for the white pine reproduction." He stayed "right in a Dalkena Lumber Company

Locals sold white pine cones to the Forest Service's Falls Ranger Station seed extraction plant, shown here. *Weber Album, Priest Lake Museum*

camp, and as far as bunking and meals were concerned we were the same as the loggers."[39] Krueger's range of experiences illustrated the efforts of the Forest Service to remake Priest Lake forests into an efficient timber crop after the devastating fires.

Expanding the Ranger Districts

For ten years Jim Ward coordinated lake activities from the Coolin ranger station, but the 1926 fire changed his career. Now the agency separated his district into two, with the Falls Ranger Station covering areas to the south. It created a new headquarters at Bismark Meadows to oversee the entire Priest Lake region. The move came as no surprise to Ward since the state land transfer a decade earlier left the Coolin station in limbo. As early as 1913, the Forest Service planned to move operations from the east side, initially to Reeder Bay. In 1933 the agency demoted the Coolin Ranger Station and began turning it over to the Priest Lake Timber Protective Association.

The Bismark Ranger Station served as the region's headquarters for thirty-six years. The agency first identified "Swedes Meadow" as a prime location in 1906. A summer guard station was built 1909 and the next season the agency constructed a mule barn to take advantage of its open meadows. The Forest Service added a bunkhouse in 1926 just in time to accommodate crews fighting devastating August blazes. The following year it expanded with a warehouse to support the growing number of fire crews who worked out of Bismark. CCC crews built an administration building, a larger bunkhouse, a garage and shop, a new water system and latrine, and an icehouse. Operations moved in 1965 with the construction of the Priest Lake Ranger Station on Highway 57.[40]

When Bismark became a ranger station after the fires of 1926, it required a residence for the new district ranger, Clarence Sutliff. With a restricted construction budget, Sutliff had to decide between a toilet and a bathtub. He opted for the toilet so his family used an old galvanized round iron tub for bathing.[41]

The Forest Service added a bunkhouse at Bismark in 1926 just in time to accommodate crews fighting devastating August blazes. The following year it expanded with a warehouse to support the growing number of fire crews who worked out of Bismark, shown here in 1930. *Priest Lake Museum*

After Bismark became a ranger station, this home was constructed for district ranger Clarence Sutliff. *Priest Lake Museum*

Civilian Conservation Corps

The Great Depression curtailed Forest Service plans at Priest Lake until President Roosevelt established the Civilian Conservation Corps (CCC) program beginning in the summer of 1933. The CCC provided the massive labor force the agency needed to remake the nation's forests. Chief Forester F. A. Silcox also believed the infusion of labor would allow the "final assault on fire."[42] While the program failed to end fires, it did transform the character of the Forest Service nationally and at Priest Lake.

Thanks to CCC manpower, "fire towers with their little glass cubicles began sprouting out of the hilltops like toadstools."[43] By the end of the decade, the Forest Service boasted permanent structures on forty prominent points around the lake and another thirteen that could be used as emergency observation points. On the east side, the PLTPA counted eighteen structures along with four tent camps.[44] Crews working for the Forest Service and the PLTPA constructed and maintained trails to the highest points around the lake. Priest Lake now could boast of a comprehensive fire suppression infrastructure of towers, trails, and roads that would have astounded early rangers.

Ironically, changes in technology rendered many of these lookouts obsolete before they were ever used. Even by the 1920s, technology to spot fires began to change. The PLTPA first supported a regional air patrol in 1924. By 1928, Jack Yost piloted a plane out of Spokane

Pack strings provided a lifeline throughout the Priest Lake region, delivering food and supplies to keep men fed and working. Packers like Barney Stone loaded the mules to balance weights of up to a hundred and seventy pounds. They hauled everything from cook stoves to crates of eggs. Trips to the lookouts took all day, starting at seven in the morning and getting back to the corral at Beaver Creek, Coolin, or Bismark by late afternoon. Here a pack string delivers timbers for a new lookout on Camels Prairie. *Ivan Painter, Weber Album, Priest Lake Museum*

and flew over the lake during fire season looking for smoke. When he spotted a fire, he circled the Coolin ranger station and dropped a message with the location in a twelve-foot length of fire hose weighted with sand sewn into one end.[45]

A RECREATION REVOLUTION

Forest Service recreational advocate Bob Marshall worked out of the Experiment Station in 1927 and observed, "Priest Lake already was a mess, recreationally, from the mistakes in development of twenty-five years."[46] Up to that point, benign neglect might best describe the agency's approach to recreation at Priest Lake. The Forest Service's initial priorities ignored recreational activities, except for the summer residences. By 1910, however, local rangers recognized the inevitable need to serve the growing number of tourists and sportsmen who came to enjoy the lake.

A 1910 lakeshore survey identified lots deemed suitable for public campgrounds. Nine years later forest examiner C. R. Clark commented, "It is hoped that a more vigorous campaign can be launched sometime in the near future pushing the recreational possibilities of this Forest." Public pressure grew for more recreational facilities at the lake and in national forests across the west in the 1920s. People from nearby urban areas like Spokane acquired automobiles and a desire to get out of the city for the weekend. At the same time, the expanding

road system the agency constructed for firefighting also opened up the forest for vacationers. The *Spokesman-Review* encouraged, "There are scores of wonderful trips by automobile…but it is doubtful if any is more pleasant than the run to Priest Lake."[47]

In response to the expanding number of campers, the agency selected seven lakeside lots for the first designated Luby Bay Public Campground. With no national guidelines or professional planners, Priest Lake rangers created a primitive camp with garbage pits, fire containment, and forest screen between sites. The lack of planning revealed both ambivalence within the Forest Service towards its role in recreation and the lack of financial support in Congress.[48] However, arrival of the CCC program in the

Luby Bay was the first public campground established at Priest Lake. *Priest Lake Museum*

1930s revolutionized the Forest Service's recreational priorities. Crews expanded the Luby Bay campground and built new ones at Reeder Bay, the Outlet, and another one nearby named Osprey. District supervisor James Ryan supported the CCC recreational efforts at Priest Lake and predicted, "More and more people, including many from Spokane, will avail themselves of the opportunity and ease with which they may relax."[49]

Bob Marshall came back to Priest Lake in the late 1930s as the Forest Service's Chief of the Division of Recreation and Land. To his surprise, "The Kaniksu is doing a really marvelous job in bringing order out of early chaotic developments." The CCC labor and resources opened up recreation areas at Priest Lake. Its attentions to "rustic design" at the campgrounds became "just about as attractive as any I have seen in the country." He found the campground at Luby Bay greatly improved with water, fire pits, and tables. However he felt the campsites too close together and the outhouses too dark. "It should be possible to find the hole of a toilet by the sense of sight instead of having to depend on the sense of smell or touch."[50]

THE ROOSEVELT GROVE OF ANCIENT CEDARS

Forest Examiner C. R. Clark wrote in 1919 that "on the Kaniksu there are some veteran cedars that may justly share the fame and consideration that is lavished on the Redwoods in California, and in order that they may be preserved for posterity, the following recommendations to consider them for a National Monument named Roosevelt Grove of Giant Cedars." Clark felt the "nicest appearing grove" was located on the North Fork of Granite Creek.[51] While lacking official status, Clark's grove began appearing on maps. The Forest Service received formal authority to use Theodore Roosevelt's name in 1937 but there was not a consensus of monument status.

In the 1910s firefighters walked from Nordman and "after the fifteen mile hike, some of the men more or less staggered in

The Roosevelt Grove of Ancient Cedars. *Priest Lake Museum*

[to the Roosevelt Grove] and someone appropriately named the camp 'Stagger Inn.' A sign from a ration box was nailed to the tree bearing this name and remained there for several years." In 1929, the Forest Service inspector found the name Stagger Inn "very incongruous with the dignity one associates with a memorial to Theodore Roosevelt and should be changed. The idea presumes the maintenance of a certain element of dignity." However, he suggested a public campground and "possibly a gas station or lunch counter."[52] The cedar grove received official designation as a scenic area in 1943, and still includes the Stagger Inn campground.

FIGHTING BLISTER RUST

Fear grasped timbermen at Priest Lake as they came to understand the white pine forests were about to be destroyed, not by fire or overcutting but by a fungus called blister rust. Unintentionally imported into British Columbia at the turn of the century, the fungus caused blisters to form on the trunks of trees, eventually killing them. The Bureau of Entomology established an experimental blister rust camp on the Upper Priest River drainage in 1924 even before the invader crossed the border. The only defense against the diseases that threatened Priest Lake forests seemed to be eradicating all the plants in the genus *Ribes*—including wild gooseberry and the edible currants—from the woods.

Every summer from 1925 through the early 1960s, armies of young men were brought in to rid the threatened white pine forests of the plants that hosted blister rust. This 1928 crew set up camp at Big Creek under the leadership of Lee White. *Weber Album, Priest Lake Museum*

These plants hosted the fungus spores until the wind blew them to the white pine needles. The spores blew past the crews along the Canadian border and the first signs of blister rust were found two years later along Binarch Creek.

The blister rust spread rapidly, so every summer from 1925 through the early 1960s, armies of young men worked the heroic task of ridding white pine forests of the *Ribes*. Crews first used paper and then cotton rope, covered with yellow paraffin, to mark their sections and keep track of areas completed. Three or four men walked abreast looking for the host plants and worked together to dig them out.

The Office of Blister Rust Control annually operated about ten area camps with thirty young men each. They worked eight hours a day, six days a week, digging out currant bushes. Crews competed for how many plants they pulled in a week and how many sports events they won. In the evenings, the men played softball, basketball, volleyball, or horseshoes.

During the Great Depression the Forest Service worked closely with the Bureau of

Entomology to assign CCC crews to blister rust projects. By 1938, the Forest Service took over the program and used the former Kalispell Bay CCC camp for the Kaniksu National Forest Blister Rust Headquarters. They operated several boats that ferried crews and supplies around the lake to the camps for the season. After World War II, it was clear that blister rust was winning the war in spite of all the efforts. The agency began experimenting with other ways to stop the spread of the disease including spraying the trunks with antibiotics and breeding disease resistant trees.

Blister rust camps ended in the early 1960s but left an economic legacy in the region. The experience also affected hundreds of men who spent their summers digging up *Ribes*. William R. Matney claimed, "A high point of teenage years to spend time in a remote wilderness area that was Priest Lake in 1943." George Grossman asserted, "Whether or not the blister rust *Ribe* eradication program saved the white pine forest I do not know but I do know that it allowed countless numbers of boys to attend college and gain worthwhile work experience."[53]

Both Marshall and district officials expressed concerns about the relationship between the public campground and the growing number of leased summer cottage sites. They encouraged no new cabin sites north of the Luby Bay campground. "The new public camp site established is a good move…but its undesirable feature is that it lies adjacent to cottage sites."[54] By the end of the 1930s, regional officials pushed to end any expansion of summer home permits on the lakeshore, feeling that public access and conservation was more important. Marshall insisted, "The most important thing for which people come to the woods is space and that it would be tragic if any attempt were made to simulate the 100% use of some suburban lake in Minneapolis in the development of Priest Lake. Whatever lakeshore in our control not needed for public forms of recreation should be preserved to provide unoccupied territory." Even with all the improvements, Marshall in 1939 foresaw that Priest Lake had "about the toughest recreation problems."[55]

World War II Brings a New Labor Force

Crowds flocking to Priest Lake turned to a trickle with the onset of World War II. The Forest Service lost its massive CCC workforce but despite the war, the agency felt they needed to continue the fight against blister rust. The agency experimented with recruiting high school boys age sixteen and up. That ended when boys as young as thirteen signed up without being asked for the required proof of age and an affidavit from parents. "Needless to say, there were many red faces from that experiment."[56]

At the front of the boat, Italian World War II detainees Captain Alex Recagno and Dr. Cuomo from Camp 127 enjoy a day on Priest Lake. *Weber Album, Priest Lake Museum*

Helmut Pitterman made up part of the next labor force the Kaniksu National Forest sent out to tackle the blister rust. His journey to pull wild currant *Ribes* at Priest Lake began in 1942 when he joined the crew of a German merchant ship sailing from Bordeaux, France. On the way to Japan, their ship was captured by American forces in the middle of the Atlantic.[57] Pitterman, a native of Herne, Germany, was officially labeled as a detainee. Under the Geneva Convention the United States needed to provide him and other detainees living conditions similar to American soldiers. They could work at jobs that did not support the war effort, so the Forest Service now used crews of men like Pitterman in the fight against blister rust. The detainees, under the control of the immigration department, required no guards as they were not officially prisoners of war. The camps provided many of the same recreational activities enjoyed by CCC workers. Trucks brought the detainees into town weekly where the men spent their wages, often on beer. While some of the men appreciated their situation, others "refused to believe U.S. newspaper accounts of how Germany was losing the war."[58]

Pitterman and others lived in former CCC camps closer to Priest River, but moved to Kalispell Bay depending on the work

assignments. During the winter, the crews removed snags from the Gleason Mountain fire burn site and in the spring they pulled *Ribes*, Pitterman's least favorite job. He earned sixty cents an hour. He thought of Priest Lake as a special place in spite of the fact he was a detainee. It was "beautiful country, lakes, mountains, and smell the fresh air and pine tree aroma."[59]

In November 1944, the 1902D Engineer Aviation Battalion from Geiger Field, near Spokane, stormed into Priest Lake as if under combat. They bivouacked near Hanna Flats on the west side road and over the next five days built an airstrip, complete with a control tower from the trees they cut down, visible on the far right. The exercise provided training for the battalion and created an airstrip for the Forest Service that increasingly used planes for fire control. The airstrip is still in use today. *Weber Album, Priest Lake Museum*

WOMEN AND THE FOREST SERVICE

Mrs. Henry Gable spent her summer in 1912 on a houseboat when her husband manned the Reeder Creek Guard Station. *Priest Lake Museum*

Forest ranger wives often found living at Priest Lake difficult. Ranger Vernon Steward took his wife and children up to his station near Chimney Rock during the summer of 1914. The next summer he went to South Baldy, but the newspaper noted, "Mrs. Steward and children are moving and will stay with her parents." Evidently for Mrs. Steward, one summer on a mountaintop was enough.[60]

Bob Marshall observed that ranger Jim Murray's wife in 1925, "Performed all the customary unpaid offices of a ranger's wife, answering the telephone at all hours of the day and night, looking for whoever might breeze in at any hour, generally unannounced, attending to the office work, while her husband and his assistants were away fighting fire, ordering supplies for the fires, and seeing that they were delivered, and dozens of other minor but annoying jobs. When the strain ends in September rains, she quite naturally suffered a nervous breakdown for performing duties for which she never received anything but a portion of her husband's meager salary check."[61]

Hank Diener believed, "Forestry women have to be rugged. They can't be afraid of the dark, storms, animals or bugs. In the old days they had to be willing to enjoy living in difficult circumstances. They really had to be the self-sufficient type." When Diener married, his wife was not the "rugged type," so he quit the Forest Service.[62]

Chapter Eight

White Pine and Water

This is the largest belt of standing white pine in the United States if not in the world. White pine lumber is almost a thing of the past from the timber lands of the East and consumers of this must, ere long, come to North Idaho for their supply.[1]
—Northern Idaho News, *1910*

A frustrated Nelson Brown addressed the annual Forest Service ranger's meeting at Coolin in spring 1911. The men literally sat in the middle of one of the finest stands of white pine in any national forest, yet timber sales floundered. Bonner County accounted for a third of the timber cut in Northern Idaho but none of that came from the Priest Lake area. Brown blamed the area's inaccessibility and the lack of transportation but promised, "In the near future we shall be able to have some timber sales running around Priest Lake."[2]

Brown used the opportunity to inculcate the rangers on the Forest Service philosophy of managing timber as a crop in preparation for the opening of commercial logging at Priest Lake. He argued, "By a systematic scheme of forest management is meant the production of the greatest amount of the best kind of timber in the shortest length of time." At the lake this meant cutting old-growth white pine to create a more efficient second-growth crop using the European forest management model. Foresters predicted that with this management the Kaniksu National Forest could increase white pine growth from thirteen thousand board feet per acre in 1911 to sixty thousand board feet per acre in 2011. The agency first needed to dispose of the region's "over-mature and decedent bodies of timber" to manage the timber as a crop. This required vigorous timber sales.[3]

Brown cautioned foresters about setting the selling price of timber, known as the stumpage value. The agency wanted to make stumpage price attractive to the mills while keeping it competitive. Most mills located in the region along the Pend Oreille River owned their own timber and shunned the national forest, where stands were more remote and the Forest Service mandated constraints like cleaning up the slash after logging. Politically the rangers could not appear too eager to support mills like the Humbird Lumber Company in Sandpoint with ties to Lakes States syndicates. Instead they encouraged regional timber companies like the Dalkena Lumber Company north of Newport. The agency also sought to guard against over-cutting for future generations while providing a constant supply of timber to economically stabilize the region. The Forest Service at Priest Lake struggled for the next fifty years to balance the range of issues Brown addressed that morning in Coolin. Its recommendations and regulations for timber evolved over the decades and transformed both public and private land.[4]

The Lack of a Railroad

Logging at Priest Lake held great promise in spite of the lake's isolation. The first step required an economical method to get the timber to the Pend Oreille River mills. When

John Leiberg surveyed the region in 1897, he observed timbermen already experimenting with floating white pine logs down the Priest River to furnish a "sample of western white pines to lumbermen in the East."[5] He cautioned profits from Priest Lake's forests depended on getting the timber from the rugged mountains and valleys to national markets.

North Idaho experienced a timber rush in the 1900s as mills sprang up, mostly underwritten with eastern money. Profits peaked in 1906 and then tumbled. However, the rush circumvented Priest Lake as companies cut along accessible rivers, focusing on the lower Priest River. This frustrated Kaniksu National Forest Supervisor Willis "Pud" Millar. The Forest Service pressured Millar to increase timber sales to generate income and create more cutover farm land for homesteaders. The agency wanted him to expand sales along the Priest River but he warned this would devoid the area of timber within ten years. It would leave the agency "open to the most serious criticism. I can see no argument in favor of increasing the cut within the Priest River division except the argument of expediency." Millar, a Yale School of Forestry alumnus, maintained the agency should force timber companies to develop a railroad to open up Priest Lake logging by not selling them the assessable timber stands along the river. Millar ordered a six-month study of logging operations, or the lack of them, south of the lake during the summer of 1911 and proclaimed, "The only barrier to sales of timber at the lake is the fact that there is no railroad transportation."[6]

Millar's Priest Lake plan included a well-managed, sustained annual timber yield that would support two large mills indefinitely. "It is assumed that the extension of large logging operations to Priest Lake will inevitably be accompanied by the erection of mills on Priest Lake itself."[7] He acknowledged it might be possible to drive logs from the lake down the Priest River to the mill on the Pend Oreille. However, "this will never be a satisfactory method of transporting forest products from the lake and

in my opinion should not be encouraged at this present time."[8] He argued instead for his scheme to force timber companies to construct a railroad to Priest Lake.

GETTING TIMBER AROUND PRIEST LAKE

Logging at Priest Lake presented such a conundrum for the Forest Service that chief forester Henry Graves came out from Washington, D.C., in the fall of 1912 to see if Millar's arguments were valid. Graves had followed Gifford Pinchot as head of the agency two years earlier. Priest Lake timber encapsulated a crucial issue for the agency—areas rich with valuable timber stands but isolated and unsalable for lack of transportation.[9] Graves believed the stability of the Forest Service depended on greater timber sales in remote areas like Priest Lake, and could be achieved by granting long-term contracts to regional timber operators. Companies would assume the risk of building railroads to reach the inaccessible timber because the contracts guaranteed lumber for a decade or more.[10]

Second-in-command William Greeley accompanied Graves on his trip to Priest Lake. Greeley oversaw the USFS Northern Region including Priest Lake before his promotion in 1911. After the men toured with Millar, they agreed to organize sales as he suggested. They mapped areas for sale "so as to promote the construction of a permanent mainline to Priest Lake." They decided on a ten-year contract for timber sales on the Upper West Branch Priest River, just south of lake. This allowed the agency to give preference to regional mills without ties to the larger syndicates. Greeley was so confident this plan would generate a railroad, he promised another long-term contract on Kalispell Creek the next year. However he drew the line at requiring a railroad. "We did not feel…we should deprive operators of the natural competition afforded by a large, drivable stream as a check upon high freight charged by rail."[11]

The Secretary of Agriculture approved the record-breaking, long-term sales on the Lower and Upper West Branches of the Priest River on December 28, 1912. The prospectus favored bids from local operators operating medium-sized mills and who needed at least ten years to cut the timber.[12] Grave assured the Agriculture Secretary James "Tama Jim" Wilson, "I feel it desirable to encourage sales to such operators who are independent of the large lumber interests and own but small amount of timber of their own." Graves and Greeley continued to orchestrate a Priest Lake railroad as the bidding procedure commenced, even meeting with the heads of the Great Northern Railway to encourage the route.[13]

Driving Logs Down the Priest River

Ed Harris shattered Henry Graves' plans for a railroad to open up Priest Lake timber. As manager of the Dalkena Lumber Company, including a mill north of Newport, Harris offered the strongest bid on the Upper West Branch timber. Harris worked out of Spokane for a group of Midwest lumber wholesalers who created the Dalkena Timber Company in 1908 and he "made the company go."[14] The company bought out a mill at Cusick, north of Newport, Washington, on the Pend Oreille River.[15] Competitors along the river included the Fidelity Lumber Company, with a mill across the river from Newport, and the Jurgen Brothers Mill in Priest River.

Harris warned the Forest Service if his company was awarded the contact, "they were considering the possibility of driving the Priest River." Harris argued that getting logs to the mill on the Pend Oreille River by railroad would be much more expensive even after covering the construction costs. A railroad also opened up the possibility of a rival mill built on Priest Lake.[16] At the same time, Harris

knew that no one had been commercially successful at driving logs from Priest Lake down the winding river to the mills. He gambled he could do it, or rather, that his woods superintendent John Schaefer could succeed.

Getting logs down the river remained elusive. In 1903, Tony Lemley tried to send logs down river from the lake. He gave up after his bateau (a flat-bottomed boat with a shallow draft) swamped only two miles downstream from the Outlet at the Binarch Creek Rapids as the logs jammed up against the rocks. His boat joined those reported by the State Engineer in 1901: "the whitened ribs of many skiffs attested to the failure of a number of previous attempts at navigation."[17]

Dalkena won the Forest Service contract in 1913 and by the next year John Schaefer successfully drove logs from Priest Lake's Outlet down to the Pend Oreille. He supervised thirty men driving the logs down the Priest River starting in April with the spring runoff. When they hit the rapids Schaefer just used "lots of powder"—dynamite—to break up the jams. He delivered the logs to the mills after driving the river for a month and half.[18] From then until 1949 logs from Priest Lake would move down the Priest River to the mills.

Ranger Rudy Fromme took this photograph of logs ready to be driven down the lower Priest River in 1907. *U.S. Forest Service, Northern Region*

World War I brought more demand and higher prices for Priest Lake timber. Ed Harris observed, "Things are looking better in the lumber business and everybody feels better. There has been little activity in these woods for some time."[19] By 1917 thirteen logging camps operated at Priest Lake and along the Upper West Branch. Dalkena ran five camps with Humbird, and Fidelity mills ran another five. Smaller operators included Joseph Lilje and Priest River's Charlie Beardmore with two.[20] Logging at Priest Lake now became as successful as Nelson Brown predicted, even without a railroad.

After World War I, more than a dozen logging camps operated around the lake. Each winter hundreds of men worked in the woods six days a week. Sawyers used cross-cut saws, shown here, to cut down the trees. *K. D. Swan, U.S. Forest Service, Northern Region*

MONSTER LOAD

The only seasons that are left in which the timber can be cut is the fall and winter. In the fall the rainy season begins and cutting is again delayed. In winter, the heavily snow covered mountains are difficult to log. But when is the best time to do logging? The summer would be the best if the forest fires didn't occur. Fall would be next best if the rainy season didn't ruin the roads. The only season left is winter.
—C. W. Beardmore

John Specht, "a hard-bitten old German," worked as foreman for the Dalkena logging camp on the Upper West Branch just south of Priest Lake in 1914. A fierce competitor, he challenged the foreman at the neighboring Humbird Lumber Company camp to see which crew could deck the largest load on a sleigh during the season. Humbird's lumberjacks nicknamed their foreman Moonlight Joe, claiming he sent them out earlier in the morning before the sun rose and he brought them back in by moonlight. He hung lanterns up in the trees as the men loaded logs on the sleighs. Specht lost that season to Moonlight Joe, who loaded a sleigh with twenty-eight thousand board feet rather than the usual twenty-two.[21]

When warm weather broke up the sleigh road in the middle of March, Specht tried to get as much timber as possible to the river before the log drive began in April. He skidded logs directly to the river and decked them up and down the bank a half a mile deep. The Forest Service assigned scaler Clyde Webb to Specht's camp. Webb determined the number of board feet in each load of logs and reported it to the ranger in charge of timber sales.[22] Dalkena's scaler measured the same loads. Scalers were crucial to logging operations, determining what was owed to the Forest Service and what was owed to the men who labored in the woods. Specht's heroic push to deck so much timber meant Webb worked ten-hour days along the riverbank with the crew and then spent evenings adding up his records. He began to consider it might have been less rigorous to be assigned to Moonlight Joe's camp.

The men cut and cleared a road with gentle grades before winter set in to take sleighs down to the river. They returned home until cold weather set in so they could pack snow on the road. Men smoothed the surface with water tanks so the horses could effectively pull heavy sleighs down to a landing on the Priest River.[23]

Through World War II logging camps depended on horse power. This picture shows the teams required to operate just one Beardmore camp. *Priest River Museum and Timber Education Center*

Priest Lake's rugged terrain meant loggers used teams of horses to skid logs from where they were cut to sleds that hauled the loads to chutes, flumes, or railroads. The first independent contractors for the timber companies, known as gyppos, were often local men who used their own teams to skid logs. *U.S. Forest Service, Northern Region*

In 1922 John Specht boasted the largest sleigh load in the region with one hundred and forty-five logs. The *Priest River Times* reported on January 26, "Many people went out to the landing on Sunday to see this monster load and many took pictures of it." *C.W. Herr, Priest Lake Museum*

"FLUNG WITH A DIVE AND A SPLASH"

The Forest Service opened up commercial logging on Priest Lake with a sale of sixty million board feet of timber along Kalispell Bay to Dalkena, which began logging operations in 1914.[24] While John Schaefer successfully drove the Priest River he now needed to overcome the lake's problematic topography for moving logs. The broad valleys on the west side meant the streams became sluggish as they neared the lake. The easiest waterways, Kalispell Creek and the Upper Priest River, "are drivable after improvements for about nine miles each." The steep valleys on the lake's east side meant the streams "have a rapid fall, and are driveable only one to three miles up from their mouths."[25] Timbermen brought a range of logging methods from the Great Lakes states but the Priest River valley's remote white pine stands demanded men like Schaefer be resourceful applying those methods to the region's valleys, streams, and mountains.

Dalkena's sawyers cut timber near Kalispell Creek while teams skidded and stacked it up along the stream bank all winter. Crews built a splash dam in front of the decked timber before the spring runoff. When the water backed up enough to float the logs they dynamited the dam and the timber washed down to the lake. The river pigs—men who moved logs on the water—corralled the logs into booms, towed them to the Outlet, and sent them down the Priest River to the mill at Cusick. In 1916, after its success on Kalispell Bay, Dalkena pulled its steamboat *E. W. Harris* out of the Pend Oreille River and put it on runners to form a sled. Teamsters then dragged the sizeable steamer up to Priest Lake when the ground froze and enough snow fell.[26]

Dalkena cut all the easily accessible white pine on Kalispell Creek by 1918, which forced the company to construct a flume to reach the timber further back from the stream. That year the company contracted with Fred Schneider's mill on Kalispell Bay to cut their unmarketable logs into lumber for the flume bed. Timber companies at Priest Lake built flumes sparingly because they were so expensive.[27] It took a quarter-million feet of lumber to build each mile of the flume in addition to the foundation timbers to support it. Dalkena also needed to build a dam at the top of the flume to store water overnight to supplement the stream's flow during the day.

When crews finished the flume in June they released the water "full blast and great monarchs of the forest came tearing and plunging down the roaring flume to be flung with a dive and a splash into the boom."[28] Otto Schneider piloted the *E. W. Harris* to keep the logs moving into the boom as they hit the lake.

Diamond Match flume on Big Creek in 1923. *Priest Lake Museum*

In 1914 Priest River timberman Charles Beardmore constructed a long, narrow bunkhouse for a hundred men, seen on the right, which inspired the name "Tunnel Camp." *Priest Lake Museum*

One Hundred and Fifteen Days without a Bath

Bill Whetsler dropped out of high school at fifteen and got a job as a grease monkey at Charlie Beardmore's logging camp south of Priest Lake in 1914. The Forest Service favored local, medium-sized operators like Beardmore and the agency awarded him white pine stumpage around the lake. Whetsler was a minority at the camp, not because of his age but he was a local boy. Most lumberjacks working at Priest Lake migrated from the Great Lakes states timber industry. Emigrants made up much of the camp crew with "Scandinavians and French-Canadians well represented." Some men labored a few days while others worked all winter in the same camp and stayed to "take in the drive." On average they earned forty dollars a month after board.[29] The men, mostly single, moved from camp to camp carrying their bedding on their backs along with their own axe heads.

Charles Beardmore's long, narrow bunkhouse housed 108 men. The lumberjacks

christened it Tunnel Camp since it had only one window at each end. Bill Whetsler remembered, "We slept two men together and two beds high. There was just a continuous row of beds with a board in between to divide each bed. We had to go out to the barn and get an armful of hay. Then we would use the hay as our mattress." Forest Service official Elers Koch said, "Logging is at best a ruthless and violent business." For him the logging camps stood as the most graphic evidence, which were "temporary and purely utilitarian, and always a scar in the midst of the forest, leaving apparent destruction behind them."[30]

Six days a week men pulled cross-cut saws, skidded logs along the frozen ground, and decked timber in the snow and mud. After nightfall, lumberjacks returned to the cold bunkhouses. They hung their wet socks, pants, coats, and underwear on wires stretched across the stoves. Most wore woolen two-piece underwear winter and summer. Beardmore provided washtubs for the men to clean their clothes on Sundays. They built fires under the tubs and boiled their clothes. Personal hygiene at the Tunnel Camp bunkhouse was limited to a wooden trough in one corner that served as the wash-up area. Whetsler worked one hundred and fifteen days "without ever having taken a bath. I just changed clothes once a week."[31] Most of the other hundred men at Tunnel Camp followed the same regimen.

Forester Elers Koch found the camps bleak, observing, "The lumberjack is rarely a light-hearted individual, but inclined to be silent if not morose."[32] Forest Service eccentric Robert "Bob" Marshall decided when he worked at the Priest River Experiment Station to study the lumberjack lifestyle to dispel romantic myths and "a great many fabulous fancies." He observed the lumberjack's language and eating habits at camps around Priest Lake. Marshall documented the most popular topics of conversations: "pornographic stories, experiences and theories." The loggers' laced about a quarter of their conversations with words "unmentionable

at church sociables" and topics of "sexual import and—excretory in nature."[33]

"Feed 'em, Feed 'em Lots"

Beardmore's Tunnel Camp bunkhouse became notorious for its size, but similar conditions could be found at all the neighboring camps. The crew tolerated conditions until Beardmore ignored the cardinal rule of logging camps. He employed a mediocre cook. The "jacks" remedied the situation themselves. They visited the cookhouse with a long rope. "We told the cook that if he was there for breakfast, we were going to hang him to the rafters. He wasn't there next morning."[34] Beardmore quickly found a better cook.

Mrs. E. M. Butler cooked for Fred Crowder's logging camp at Priest Lake for seven years starting in 1918. Crowder told her "I'll get anything you ask for, Mrs. Butler. Order it and I'll get it in the house. Feed 'em, feed 'em lots." She baked all the bread, cookies, pies, and doughnuts the crew consumed. When half-sides of beef and pork

This 1908 Beardmore summer dining tent could seat fifty men. *Bonner County Historical Society*

arrived at camp, Butler herself cut them up. With no refrigeration, or even ice, she kept the meat in a shaded shed with screens to keep the flies out. Butler added, "Of course a half of beef won't last very long with fifty men."[35]

Logging camps restricted talking during meals. The lumberjacks gulped their enormous meals down and, on average, finished dinner in thirteen minutes during a "mad dash for sustenance." Their knives served as harpoons for the slices of bread piled upon the table. They slurped soup with the "average auditory range" of nine feet. While void of conversation, the dining hall still reverberated with sound.[36]

Men entertained themselves with music and singing in the evenings. "A lot of times they just lazed around and told stories to one another."[37] Occasionally special events broke up the winter monotony. The Dalkena camp in Squaw Valley held a "hard-time dance" in January 1922. A sleigh load of loggers from the neighboring Beardmore camp joined them along with the "home folk. There was a splendid crowd, good music and plenty of good eats." The end of the season often brought celebrations and an opportunity to settle rivalries. Coolin held a three-day celebration in 1930 when logging camps held contests of skill and "pitted their finest river pigs. Many have driven Wisconsin and Michigan streams over forty years ago and are still catty on a log."[38]

With camps operating seasonally around the lake, logging companies often moved facilities

Sam Byars towed the Schaefer-Hitchcock Company's cook house and houseboat up lake, shown here. *University of Idaho, Simpson Collection*

from camp to camp by water. In 1923, the *W. W. Slee* moved Diamond Match's floating kitchen from their winter camp at Caribou Creek to the Outlet for the drive down the Priest River.[39] Some weeks later, the steamboat towed it back up lake to the summer camp at Huckleberry Bay.

"Outrages of Capitalism"

The men at Tunnel Camp accepted the rough conditions until April 1917. They grew angry after Beardmore dismissed a lumberjack with ties to the Industrial Workers of the World (IWW), known as the Wobblies. Bill Whetsler recalled, "About that time the Wobbly union got started, they were pulling for real beds and shorter hours."[40] A month earlier the IWW organized the Lumber Workers' Industrial Union No. 500 in Spokane. The Wobblies in the Priest Lake region demanded an eight-hour day and a minimum wage of sixty dollars a month with free board. They pushed for wholesome food, sanitary sleeping quarters with not more than twelve men per bunkhouse, free hospital service, pay twice a month, and no discrimination against members of the IWW.[41] Leaders espoused a socialist message and embraced sabotage as a means to an end. Most lumberjacks expressed little interest in IWW politics but they often became frustrated by the "outrages of capitalism."[42] The campaign to end the dreadful conditions in the camps and mills sparked action from the loggers across the Idaho panhandle including the hundred at Beardmore's camp who went out on strike. He replaced them in two days with men from Spokane's skid row.[43]

Paranoid reactions to IWW activity spread as local businessmen organized the Priest River Home Guard to "see that the laws are enforced and to protect life and property during the war."[44] For the next two years, northern Idaho lumbermen joined with local and state authorities to fight against the Wobblies. They pushed to get the Idaho legislature to pass a criminal syndicalism and anti-sabotage bills.

The IWW pushed timbermen to improve the traditional logging culture transplanted to Northern Idaho from the Great Lakes states. Those familiar with the conditions agreed the arcane system needed to be modernized.[45] Priest Lake ranger Hank Peterson conceded, "Some were radicals but most were only trying to better their working conditions. Lumberjacks joined the IWW for the simple reason that it advocated that the companies furnish bedding, mattresses, and steel cots; smaller and more sanitary bunkhouses, separate drying rooms and bath and laundry facilities."[46] Such sympathies left many uncomfortable with the criminal syndication laws applied to the striking men.

"It Was a Hard Thing to Change"

The next fall Charlie Beardmore rebuilt his Tunnel Camp on the Upper West Branch of the Priest River. The *Priest River Times* reported, "[Beardmore] has the finest camp that was ever put up in this section. Everything is up to date. He has twenty-one stoves in the camp, a drying room, bath house and shower baths at that and no upper bunks." Beardmore even added a bull cook to keep the bunkhouse clean and a fire going so it was warm when the men returned at night. He gave no credit to the Wobblies for the long overdue improvements but he met many of their demands with his new camp. Beardmore "was a good guy" according to Whetsler but the Wobblies "had to put him in his place because he would never give us nothing."[47]

In spite of Beardmore's improvements, a "Wobbly agitator succeeded in stirring up a little trouble" at the camp by February. The marshal and sheriff took him to Sandpoint "where he will answer to the charge of being a slacker" under the criminal syndicalism law. Some months later the Bonner County sheriff and the county commissioners went through the Priest Lake camps appealing to the loggers as patriots. They urged the loggers to sign an oath of allegiance to the United States and to reject the IWW.[48] They played on the patriotic fervor of war and cast the Wobblies as a national threat.

When officials found a "red card" signifying IWW membership at a camp near the lake they intimidated the lumberjack so much that he bought fifty dollars of war bonds.[49]

Timbermen increased wages to neutralize the efforts of the Wobblies but the IWW continued to interrupt Priest Lake camps through 1919. Beardmore's crew walked out that May when he fired a Wobbly. In October lumberjacks struck the nearby Humbird camp over a twenty-five cent increase in board to a dollar and a quarter. Camp operators argued it cost them a dollar thirty-five just to feed the men each day. The union brazenly set up headquarters a block off Main Street in Priest River to coordinate their efforts at the camps all the way to the lake. Whetsler recalled, "We had walk out after walk out. However, it was a hard thing to change." A bloody confrontation in Centralia, Washington, between the American Legion and the IWW "outraged" local officials who used the conflict to justify rounding up all union members.[50]

The Wobblies helped reform conditions in Priest Lake camps but they also hastened the expansion of the "gyppo," the independent logger who worked on contract. The union claimed, "The gyppo is a man who 'gyps' his fellow workers and finally himself, out of the fruits of all our organized victories in the class war." Ike Elkins defined the term for loggers as meaning, "How much you pay him to do the work and that's the fee taken by contract." Timber companies in the Inland Northwest increasingly contracted local men to handle some of the logging procedures in the woods. This piece-work system functioned well at Priest Lake and encouraged more contracts. It also meant strikes became less effective.[51] When the IWW regrouped in 1922, area lumberjacks responded less enthusiastically.[52]

Heyday of the Lumber Industry

Northern Idaho experienced the "heyday of the lumber industry in the twentieth century" during the early 1920s. Timber prices finally rose after World War I and forest product

The Elkins Brothers constructed a gas loader onto a truck with a wooden boom. They could use it to pull logs into the road and also to load the truck. *K. D. Swan, U.S. Forest Service, Northern Region*

companies began making strong profits. Expanding technology accelerated by the war began changing logging practices. Heavier trucks allowed timbermen to mix old and new strategies to get logs out of isolated patches around the lake beginning with Humbird Lumber Company during the winter of 1922 at Priest Lake. The solid rubber tires on early logging trucks chewed up dirt roads so much that the hauling was still limited to winter. Swampy areas along Granite and Lamb creeks required Dalkena crews to build pole roads for the trucks. The men laid two hewn logs side by side with long poles spiked to the inside of the inner log to serve as a guard rail.[53]

Dalkena used logging trucks instead of sleds to haul timber to Kalispell Creek for the spring drive in 1923. When the creek became too shallow in July to float the logs the men trucked them down to the lake instead. However, when the foreman became frustrated with the slow progress he reverted to traditional methods. He built a dam at the mouth of the creek "so as to float the logs in to the lake instead of having to haul them part of the way as at present."[54] Soon there were many other improvements, such as skidding with Caterpillar tractors, and using bulldozers for building roads. More mechanization, however, meant fewer jobs for the lumberjacks.

Swampy areas required crews to build pole roads for the trucks. The narrow track required one-way traffic and a skilled driver. *Priest Lake Museum*

Moving Logs from the Stump to the Sleigh Roads

Fred Forsythe came back to Priest Lake after serving in World War I but instead of rejoining the Forest Service, he signed on as the woods superintendent for Dalkena Lumber Company. He replaced John Schaefer who quit to establish his own pole company. Dalkena operated camps on private and government land around Priest Lake including on Reeder Bay where Forsythe oversaw Camp Three with seventy men in 1920.[55]

Company lumberjacks worked for Dalkena but Forsythe increasingly relied on men like Frank Sutliff, "a true prototype of the working gyppo."[56] Sutliff and other local men with teams contracted to skid logs from "stump to the sleigh roads." Sutliff used his two brothers, six horses, and a heavy-duty wagon to move logs at Reeder Creek. The independent and self-reliant nature of gyppo work fit well with the earlier patterns of crafting a living at Priest Lake. It relied on families like the Sutliffs working together and using their ingenuity in the woods.[57] It also allowed them to stay closer to home.

Four-horse teams hauled the loaded sleighs down to the landing on Reeder Bay. Crews decked logs on the frozen bay, stretching out two hundred and fifty feet on the ice. The decks soon became solid masses of logs and ice because of melting and freezing snow. In the spring Dalkena used dynamite to break up the frozen mountains of logs so they could tow them down lake in time for the "driving stage of water out over the outlet." By 1924 Dalkena towed booms from logging camps at Caribou Creek, Distillery Bay, Reeder Creek landing, and Kalispell Bay to the Outlet. In the spring, crews floated the logs about one hundred and forty miles from Priest Lake to their mill at Cusick. Dalkena built Camp Eight higher up on Reeder Creek after exhausting lower stands. The steeper terrain required a chute to get the white pine to the creek landing.[58] With the help of gravity, and at times grease, horses skidded strings of logs down the chute to Reeder Creek.

Logging companies around the lake made use of chutes because they allowed access to remote stands of white pine for a modest investment. Crews placed "logs on cross timbers and spiked them down. Then they hewed them until they are a trough or V shape." They worked on the steep terrain although they had to use horses to pull strings of logs down to the lake. Bill Whetsler worked as a grease monkey on the chute for Beardmore in 1914. "I had a

Logging companies used chutes to move cut logs from remote stands down to the lake. *Museum of Northern Idaho*

Timbermen used the larger streams to drive logs down to Priest Lake or River. Here the Beardmore sleds unloaded logs along the Upper West Branch of the Priest River waiting for the spring runoff. *K. D. Swan, U.S. Forest Service, Northern Region*

barrel of crude oil with a fire built under it to keep it hot," he recalled. "I'd take a five-gallon can and fill it about full. Then I'd use an ax handle with a piece of gunny sack tied on it for a swab. I walked up and down and greased the chute so the horses could take about twelve or fifteen logs."[59]

A FLUME OR A RAILROAD?

Fred Forsythe faced pressure from his old employer, the Forest Service. Ten years earlier he helped the agency negotiate Dalkena's recording-breaking timber sale on the Upper West Branch. Now as woods superintendent he became responsible for finishing the contract the company signed in 1913. The Forest Service grew impatient with Dalkena's continual requests for extensions and urged the company to quickly "complete the harvest of the sale."[60] Forsythe found himself with few options because years of logging on the Upper West Branch created an environmental mess that forced the company to make the sizable investment it had avoided a decade earlier. Forsythe needed to either construct a flume or a railroad to complete Dalkena's contract.

Dalkena and other timber companies brought millions of feet of logs down the Upper West Branch to the Priest River using splash dams. Crews constructed dams across

Crews constructed splash dams across the streams with slash and logs so in the spring the water would rise and float the logs, as shown here. *Red Gastineau, Weber Album, Priest Lake Museum*

After C. W. Beardmore dynamited his first dam, the rushing West Branch waters drove most of the logs toward the Priest River. This image showed logs left behind along the flooded stream bank. Area streams provided logging companies with cheap transportation but the operations took a toll on the environment. *K. D. Swan, U.S. Forest Service, Northern Region*

the streams with slash and logs so in the spring they could "build up a sizable head big enough to float logs." When the decked logs began to float, they dynamited the dam. "Where the logs stopped, another dam would be constructed. Somewhere around one per mile usually did the trick."[61] This complicated operations as Dalkena moved the camps further up the watershed, lengthening the distance to the Priest River. The Forest Service urged the company to build a flume. Instead, the company that helped to squash a railroad to Priest Lake a decade earlier decided to build the first line in the region. By 1923 the company was forced to build a six-mile logging railroad to finish their contract, and brought in a Shay locomotive from the Lima Locomotive Works in Ohio. Crews waited for snow so they could sled the thirty-six ton engine from town to the Dickensheet.[62]

Forsythe supervised construction of standard gauge railroad six miles along the Upper West Branch. He began on the Priest River just south of the Dickensheet Bridge. He engineered a route with a gentle grade and few bridges. Along the swampy areas of Big Meadow, he elevated the tracks on a low trestle. Dalkena constructed a sizeable camp at the west end of the line. Crews built twenty-five buildings

including a modest roundhouse, a light plant, a water system, a bathhouse with two showers, and a storehouse for the men's bedding. Thanks to the earlier efforts of the Wobblies, the camp consisted of six bunkhouses, with twenty men in each one. Dalkena furnished men with metal beds and linens that were cleaned regularly.[63]

Lumberjacks still worked mostly in the winter even with the railroad. Eighteen teams of horses skidded logs to cars waiting along the line. The Shay locomotive brought the timber

Dalkena ordered a Shay locomotive from the Lima Locomotive Works in Ohio and it arrived in the late fall of 1923, shown here. *Priest Lake Museum*

down to the landing a hundred feet above the Priest River. "To unload [the logs]…workers only needed to roll them off the log cars and over the edge of the bank." The railroad increased Dalkena's daily output 100 percent as crews kept "their Shay engine busy practically every hour of the day."[64] The railroad operated six years and allowed the company to finish harvesting the sale before the Great Depression. Dalkena cut two hundred and forty million board feet of white pine on the Upper West Branch over seventeen years.[65]

Diamond Match Growth

World War I embargos created a new industry for Priest Lake white pine that would come to dominate the region's economy. The government used square wooden matches imported from Europe but with the war it turned to the Diamond Match Company to furnish them instead.[66] The company obliged but faced a shortage of eastern yellow pine. It shifted to western white pine after experimenting with making the wood suitable with new methods of cutting, drying, and treating.

During the war the company used local timbermen like Charlie Beardmore to cut "planks" of white pine and ship them east to their factories. In 1919 Diamond Match changed its strategy and began moving its own facilities to the Inland Northwest instead of relying on locals to supply them with pine. The company built a factory in Spokane to process blocks of wood for matches and then quietly began buying timber claims from homesteaders at Priest Lake. Diamond's presence became evident when it acquired twenty-five thousand acres from the state of Idaho on the east side of Priest Lake in 1920 and the next year bought another fourteen thousand acres from the Northern Pacific Railroad.[67] At the same time the Forest Service softened its policy toward awarding sales to large eastern companies and began accepting the match company's bids at Priest Lake. The agency lamented the waste of lumber in the manufacturing of match stock but conceded the steady payroll for local communities the company provided made up for the "poor utilization."[68]

Diamond Match became one of the largest timber owners in the Priest Lake area in just three years. Regional companies who sold white pine to Diamond in the past now found themselves in competition with the match giant as it began operating its own mills and camps. E. C. "Charlie" Olson managed the three large camps Diamond operated at Priest Lake most seasons. He cut the highest grade of white pine and floated it down to mills on the Pend Oreille River. The mills sawed the timber into planks, seasoned them for two years, and sent them on to the match block factory in Spokane. There the planks were reduced to blocks the length of matches, cured, and shipped to the eastern factories to be made into matches.[69]

Diamond Match "vaulted to a major place in the Inland Empire's lumber business" when it bought Northern Pacific Railway timber in the Kalispell Creek drainage in 1926.[70] A few months later the expansive sale seemed a poor gamble when fierce fire swept through their newly acquired forests. The Forest Service offered stumpage on its adjoining lands to encourage the company to salvage the white pine instead of abandoning it.

After the fires of 1926, Diamond Match Company subcontracted the Kalispell salvage job to Charlie Olson. He decided to construct a logging railroad to reach the upper areas of the drainage, almost seventeen miles from the lake. He hired crews of "Swedish and White Russians" to lay the narrow gauge tracks and brought in modern equipment designed to mechanize skidding and loading logs.

The Forest Service prohibited steam engines on public land so the company bought two eighteen-ton Plymouth gasoline mechanical locomotives. The engines weighed about half of what a steam engine would and this made it easier to transport them from Priest River on sleds over late winter snow drawn by tractors.[71] At Coolin they loaded the locomotives, cars, and

One of the two Plymouth gasoline mechanical locomotives used by Diamond Match Company on Kalispell Bay. *A. Haines, Priest Lake Museum*

railroad or the chutes and gyppos negotiated a price to cut and skid the timber. The company contracted for the gyppos' horses but furnished the tools. Some crews used a Holt Caterpillar to skid logs from the stump to chutes. Olson also hired gyppos with draft horses to skid the logs down the chutes to the spur lines of the railroad. The Forest Service followed behind crews providing the manpower to clear the brush. "These were mostly older men who still could handle the work. Lumberjacks in those days scorned that type of work."[72] The Diamond Match completed the sale in 1930 and hauled all the equipment out by the next summer.

The Great Depression

The Great Depression hit just as Dalkena and Diamond finished railroad logging operations on the Upper West Branch and Kalispell Creek. Ironically the successful harvests of both companies contributed to overproduction of cut timber and prices begin dropping in 1926. In 1925 companies cut 236 million board feet at Priest Lake and the surrounding region. Seven years later they only cut 11 million board feet. Priest Lake

rails on barges and towed them to Kalispell Bay. After the company completed the sale in 1930, they hauled all the equipment back out.

Crews began cutting in June 1927 and worked twelve-hour days for much of the next two years. Olson orchestrated a combination of old and new technologies to accomplish the scale of such a large harvest. The camp foreman laid out strips of forest at right angles to the

Each Diamond Match locomotive hauled eight log cars and, on average, dumped twenty-four loads into Kalispell Bay each day. Booms corralled the timber until spring when the *W. W. Slee*, seen in the distance, towed them to the Outlet to be driven down the river. *Weber Album, Priest Lake Museum*

The Kalispell Creek Plantation, shown here in 1945, area included an island of green timber that escaped the 1926 and 1939 fires. The Kalispell Creek drainage "experienced the most complete and drastic face lifting of any comparable drainage within any forest in Region One," according to ranger Henry Peterson. The area became one of the first clear cuts in the Priest Lake region as a result of the fires, salvage work by Diamond Match, Forest Service-prescribed burns, and work later done by the Civilian Conservation Corps. *Weber Album, Priest Lake Museum*

timber profits peaked in 1926 and by the next year the Forest Service began scaling back timber sales over concerns about falling prices. The agency all but suspended sales as the depression sent prices even lower. By 1932, stumpage prices tumbled to the lowest since 1904.[73]

The depression knocked out both large and modest operations at Priest Lake. Priest River's Charles Beardmore incorporated a planned pulp mill in 1929. He leveraged his mill and was left limping with small logging operations until he died in 1936. Dalkena tried to keep logging south of Priest Lake but when its mill at Cusick burned in 1935, the company collapsed.[74] The economy also forced their massive rival, the Humbird Lumber Company in Sandpoint, to fold in 1931.

Humbird's demise helped Diamond Match weather the depression.[75] The match company bought Humbird's land on the east side of Priest Lake and in 1935 acquired its Albeni Falls mill across the river from Newport. Idaho state laws required three dollars for

every log cut on state land but sent to a mill outside the state. Now Diamond could avoid the state fee along with the extra expense of driving Priest Lake logs all the way to Cusick.[76] In 1932 Diamond's logging superintendent Charlie Olson resigned to organize a subsidiary, the Kaniksu Timber Company. He bought Humbird timber west of Torrelle Falls, constructed a mill at Four Corners in 1933 and cut match planks to sell to the Diamond match block factory in Spokane.

Unlike his former employer, John Schaefer also survived the Great Depression. He quit Dalkena in 1919 and formed the Kaniksu Cedar Company with partner Beecher Hitchcock in Priest River. Schaefer expanded the company's presence at Priest Lake during the 1920s. He reincorporated in 1930 as the Schaefer-Hitchcock Company when he bought a Sandpoint pole company held in part by the Joslyn Manufacturing and Supply Company of Chicago. Eventually, the company became a subsidiary of the Joslyn Company.[77]

Hunters on Upper Priest Lake in the autumn. *Priest Lake Museum*

Nell Shipman canoeing on Priest Lake, c. 1924. *Northwest Museum of Arts and Culture*

at Bear Creek. With another twelve miles to go, Gumaer used the dog sled during the night to haul a small boat with a motor three miles down the ice to open water.

The next morning they got Van Tuyle to the boat and continued down lake. Running into rotten ice, they used an oar to break a channel for another six miles until they cleared Four Mile Island. The ice again turned solid so Shipman left the boat and walked down to Coolin for a sled to rescue Van Tuyle. The producer survived, but his relationship with Shipman proved irreparably damaged and by the next year they had separated. Shipman parlayed the adventure into national press.[34]

to find the unconscious Van Tuyle. Shipman believed, "We would have died out there that first day had not Joe Gumaer saved us." They managed to get to the Lone Starr Ranche

Nell Shipman insisted on moving her zoo to Priest Lake to use in her films. It took two hundred cages to move the animals from Hollywood to the lake via Spokane. Feeding the forty bears, dozens of dogs, bobcats, eagles, and others animals strained the finances of the company and during the winter made logistics a nightmare. A bankrupt Shipman left Priest Lake by April 1925, leaving sourdough "Daddy" Duffill in charge of the animals with few resources. A neighbor recalled, "He was there for a long, long time with very little food for the animals. In fact, Billy only had what he could scrounge to feed himself. I remember Bill feeling so sad because he didn't have anything to feed some of the animals." Forest Service personnel and lake residents organized fundraising to ship the remaining animals to the San Diego Zoo. *Northwest Museum of Arts and Culture*

Teams of horses pulling an early visitor out of the mud at Priest Lake in 1913. *Frank W. Guilbert, Northwest Museum of Arts and Culture*

❧

SPRING

The spring rush is on. Coolin is fairly flying making ready for guests. Mr. Paul, our well known merchant, is back on the job. The Hodges, proprietors of the Idaho Inn, are cleaning from garret to garret. Mrs. Handy of the Bungalow and the Northern Hotel is turning everything upside down. If you wish to speak to Arthur Moore of the Priest Lake Boat Livery you've got to trot along with his long strides and talk as best you can. Ed Stevens is working hard every day on the Byars boats and a smell of fresh paint permeates the air from both the Emily and Byars docks. Yep, things are picking up and only a little over two weeks until the opening of fishing season.

—Priest River Times, *April 18, 1931*

UNCLE PETE'S MONOGRAM

A sure sign of spring in Coolin was when sourdough, trapper, and bootlegger Pete Chase showed up on the Priest River stage and greeted his old friends with a wink proclaiming, "Well, I'm back from college." Chase acknowledged that as he got older, he often allowed himself to be found by the revenuers in late fall, and

"college" was his euphemism for a winter jail stay complete with hot meals. Chase asked Art Moore to service his boat as he visited the Leonard Paul store to pick up a "few sacks of sugar, cracked corn, and new oak casks." Chase would unearth a "fiver," a five-gallon keg he had set back, and share his year-old aged whiskey with his friends to celebrate the beginning of a new season. Thanks to Prohibition, which went into effect in Bonner County in 1910, in Washington State in 1915, and in Idaho a year later, Chase and other Priest Lake sourdoughs came to enjoy expanded economic opportunities.[35]

Chase fired up his hundred-gallon still back up at Trapper Creek on the Upper Priest Lake. He made 140-proof whiskey by double distilling his spirits. He filtered it to 100 proof and aged it in fifteen-gallon white oak casks. When Chase deemed it ready, he brought the casks down lake and stashed them in the sawdust pile at Art Marston's mill across from Coolin until they could be moved safely to Spokane. At the fashionable Davenport Hotel the head desk clerk facilitated access of Uncle Pete's Monogram whiskey to their favored cliental.[36]

The business of distilling, referred to locally as bootlegging, congregated around the upper lake. The length of Priest Lake and the meandering Thorofare protected bootleggers, who could track the county or federal "revenuers" as they left Coolin. At the Thorofare Sam Byars watched officials negotiate the narrow channel and sent a warning to his partner at their still on the upper lake. Pete Chase relied on a supportive network, his familiarity with the woods, and his boat, which boasted one of the fastest outboard motors on the lake. If bootleggers "did want to be found, they'd be found. But if they didn't want to be found, they didn't find them."[37] One exception occurred in 1930 when the Bonner County sheriff "knocked over" Pete Chase unexpectedly and arrested him for possession and sale of intoxicating liquor because he refused to pay a protection bribe of fifty dollars. He protested that the Italian bootleggers in Priest River escaped the sheriff's shakedown because they could provide a large, supportive voting block, but Priest Lake sourdoughs lacked such political clout.[38]

Chase was known as a generous host and often received visitors at his Trapper Creek cabin. One guest confirmed, "When we got to Pete Chase's I remember him taking us out to his spring house and dipped into a can or crock and offered it to us. It burned all the way to my toes and back again." Thanks to Chase and the other bootleggers, there was never a shortage of whiskey so residents and visitors found it freely available at establishments around the lake.[39] Even Leonard Paul kept a bottle behind his counter to treat old friends and make new ones.

Distilling opportunities at Priest Lake attracted newcomers and rivalries. On Reeder Creek in 1926 Sam Roland distilled moonshine from corn. He gave his mash to his neighbors, the Kerrs, who fed it to their poultry. Intoxicated farm animals often tipped off north Idaho revenuers to the presence of a still. Up the hill from Roland another moonshiner named Liscomb established a camp. An increasingly agitated Roland warned Liscomb off a trail that ran by his place. The men sparred, fueled by their own liquor, and Roland fetched his rifle. He shot Liscomb in the back of the head, briefly tried to escape capture, and ended up in the penitentiary.[40]

The profusion of moonshine around the lake increased abuse and abandonment among marginalized Priest Lake families. Teachers at the lake's schools could observe the effects on their students. Recalling one moonshiner's family, a classmate noted, "Sometimes one of the boys would come to school with a hangover and they never could quite make it down the aisle without throwing up. Their mother left them and their father tried to take care of them."[41] Alcohol contributed to the deaths of several sourdoughs whose obituaries listed a "disordered liver." Pete Chase continued offering his brew to guests on the upper lake after prohibition, but in 1941 he drowned in the Thorofare, probably while intoxicated. More than thirty friends contributed to honoring the Priest Lake pioneer by hiring a plane to scatter his ashes over the little lake.[42]

Pete Chase's still on the Upper Lake. *Priest Lake Museum*

Men and some women ran trap lines at Priest Lake for meat and pelts, as well as the bounty offered for unwanted game, like the coyotes whose pelts are shown here. Trappers used snowshoes and skis, also shown, to check their traps lines in the deep winter snow. *Priest Lake Museum*

TRAPPING FOR CASH

Sourdoughs and homesteaders at Priest Lake followed the traditions established by Hudson's Bay trappers a century earlier. They ran trap lines all winter and in the spring shipped out the pelts for well-earned cash. For a couple of decades, Pete Chase ran over two hundred traps that "kept him pretty busy." In February 1926, Chase sold twenty-one martins and two lynx and received $2.50 bounty each for several coyotes. He and others relied on Leonard Paul to ship their furs to the East. Some trappers dealt directly with buyers like Seidel and Son in Sedro-Woolley, Washington. The firm with Priest Lake connections promised, "We want your coyote, lynx, mink, marten. In fact all kinds of skins."[43]

Some trappers secured permits but others like Cougar Gus Johnson became skilled at evading game wardens by moving around the lake to his various lean-tos. Trapper Bill Hutchin headed high up in the mountains and came out in the spring with two lynx and several martins. He reported the weather cooperated, making it "a great year for trapping." When Elmer Stone and Charles Lund tried their hands on North Baldy and up Granite Creek, heavy snows hampered their success.

Professional trappers sometimes drifted into Priest Lake, but failed without local knowledge. One season a trapper from St. Maries, Idaho, tried his luck and built a cabin at Granite Creek. He grew frustrated with his catch and soon abandoned his efforts. He took a dugout canoe down lake and then tried to run the Priest River. He made it nine miles before the rapids ended his trip.[44]

Bounty hunting for coyotes, bears, and especially cougars provided extra income. One spring during the Depression, the Winslows turned in eight cougar pelts for a bounty of fifteen dollars each. They remarked that while trapping the cats around the head of the lake, they found more than thirty deer killed by the cougars. Pete Chase trapped a cub but a grizzly "beat Pete to it." He reset the trap and according to the *Priest River Times* "now has two bears in one. He will get only one bounty and that's what bothers him." Beaver pelt were illegal but some trappers, including "Daddy" Duffill and Pete Chase, "bootlegged" them to sell in Spokane through connections. Duffill's daughter recalled he "knew how to get rid of the hides for money. We got between $20 and $39 per hide and the cash always went for food."[45]

Haying in Squaw Valley. *Lee White, Weber Album, Priest Lake Museum*

SUMMER

HAYING WIDOWS

Hilma Sherman spent more than forty summers taking care of vacationers at Priest Lake resorts. In the spring, she cleaned, painted, and dusted at the Northern Inn and the Idaho Inn getting ready for guests. With the start of the fishing season, she worked long, hot days, washing, ironing, cleaning, and serving vacationers. Her husband often spent summers working at Art Marston's sawmill and her son worked in the woods, for the Forest Service, or at the Woodrat mine. The Shermans counted on the summer months for a cash income that would see them through the rest of the year.

Winter supplies required cash. The Kerr family north of Nordman estimated that in the 1910s it took about four hundred dollars to get through the winter months. They bought flour, sugar,

Earl Olmstead was one of the many Priest Lake men who earned cash working the Palouse wheat harvest, while his wife Nellie managed the farm. *Priest Lake Museum*

and other staples from the Leonard Paul store and shipped it up lake to Reeder Bay before the *W. W. Slee*'s final voyage of the season.[46] For the Kerrs, the Shermans, and the other homesteading families, survival required both husband and wife to generate "cash money."

In 1914 Earl Olmstead left his Outlet homestead for the summer to earn money working for the Forest Service. His wife Nellie managed the farm, putting in a half-acre of potatoes along with other produce they could grow. She operated their launch back and forth across to Coolin, and sometimes took it out fishing. Olmstead returned home in August long enough to clear some brush and then left again to work the harvest on the Palouse along with scores of men from Priest Lake. The newspaper commented on the number of Priest Lake husbands leaving for the Palouse and celebrated their "haying widows. The spirit of the pioneer woman is still displayed by some of the rancher's wives around here."[47]

Astor Calfee, shown here on the road to the family cabin in Coolin in the 1920s, supplied baked goods and dairy products to summer cabins. *Priest Lake Museum*

"Aunt" Sarah Fish, shown here in 1911, contributed to the family's summer operation near the Twin Islands. They offered vacationers lunch or dinner in a large tent set up near the shoreline. *Museum of Northern Idaho*

For Priest Lake women, cash money often meant peddling their produce and wage labor during the summer months. Each season Nelle Schurr loaded up her rowboat with strawberries, blueberries, and gooseberries along with vegetables grown on her family's homestead at the mouth of the Upper Priest River. She worked her way down the shoreline selling her produce to the cabins and campers along the way.[48] She rowed through the Thorofare and some days went as far south as Canoe Point looking for buyers.

Vacationers who stayed for weeks provided livelihoods for Priest Lake women like Nelle Schurr. Families going up lake often stopped at Cavanaugh Bay to buy milk, eggs, cheese, and bread from homesteader Nelle Fenton. Astor Calfee delivered her dairy products to summer cabins around Coolin. She also baked bread, cakes, and pies to sell. Her ability to supplement her family income improved significantly in 1925 when her husband Wirt brought a massive cook stove down lake after filmmaker Nell Shipman abandoned Lionhead Lodge. Shipman had used the huge stove to provide for both her crew and zoo. Calfee installed it in the woodshed where Astor could bake two dozen

loaves of bread at a time, thus expanding sales and the family's income. Although her family raised cattle, the Calfees never enjoyed the beef. In the spring, they fattened a calf to sell in Priest River for veal and used the money to pay for the year's supply of baking ingredients. Calfee hung up the sacks of flour and sugar by bailing wire to the rafters in the attic to protect them from mice.[49]

"Lived like Hell Ever After"

When Mary Smith came from the Midwest to work as a barmaid in Coolin, Tony Lemley took to frequenting the saloon even more than usual. With encouragement from his fellow drinking buddies, he eventually proposed to Mary. They married and moved to Lemley's homestead at the Outlet. Young women like Vera Paul and Mary Lemley working domestic jobs at Priest Lake often found husbands. Even with the arrival of the homesteaders in the late 1910s and '20s, men still outnumbered women in the region.

Pearl Mack started cooking at the Nickel Plate Mine near her family's homestead, where she met "Six Shooter" Jack Mayer. Unfortunately both the mine and their marriage proved ill-fated, but many of Priest Lake's matches withstood the area's hardships and the test of time.[50]

Leonard Paul offered advice for lonely men unable to catch a schoolteacher or the summer help: "if a fella wanted a wife he'd get a 'Heart in Hand' book from Michigan and write a couple letters and then go down to Priest River and meet her and bring her up here and marry her. Old man Handy was a justice of the peace. He could marry them and they lived like hell ever after."[51]

Priest Lake women at times struggled with the responsibility and isolation. Homesteader Lillian Johnson found life at Granite Creek to be the "loneliest spot on the face of the earth." When Barbara Seymour's husband Walter left Nordman and headed to Boise as the state representative, she insisted schoolteacher Rose Chermak move in with her "because she didn't want to stay alone." Seymour's Pennsylvania roots left her ill prepared for the West. When Tony Lemley headed to the Palouse to work harvest, his wife Mary lamented she would be glad when harvest days were over "for it is mighty lonesome when you are really alone on 160 acres, no matter where it is situated."[52]

The Priest Lake social event of the century occurred in July 1923 when movie star Nell Shipman invited the community to her Lionhead Lodge. Steamboats ran excursion rates including a barge which brought up two hundred people. Barbecued beef sandwiches for lunch and an afternoon of games and contests left the crowds well-satisfied. *Jim Parsons, Priest Lake Museum*

Henry Sorg built his cabin along the "picturesque driveway" Richard Handy constructed to his Camp Sherwood north of Coolin. Handy hoped to attract wealthy clients like Sorg to establish an enclave of fashionable summer cottages. *University of Idaho Library, Simpson Collection*

Families set up vacation camps like the one shown here. *Northwest Museum of Arts and Culture*

increasingly outnumbered the sportsmen on the lake's beaches. Some groups pitched simple tents, but others created small settlements. When the extended Beardmore family camped on the sand bar at the Thorofare, the party included a "girl" to watch the children and a cook with a stove.

Some families stored camping equipment with Joseph Slee in Coolin. When they arrived for the season the men used a large wooden wheelbarrow to bring the gear down to the dock from the storage sheds. Equipment often included "sheet iron camp stoves, roped tent rolls, camp cots, bucket, axes, shovels and blackened coffee pots."[19] With rented rowboats bobbing behind, the *W. W. Slee* delivered vacationers to their favorite beaches.

The Forest Service reserved the big beaches around the lake for camping and families often set up campsites for weeks. Coolin storekeeper Leonard Paul sent his wife and three daughters, along with a hired girl, to camp on the sandbar at the Thorofare for a month every summer. They set up two sleeping tents and a billowy

cooking fly. The group enjoyed lazy days rowing the boat up the Thorofare and letting it drift back down. "Any company who showed up just came and joined us," recalled daughter Marjorie.[20]

Richard Stejer worked with a colleague in Spokane who effusively extolled the beauties of Squaw Bay, so in 1924 he launched his boat with a twelve-horsepower Evinrude motor from Luby Bay and headed up lake to see for himself. He pitched his tent down the beach from a large family campsite and "let it sit there all summer long," coming up every weekend. Toward the end of the season, he ran into Raymond Vincent "Nig" Borleske, a coach at Whitman College, who since 1917 had camped all summer, usually near the mouth of Lion Creek. Borleske constructed an elaborate windbreak wrapped around the trees to protect his campsite. He stored his gear in the winter with Elmer Berg at the Shady Rest Resort. Borleske never transitioned from beach camping to cabin ownership, but Stejer and dozens of other campers migrated to more substantial accommodations.[21]

Coolin storekeeper Leonard Paul and his family, seen here c. 1925, camped at the Thorofare for a month every summer. *Priest Lake Museum*

FROM TENT TO CABIN

The first time Joe and Nona Hungate camped at the lake in 1913, they took the trolley from Cheney to Spokane. They caught the Great Northern train to Priest River and then the Beardmore stage to Coolin. They spent the night at Mrs. Handy's Idaho Inn, bought groceries from Leonard Paul, and boarded the *W. W. Slee* with their rented rowboat tied on

behind. Hungate's position as professor at the State Normal School at Cheney allowed the family to spend weeks camping. Toward the end of their vacation, they rowed down lake, camping along the way. Over the years they became acquainted with Diamond Match timber cruiser Jack Barron, who gave them permission to build a cabin on the company's land on Canoe Point. They built a shed on the site to store their gear and it eventually evolved into a bedroom. By 1924 they enlarged it into a hip-roofed, twenty-by-twenty-foot cabin with walls made of unpeeled cedar logs, complete with a kitchen and fireplace.[22]

Priest Lake vacationers replicated the Hungate's pattern of camping and then building a cabin over and over again.

The Hungate family camped annually on Canoe Point after 1914 and each year added a few more amenities like the table and shelves shown here. *Priest Lake Museum*

Spokane mechanic Tom Moar camped at Priest Lake in 1920, enjoyed the fishing, and returned every summer. In 1930 he decided to lease a lot from the state on Cavanaugh Bay. The resourceful Moar and his relatives built a cabin over the Fourth of July weekend. Moar's mechanic friends from Spokane soon joined him around the bay in their own cabins.[23] The state, which took over the east side of the lake in 1917, continued with leasing policies for summer cottages that mirrored the Forest Service on the west side but it did not monitor construction and expansion as rigorously.

"Things Ornate, Elaborate, Pretentious, Showy, Tricky, Fussy or Peculiar"

Unlike the Sorg vacation home in Sherwood Beach, most early cottages at Priest Lake, whether on leased or deeded land, were shaped by the Priest Lake environment rather than imposed by a Spokane architect. In 1923, permittees built sixty-four cabins; just two years later the number jumped to eighty-nine, the highest concentration of summer residences in USFS Region One. As the number of cabins rose exponentially, especially on Forest Service land, some rangers raised alarm about their impact on the natural environment along the shoreline. The agency encouraged conservation ideals, advocating that the cabins should blend in with the shoreline by using organic materials. "As evidences of man increase in the forest, so decrease many of the attractions sought by those visiting the forest for recreation. The Forest Service seeks to save these attractions, to preserve an environment as nearly natural as possible."[24]

Guy Heatfield's slapdash cabin allowed under the 1912 special use permit needed no screening with trees, no sanitation provisions, or architectural restraint. By the late 1920s the Forest Service implemented regulations mandating buildings be screened from sight, set back from the shoreline, and constructed with local materials. "It is our desire to discontinue the practice of allowing the construction of unsightly buildings and do away with those already constructed as rapidly as possible."[25]

Priest River resident Ralph Clintsman's cabin for his family in the Shoshone Bay tract needed to "be inconspicuously located and limited" and "fit the ground." Clintsman's cabin was up the hill from the shoreline, well-screened from view either by the lake or the road. As the Forest Service regulated, he used unplaned lumber and stain. When he painted, he found that "Sienna browns, nature greens or battleship grays are best." Clintsman complied with the Forest Service's admonishment that "doodads, scroll work or curlicues of any kind are unsuited to a forest residence. Simplicity is the keynote of good design. Things ornate, elaborate, pretentious, showy, tricky, fussy or peculiar are bad."[26]

Many permittees brought building supplies from Spokane, but the Forest Service encouraged the use of native materials such as local stone to construct chimneys. "Brick chimneys are least appropriate."[27] Fireplaces were crucial aesthetic elements for vacation cabins, along with providing heat that was needed even in the summer. Some families collected stones for their chimneys and fashioned mortar from beach sand and blue clay mined from the Thorofare. The Hungates at Canoe Point used cedar shakes to form a tapered chimney, and when they inaugurated their fireplace, the shakes went up in flames. Their entire cabin cost less than thirty dollars, mostly spent on concrete. Almost all the other materials were native.[28]

Early cabins were constructed with timber cut from the lots on which they stood, or with rough-cut lumber purchased from the Art Marston or Fred Schneider mills. Indoor plumbing remained rare, but many resourceful owners used gravity to divert water to their cabins. Edward Blanchard brought water from a spring to his cabin on the Outlet with "an ingenious system of taps, one on the back porch with soap and a basin and one which dripped into the big copper tank on the back of the range for hot water." Don James piped water from Hunt Creek using metal filters to strain

Don James's system of pipes even delivered water to a wringer washing machine. On washdays his daughter-in-law Betty, shown here with her daughter Ann, only needed to carry hot water from the wood stove. Even during Priest Lake summers, mothers starched cottons and used flat irons to press both adult and children's clothes. *Priest Lake Museum*

Cabin owners shared their lots with the wildlife. At the Hungate family's cabin, their washtubs doubled as a "bear scare" when piled up against the root cellar door. *Priest Lake Museum*

Chapter Eleven

Fishing Camps to Resorts: Tourism at Priest Lake

Logger Ike Elkins started a new era in modern tourism at Priest Lake when he tore up the mortgage note from Tom and Bud Jarrett on a fishing camp at Reeder Bay in 1931. The Tennessee native first came to the lake in 1912 to fish at Granite Creek. He built up a successful contract logging operation out of Newport so when fellow loggers, the Jarretts, asked him for a loan to acquire the Winslow fishing camp he readily complied. The camp included Bert Winslow's homestead near the mouth of Reeder Creek along with a summer residence permit on a waterfront lot.

The Forest Service, eager to encourage more public access to the lake, had approved a resort for Winslow's son Graydon in 1930 on the cottage permit site.[1] The Forest Service inspector expressed little enthusiasm for the location, deeming it "not very desirable to resort development. The beach is poor." The dilapidated homestead cabin and abandoned fields marred the scenery and a shabby houseboat moored at the mouth of Reeder Creek contributed to the woebegone scene. The agency mandated Winslow move his houseboat upstream and provide a screen of trees. On the government land, he needed to remodel the cabins he had already built, and for the three he proposed, he had to extend the windows, add screened porches, and shake the roofs to fit into the landscape. When Winslow proposed expanding a building to create a store and office, the inspector instructed, "The additions should be of log construction so as to harmonize with the present type of

architecture." The Forest Service encouraged owners of small, family-run fishing resorts on federal permit lands to respect an environmental aesthetic and hoped to get Winslow on the right track early in the relationship. The inspector concluded that for all the problems with the Winslow site, "there is a demand for a small resort at this point."[2]

To encourage tourist activity on Priest Lake the Forest Service agreed to grant a resort permit to Graydon Winslow on Reeder Bay in 1930. Winslow planned to transform his family's homestead, shown here ten years earlier, and the adjoining federal land into a fishing camp. The site later became Elkins Resort. *Priest Lake Museum*

129

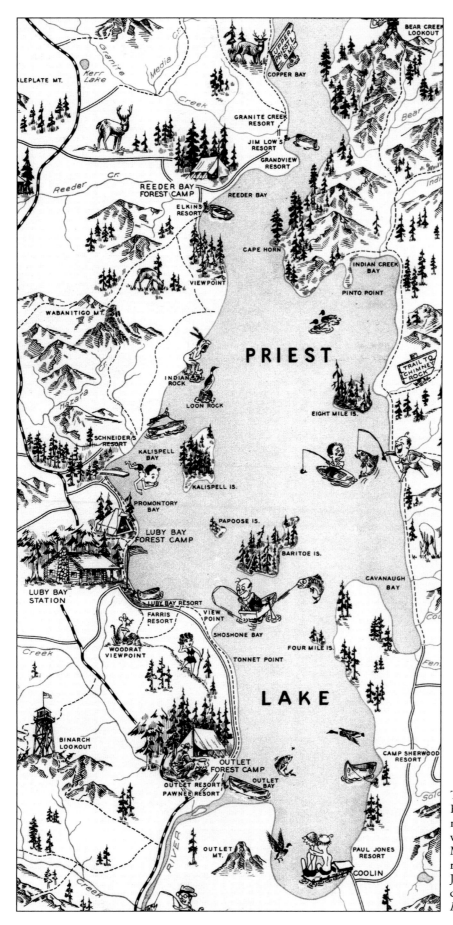

This 1937 map featured resorts and Forest Service sites including the newly completed Luby Bay Station, which is now home to the Priest Lake Museum. It also showed the limited road access. Forest Service illustrator John Lacasse created the map and continued to modify it over the years. *Priest Lake Museum*

Winslow labored on his resort for a year before giving up on the scheme. He sold it to his sister, Dot Overmeyer, and the Jarrett brothers for $5,000 with money borrowed from Ike Elkins. According to Elkins, "I loaned them some money on the resort down there and they didn't take no care of it. When the mortgage come due they told me if I'd tear up the mortgage they'd turn the thing over to me then." Elkins found himself owner of five old cabins and a few boats. "But the fishing was good and I liked to fish and stuff so I figured it would be a good investment like that."[3]

"Everything the Sportsman Desires"

The same summer Elkins acquired the Reeder Bay fishing camp, Coolin hotel owner Ida Handy noted "more people have been to Priest than ever before and of the great number, scores admitted they were visiting Priest Lake for the first time." A Spokane newspaperman explained tourism growth in the middle of the Depression, arguing that the lake is "far enough removed from towns and cities it has retained its wild state and continues year after year to hold the same lure for sportsmen."[4] Sportsmen considered Priest Lake as "the last stand for real sport" in the Inland Empire so seasonally they reserved their favorite cabins at their favorite resorts located near their favorite fishing spots. Some brought families but the focus for the resorts and their guests remained on fishing. Tellingly, Priest Lake promoters freely interchanged the term sportsman with tourist and vacationer.

Ike Elkins began to transform his fishing camp to "provide everything the sportsman desires." He acquired fire-damaged timber south of the lake so he and his brother leased a small sawmill, sold the white pine to the Dalkena mill, and salvaged the remaining cedar to build up his resort.[5] Elkins kept his crew employed during the first winter to construct thirteen new cabins. He housed some men in Winslow's old houseboat and put up a bunkhouse to accommodate the rest. He filled two big root cellars with canned food and also hunted deer

to feed his crew. The following fall, he added eight more cabins and a long floating dock for bathers.

Elkins opened every April 15, the first day of fishing season. Their cedar cabins came equipped with wood burning ranges, ice boxes, and beds with new Simmons mattresses. They rented "complete except bedding for $1.00 a day." During the summer son Al hauled ice and wood to each cabin while daughters Jan and Joan helped clean the cabins and wash dishes. Elkins even installed an electrical plant that ran on gasoline powered motors. "Getting electricity took a lot of responsibility of all of us and it was hard to keep them up." Ike Elkins turned the electricity off at night, leaving guests with only kerosene lamps and they would "squawk a lot of times."[6]

Ike Elkins envisioned his resort as a fishing camp but "the women got it in their hat to remodel the camp and modernize everything to satisfy them." As he expanded his logging business, he turned over much of the resort operations to "the women." Gradually Elkins' wife Sue would "take care of it when I was in the woods a loggin'." They also retained Dottie Winslow Overmeyer, who had grown up on the homestead, as general manager and bookkeeper.

Elkins ordered his first five "resort boats" from a fellow Newport entrepreneur who

Shown here from left to right is the Elkins resort crew in 1940: Dottie Winslow, Olga, daughter Jan Elkins, Denise Overmeyer, Sue Elkins, son Al Elkins, Sue's sister Hazel Mill, Joan Elkins, and the handy man Raymond "Slim" Jones. *Priest Lake Museum*

The cedar cabins at the Elkins Resort came equipped with wood burning ranges, fireplaces, ice boxes, and comfortable furniture. *Priest Lake Museum*

launched the Carter Craft Company. Although more expensive than the poplar Kant Sink 'Em metal boats made in Spokane, Elkins found Carter Crafts leaked less, were more stable for fishing, and with their v-bottom hulls handled the new outboard motors better. The first boats proved so popular Elkins quickly ordered five more. Sue Elkins recalled, "We had to have a cabin, a boat to go with the cabin, and motor to go with the boat. Nobody ever brought up a boat in those days, let alone keep one at the lake."[7]

Tourism as a Family Business

Sue Elkins and Dot Winslow Overmeyer joined other women around the lake who contributed to their family incomes by providing food and lodging to vacationers. As rustic fishing and hunting camps evolved after World War I, Priest Lake families found seasonal resorts vital to their economic survival. Mary Lemley at the Outlet offered "four bedrooms for guest, immaculate and ready for guest any time after 6 a.m." Nelle Fenton at Cavanaugh Bay rented a couple of cabins in addition to selling milk and bread to summer people.

Homesteader Sam Byars married Grace Hamm and together they built Forest Lodge in 1919 at the mouth of the Thorofare and "met

a need of fishermen, hunters, and vacationers who were beginning to explore the possibilities of the beautiful area." Byars operated a steamboat to bring sportsmen up to the head of the lake. They enjoyed his wife's cooking in the spacious dining room and slept in one of the seven rooms upstairs or in a guest cabin. The Byars kept a couple of cows and a big garden to support the kitchen. The barn held horses that guests used for packing and riding. Wild hay from the nearby meadow fed them. Actress Nell Shipman leased Forest Lodge the first season her company arrived at Priest Lake in 1922. Byars, unhappy over unpaid bills, evicted the company along with their zoo the following spring. This expedited their move across the bay to Lionhead Lodge. After Byars died in 1930, his wife leased Forest Lodge to a couple from Boston, the Pattees, who modernized the lodge but soon fell victim to the Depression and lack of regular boat service. Slee family members leased the lodge next until it burned in 1938.[8]

The Lone Star Ranche stood on a hill above Bear Creek. Harry Angstadt homesteaded the land in the 1890s. In 1910 he married the notorious Belle Hall. Belle, the former mistress of the first owner of the Northern Inn, had been acquitted of shooting another lover in

Forest Lodge, at the mouth of the Thorofare, welcomed guests—including Nell Shipman, shown here at far right—from 1919 to the 1930s. *Northwest Museum of Arts and Culture*

Priest River in 1907. Angstadt and Hall used the alimony money from her first marriage to a wealthy St. Louis man to create a resort. They expanded the original home, built five cabins, and added other embellishments including a gazebo. The Lone Star served sportsmen but also acted as a halfway house for people going up and down the lake. Belle Angstadt always kept a big kettle with venison stew on the back of her stove to which guests helped themselves, washing their bowls when they finished, leaving them for the next person.

"Aunt" Belle spent a lifetime entertaining and even in her old age, stout and bug-eyed from an enlarged goiter, she remained the life of the party. One frequent visitor exclaimed, "Aunt Belle was loved by everyone. She was talented, clever, quick-witted, wrote poetry and could really entertain people."[9]

Luby Bay homesteader Jim Low opened a fishing camp with four rental cabins spread across three Forest Service waterfront lots in 1924. He paid yearly for a special use permit and faced a number of mandated regulations

The notorious Belle Angstadt is seen here in 1924 by the gazebo at the Lone Star Ranche resort. *Boise State University Library, Hein-Matlock Scrapbook*

In 1938, Jim Low bought land near Granite Creek and built cabins for a new resort free from Forest Service guidelines. *Priest Lake Museum*

Luby Bay resort owner Will Schneider (not related to Fred Schneider who rented cabins in Kalispell Bay) is shown here with his mother Margaret and young Mary Dostert. *Priest Lake Museum*

for resorts including a prohibition on the sale of intoxicating liquors. The Forest Service inspector in 1930 found conditions "rather unsatisfactory." He urged Low to improve buildings considered eyesores "in order that harmony of all structures will be had." Low chafed under Forest Service directives so he moved his family up lake in 1938 to open a new resort.[10] He sold his Luby Bay cabins to Earl and Lauren Farris who operated them for the next eight years.

Low's neighbors to the north on Luby Bay, Will and Pauline Schneider, tolerated Forest Service supervision better. When the Schneiders bought a rustic resort camp in 1930 from the Hampton family who moved back to Walla Walla, the Forest Service eagerly transferred the special use permit to the better-financed and more hospitable family. Schneider embraced the agency's concerns about architectural integrity

along the shoreline. He strove to make his store, boat house, icehouse, and growing number of cottages blend into the landscape. In their inaugural season, the Schneiders hosted a July Fourth celebration complete with a dance.[11] In 1939 they sold their Luby Bay Resort to Spokane grocery store owner George Richter and his brother-in-law Carter Carson, who added a lodge and more cabins. After the war Bob and Mary Timm bought the business about the same time George Hill acquired the Farris Resort next door.

IDA HANDY, BUSINESSWOMAN

When Ida Handy's husband died unexpectedly she turned to the tourism industry for her livelihood. She bought the newly constructed Idaho Inn at Coolin in 1907 but, unlike the seasonal fishing camps around the lake, Handy kept it open all year. The inn featured a large dining room with white tablecloths and Handy's own fireweed honey with freshly made biscuits. It hosted vacationers, businessmen, and Forest Service personnel, and boarded schoolteachers.

Ida Handy's Idaho Inn featured upstairs rooms as well as tents around the grounds, shown here in the foreground. *Priest Lake Museum*

Her successful business approach to tourism allowed Handy to purchase the Northern Hotel, just up the hill, in 1917. Four years later she again responded to changes in tourism and transportation by opening The Bungalow, a more casual restaurant across from the Idaho Inn on the waterfront.[12] Handy developed the largest tourist operation on the lake, eventually operating two inns, two restaurants, a dance pavilion, and cabins at Sherwood Beach. She sold the Idaho Inn to Mary and Bill Hodges, former cooks for the Schaefer-Hitchcock Lumber Company in 1924. The Coolin landmark burned in 1942.

For more than twenty years until her death in 1935, Ida Handy oversaw one of the most successful tourist operations at Priest Lake.[13] She and other regional women contributed to a stable tourist industry that tempered the region's seasonal incomes from logging, mining, and trapping. These women helped knit together a Priest Lake economy that supported increased settlement and provided an infrastructure for growth.

Coolin's Northern Inn passed rapidly through a number of hands after its construction at the turn of the century and at times acquired an unsavory reputation. Ida Handy bought the inn in 1917, remodeled it and maintained it as an upstanding establishment. Shown here in 1910, the inn still welcomes guests in 2015. *Priest Lake Museum*

At Ida Handy's casual restaurant, The Bungalow, families enjoyed the large screened porches in front while men played pool or gambled in the backroom. Here the Beardmore family and friends gathered at the Coolin waterfront establishment. *Priest Lake Museum*

"Good Auto Roads to All Cottages"

Coolin storeowner Leonard Paul partnered with Priest River garage operator Stanley Jones to take advantage of increasing numbers of vacationers bringing families to the lake in their first automobiles. The men purchased lakefront land north of Paul's store in 1923. They opened a tourist park and campground on one of the few sites cars could reach with relative ease. They appealed to families by providing more modern options than the fishing camps, and Paul offered grocery delivery to the cabins that included

To appeal to families, Leonard Paul and Stanley Jones anchored a large diving raft in the deep water off their tourist park. Near shore they constructed a two-deck water slide. *Bonner County Historical Society*

Each winter during the 1920s at Paul-Jones Beach, Swedish builder Elmer Berg, shown here with Marjorie Paul, added another log cabin complete with running water and even some with indoor plumbing. *Priest Lake Museum*

local vegetables and dairy products. At Paul-Jones Beach, there were "good auto roads to all cottages spaciously set apart among the shady evergreen trees assuring privacy and comfort."[14] The men built a long dock to moor the Kant Sink 'Em boats that came with each cabin.

In the evenings after closing his store, Paul wandered down to the beach to check on guests, many of whom booked the same cabins for the same weeks every summer. Vera Paul hosted a weekly potluck wiener roast "for anyone in the cabins who wanted to come. It ended with an evening sing along and swim." On nights when the northern lights shimmered, Paul woke up his sleeping guests to see the sight from the dock. "Not all of them appreciated it but none of them forgot it."[15]

SUMMER DANCES

Paul promoted activities that expanded Priest Lake's vacation appeal, as did Ida Handy, who built a dance pavilion with a large covered dance floor behind the hotel in 1914. She hired a three-piece orchestra and charged fifty cents per person for Saturday dances. Since Handy served no alcohol, whole families came out. Tourists and residents danced the fox trot and waltzed. Talented guests like Edgar Stevens contributed Scott Joplin rags. Tired children fell asleep on the benches lining the walls as the evenings grew late. For more than ten years, Handy hosted summer dances, some years offering both afternoon and evening sessions.[16] Steamboat owners sponsored special excursions to bring vacationers from around the lake to the dances and deliver them home at the end of the evening.

When Leonard Paul outgrew his original log store in 1926, he moved closer to the waterfront and dug into the hillside to construct a two-story concrete building in 1926. Upstairs his new dance pavilion became "one of the finest in the Inland Empire." Dancers enjoyed the smooth maple floor and in between songs people gathered around the expansive windows offering a "wonderful view of the lake." On opening night three hundred people crowded the dance floor, swaying to Spokane's Washingtonian Orchestra.[17]

During the summer of 1934 Bill Warren and his brother organized the dances above the store. "Leonard Paul provided a dance hall above the store and it was the hub of activity especially in the summer season. Year round residents and summer visitors mingled to the music of the piano and fiddles and no introductions were necessary." Warren related, "My brother played trumpet and I played saxophone and we went up to the CCC camp at Cavanaugh and found a boy from New Jersey that played the piano. We had some good dances up there all that summer."[18] The successful season ended just before Labor Day when a polio scare resulted in a quarantine.

Leonard Paul built a new store in 1926, with a new dance pavilion above. Dances were held here up into the 1950s. *Priest Lake Museum*

BOATS ON PRIEST LAKE

The colorful "Cap" Markham in his launch, *Seneaquoteen,* picked up couples around the lake and took them home after the dances at Leonard Paul's. In the early years vacationers depended on regular boat routes to navigate the lake. After Walter Slee died in 1919, Bert Winslow bought his boat and piloted it for a number of years. Sam Byars acquired Mose Fish's steamboat in 1918 and began his own service. Instead of competing, the men collaborated to set prices for passengers and freight, but Winslow often irritated Byars by cutting his rates. Byars held the contract to deliver mail around the lake and used his boat to ferry guests to his Forest Lodge.[19]

The need for wood-burning steamboats on Priest Lake declined after the introduction of Evinrude outboard motors mounted on rowboats along with a growing number of larger launches powered by combustible engines. The Pattee family took over Forest Lodge and used the thirty-foot launch, *The Rainbow,* to transport guests up lake. Elmer Berg, at his Shady Rest Resort, brought a twenty-six foot launch up from Lake Coeur d'Alene in 1939 to accommodate his guests at Beaver Creek. Art Moore, Leonard Paul's brother-in-law, returned from World War I and set up a boat livery next to Slee's dilapidated docks at Coolin. He rented boats with motors and traveled back East for special training on pioneering Evinrude motors.

Mechanic Art Moore, shown here with an Evinrude motor, opened a boat livery in Coolin after World War I. *Priest Lake Museum*

In 1948, Art Moore built a large marina at the south end of the lake that later become known as Bishop's Marina. *Priest Lake Museum*

He later added the lighter weight Johnson motors to rent to fisherman after they were introduced in the 1920s. Moore became good at taking "care of individually owned boats and motors, having them ready when anxious fisherman wanted to go."[20]

Moore faced a setback in 1932 when a can of tar heating on the stove exploded and burned down the old Warren and Burch store he used as a workroom and boat storage.[21] In 1948, after World War II, he catered to the growing number of speedboats and built slips with a massive boat storage barn overhead on pilings, creating a landmark on the south end of the lake in 1948, known later as Bishop's Marina.[22] Moore faced little competition until Bryon and Betty Stephan started a marina at Kalispell Bay.

During the Great Depression Priest Lake enjoyed an increase in tourism activities, but World War II brought the influx of visitors to a halt. Rationed gasoline and rubber tires meant trips to the lake became a luxury, even for cabin owners. In response, the newly formed Priest Lake Resort Owners Association tried to organize a daily bus schedule from Spokane during the summer of 1944 to encourage more vacationers.[23] Wartime restrictions also meant no materials for expansion but then again there was little demand. While their Priest Lake business slowed, resort owners like Ike Elkins and Willard Stevens turned to construction work supporting the war effort. The end of the war would bring a new era for tourism to Priest Lake.

Postcards Popularizing Priest Lake

The earliest photographs of Priest Lake date to 1889 but three twentieth-century photographers in particular—Frank Palmer, Leo Ostreicher, and Ross Hall—helped to promote tourism at the lake.[24]

Thoroughfare between Upper and Lower, Priest Lake, Idaho.

Spokane photographer Frank Palmer advertised that with his glass plate negatives he captured "Inland Empire Wonderland Scenery." In the summer of 1910 he took a handsome series of images around Priest Lake that he turned into postcards like the one of the Thorofare shown here. His photographs were also converted into colored lithographic cards sold at the Leonard Paul Store to tourists eager to share the beauty of the lake. *Priest Lake Museum*

60-010 Luby Bay Resort on Priest Lake Idaho.

Leo Ostreicher operated a photography studio in Spokane that specialized in school and group portraits. He first came to the lake in the 1930s to take postcard pictures for CCC men to send back East to show off their Idaho experience. He expanded with images of local businesses and sites popular with tourists. The prolific Leo's Studio continued to produce Priest Lake postcards like this Luby Bay scene through the 1950s. *Priest Lake Museum*

H-134 Priest Lake for fun!

The Kodak Company listed Ross Hall as one of the top ten scenic photographers in the country in the 1940s and many of his images featured Priest Lake. The Sandpoint photographer developed a striking black and white look that gained him national attention and helped to promote regional tourism. *Priest Lake Museum*

CHAPTER TWELVE

Civilian Conservation Corps

SIX MONTHS IN IDAHO

*Six months in Idaho
Is all that I can take
If I stay here any longer,
I am afraid that I will break.*

*When we left California
We thought we'd have it nice;
But now our only pastime,
Is cards and shooting dice.*

*We're forty miles from town
And just twice a week we can go;
The roads are so dusty, when we get there we're crusty,
That's the way with old Idaho.*

—Alton Ponco, CCC Co. 572
Cavanaugh Breeze Newsletter, September 1935

Bismark District Ranger Henry Peterson drove into Priest River to meet a special train coming from Fort Dix, New Jersey, in June 1933. He greeted two hundred young men from Civilian Conservation Corps (CCC) Company 1269 as they disembarked at the station and directed them into the waiting Dodge trucks that hauled them north to Kalispell Bay. Over the next nine years, hundreds of these CCC men profoundly transformed the Priest Lake region. They worked on fire prevention, improving timber stands, and expanding recreational opportunities. The Forest Service and the Idaho State Land Board could not have imagined the scale of the projects undertaken.

President Franklin Roosevelt created the CCC within ten days of his inauguration in March 1933 as one of the centerpieces of his New Deal program to help the country recover from the Great Depression. Just two months later ranger Peterson found himself serving as a camp superintendent. He coordinated Forest Service projects with the military commander assigned to the company. The commander supervised day-to-day camp operations and its logistics for the two hundred men stationed at Priest Lake for six months. For Peterson, this joint experiment proved to be "a very busy and sometimes frustrating year for me."[1]

Ultimately, the Priest Lake region supported one of the greatest concentrations of CCC camps in the country. Along with the camp at Kalispell Bay (F-142), the Kaniksu National Forest also included Blowdown #2 (F-159), a mile away on Reynolds Creek near Hanna Flats. Kalispell Creek camp (F-102) lay eight miles west up the watershed just over the Washington state line. South of the lake, Forest Service camps opened at the Experiment Station, at Four Corners, and in Boswell Canyon.[2]

The CCC program partnered with the U.S. Forest Service and with the forest products industry and state agencies. This meant that the Priest Lake Timber Protection Association (PLTPA) also coordinated CCC camps on the east side of the lake. The association struggled to organize its camps as it lacked the long term planning and resources of the Forest Service. Captain Ed Elliot ferried the CCC men on his boat the *Tyee* to the first camp at Indian Creek in June 1933. The challenges of supporting 213 men with access only via water quickly became apparent. The association then had Elliot move the men across the lake to Kalispell Bay and trucks took them south to set up another camp along the Priest River. The PLTPA eventually made use of CCC crews at the Cavanaugh Bay camp (S-263). By 1940, the camp moved just southeast of Coolin where it was rechristened Camp Priest Lake.[3]

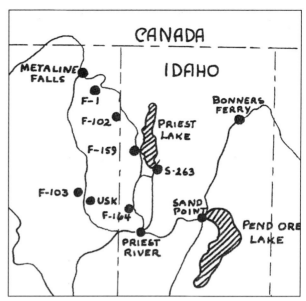

Civilian Conservation Corps camps near Priest Lake, 1944. *Priest Lake Museum*

"Joining an Army without Guns"

When George Cannata climbed out the back of the truck at Kalispell Bay in June 1933, he discovered "it was a beautiful place." He had worked in a barbershop in New York City's tough Bowery district, but his commuting costs ate up his meager pay. His unemployed friend Sal Marsala suggested they join President Roosevelt's newly inaugurated Civilian Conservation Corp and Cannata agreed. The first requirement at the CCC recruiting station near Broadway involved getting a shot in the arm.

Captain Ed Elliott ferried CCC workers on the *Tyee* to the first camp at Indian Creek in June 1933. Here he is docked at the Beaver Creek Ranger Station. *Ernie Grambo, Priest Lake Museum*

The PTLPA made use of CCC crews at the Cavanaugh Bay camp (S-263), shown here, until 1940 when it was moved closer to Coolin. *Leo's Studio, Priest Lake Museum*

Afraid of needles, Marsala deserted the line but Cannata decided to sign up. He quickly found himself in the back of an army truck going to Camp Dix, New Jersey. When he arrived there, he called home to let his shocked family know he would not be back for a year. He was assigned to Company 1266 along with other men recruited from New York and New Jersey. He received a GI-issue uniform from World War I, "just like I was joining the army without guns. We were to fight forest fires, build roads, create huge fire lanes, and plant new trees."[4]

George Cannata's company was the first to arrive at Priest Lake so they built their own barracks in the burned-over area on Kalispell

Company 1266, the first to arrive at Priest Lake, built Kalispell Bay camp from the ground up. *U.S. Forest Service, Northern Region*

Bay. They slept in tents on mattresses they filled with hay, and used pit toilets and drank water from a nearby spring delivered through log pipes they hollowed out. The two hundred men constructed rows of wooden barracks, a mess hall, a recreation hall, and latrines, as well as numerous support buildings.

Cannata put his New York City barbershop experience to good use. After he finished working in the woods each afternoon at 4:00, he set up a barrel for a barber chair and charged fifteen cents a haircut. He made about fifty dollars a month, "big money in those tough days."[5] He sent the money home to his family in New York. Cannata and the

New York City barber George Cannata made extra cash cutting hair for his fellow CCC recruits. *Weber Album, Priest Lake Museum*

other CCC recruits got paid thirty dollars a month but twenty-five of it went directly home to help support their families. Cecil Wylie, who lied about his age and joined up with the CCC at the age of fifteen, remembered using his monthly five dollars "to buy our beer and cigarettes. I went down to Joe's on Luby Bay. He had a little convenient store and pool hall with pool tables and stuff."[6]

"Reveille and All That Stuff"

Recruit Cecil Wylie observed, "The CCC was like being in the army actually. We had captains and everything. We had to make our beds, we had to do reveille and all that stuff."[7] Roosevelt's administration became mindful of the growing militancy in Germany so took care to create a program for young men that balanced the army's role with that of the Forest Service and the other agencies who oversaw the actual work. The Forest Service administered about half of all the CCC projects nationwide.[8]

The army provided structure and discipline to keep order for the men who were between the ages of eighteen and twenty-five. Rules included no alcohol, no profanity, and "scuffling [was] not permitted unless under proper supervision." Camp leaders strove to create a supportive environment to keep the enrollees engaged by providing abundant good food, extensive athletic competitions, educational opportunities, and job training. They encouraged leisure activities during the week and granted time away from the camps on the weekends. At Kalispell Bay this mixture of work, discipline, and recreation seemed to keep most men satisfied, especially in the early years of the program. Cannata proclaimed, "The food was out of this world. I gained ten pounds and was in great physical shape." By 1938, out of the two hundred men in the camp, "there are only about ten of these habitual sick list enrollees." This handful of men used illness as an excuse to get out of work assignments but "the records show that they are not sick on Saturdays and Sundays."[9]

The Kalispell Bay camp, like the others in the Priest Lake area, featured a long, narrow recreation hall with a library at one end and a company store. The men enjoyed the radio or "someone will be playing a guitar and still others will be playing harmonicas and violins. Many of the boys will be singing the most favorite cowboy songs." Men played cards, ping pong, or enjoyed the pool tables with "the endless click of balls for several hours during each evening." Once a week the men watched talking movies shown with a projector. Cavanaugh Bay Camp set up an outdoor movie screen. The state camp lacked the amenities enjoyed at the Forest Service camps on the west side. "Summer evenings have seemed awfully long to some of us and the week-ends have been rather dull." The men built an outdoor theater and organized a "hillbilly band."[10] It proved so successful, the group performed at the other camps in the area.

"We made buddies according to the area you came from," Cannata explained. "One latched onto me because the boys made fun of him due to his Lower East Side dialect. I came from his hometown and we got along great." Cannata's friend encouraged him to participate in the inter-camp track meets. He discovered a talent for running the mile and won at a meet with the six neighboring camps. Spokane papers followed CCC sports and reported on Cannata's remarkable success even though he

The CCC camps sponsored a range of sporting events including boxing, seen here at the Kalispell Bay camp. *Quentin Larson, Weber Album, Priest Lake Museum*

"ran with chamois moccasins for foot covering," the only footwear he owned besides his Army issue boots. His natural talent failed him when his buddies signed him up for a boxing match. When Cannata faced a Golden Glove veteran, "for three rounds I would jab, hold and dance backwards. I survived but I told them not to ask me again."[11]

The men at the Experiment Station camp competed against each other's barracks in softball games at the end of the workday. The commander reported, "Each game seems to bring out all the 'wisecracks' which have been stored up during the day." The camp's baseball team "pounded its way to the district championship in 1938," and produced two district winners in boxing.[12] During the winter, camps played each other in basketball when the roads allowed and the Priest River High School gym was available.

On weekends, trucks took the young men into Priest River. From there Cannata and his buddies hitchhiked "to see the country around us." Once they went to Spokane but arrived back in Priest River after the last truck left for camp. They walked the thirty miles to the lake, "singing to scare away mountain lions and

bears. We made sure we never missed the truck again."

Education at CCC camps often came in the form of vocational training. The Forest Service reported, "The foremen all appear to be very alive in teaching enrollees how to improve their skill on the job." At Kalispell Creek, "The boys are trained in the art of tool sharpening, axe work, sawing, powder, and road work." An engineer taught enrollees to survey and locate a route so crews could replace the primitive telephone lines from Priest River. Foreman John "Snick" Sudnickovich taught a class on "procurement of telephone poles and use of tools" before the men began stringing the line on to the Bismark Station.[13]

At the camps, enrollees had the opportunity to take classes to complete their grade school or high school education. The faculty at Priest River High School tested men ready to receive their diplomas. The New Deal added more formal educational opportunities at the CCC when Eleanor Roosevelt pointed out that as the men returned to their urban neighborhoods, very few would find employment as foresters. Enrollees could take correspondence college courses, including aeronautics, business law, English, psychology, and forestry.[14] At Cavanaugh Bay, the men reserved time at the camp's typewriters to complete their assignments.

The camps also provided classes in "foremanship" to build leadership skills among promising young men. "Those who show special abilities are given an opportunity as far as is possible, to cultivate them."[15] In 1935 "Snick" Sudnickovich joined the CCC in New Jersey and eventually his company came to the Kalispell Creek camp. He recalled, "I started to work with the other kids and I don't know, I guess it was I had some ambition or some damn thinking, I got to be a corporal, and assistant leader. Then I got to be a sergeant."[16] When he left the program, the Forest Service hired him as a technician, who in turn trained CCC enrollees at the Experiment Station camp.

For all the planning and activities, trouble found its way into the camps. Hazing was not uncommon among men from different regions.

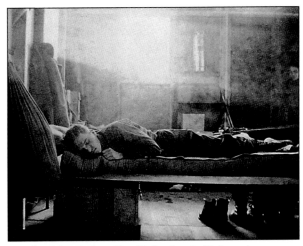

John Cihanek from New York asleep in his barrack at Priest River Camp F-164. *Priest Lake Museum*

Racial tensions led black recruits from Chicago to hike out of a camp to a Spokane police station. Harlem recruits at the Kalispell Bay camp found the experience lonely and "there aint' much to listen to." Racism and discrimination affected the workforce also. Foremen, especially those hired locally, favored boys from rural or

"Snick" Sudnickovich, second from the left, joined the CCC in New Jersey and ended up at the Kalispell Creek camp. Hired by the Forest Service at the end of his program, he spent the rest of his life at Priest Lake. *Priest Lake Museum*

Western backgrounds. "If there was a high percentage of blondes among the boys I expected good results; if they were mostly brunettes, not so good," said one, demonstrating how blonde country boys were often preferred to the Jewish and Italian boys from the East Coast.[17]

INTRODUCING WINTER CAMPS

When George Cannata's six-month enlistment ended in October, he re-upped for another stint. His company and the others stationed at camps in the Kaniksu transferred for the winter to work on projects in sunny California.[18] The next spring assistant forester Elers Koch began planning for winter camps at Priest Lake. He decided there was "sufficient work within easy reach to keep them busy" at Kalispell Bay and Blowdown camp. Company 1994 moved to Kalispell Bay for the first winter in October 1934. The lake was "frozen over in the bays and the boys had ideal skating," along with skiing and tobogganing.[19] They spent the winter working at Granite Creek cutting,

clearing, piling, and burning brush. By 1936, the Kaniksu National Forest maintained six winter camps and the other Panhandle forests hosted several others. Now only about two thousand men left seasonally for the south instead of the twelve thousand transferred the first year.[20]

Earlier that spring Company 1235 constructed Blowdown #2 camp (F-159), named for its location surrounded by downed timber from the 1926 fires. Crews redeveloped a site along Reynolds Creek near Hanna Flats that only a year earlier had served as the Beardmore logging camp. The men found "it was necessary to accept rough conditions, eating meals from mess kits and sleeping in tents on snappy nights." They spent much of their summer fighting fires instead of developing the camp and "were unusually happy" to be assigned winter projects in California. When Company 1924 arrived to take their place, they found the camp lacking and worked quickly to make it a "sightly and livable place."

At Blowdown #2, seasoned timbermen made up much of Company 1924 so the Forest Service assigned them the task of fire hazard reduction. This included removing snags on the fourteen thousand acres that surrounded the camp shown here. Veterans sometimes worked in −26° temperatures in five feet of snow. *Lee White, Weber Album, Priest Lake Museum*

Unfortunately, winter arrived early and the men spent a miserable season battling the elements.[21]

Unlike the other CCC companies around Priest Lake, Company 1924 was made up of World War I veterans. When President Roosevelt expanded the CCC program to include veterans, district headquarters at Fort George Wright in Spokane recruited men from the surrounding region. The administration decided to keep the veterans—most in their forties—at separate camps, which meant that Blowdown #2 operated much more casually than the nearby Kalispell Bay camp housing younger men. The veterans even enjoyed beer in camp.

Keeping the road open to Priest River proved to be an ongoing challenge during the winter; nevertheless, the men hosted two dances at the camp. Trucks picked up their families and guests from Sandpoint and Priest River and took them home at the end of the evening.[22] At Christmas, the veterans decorated a large tree in the mess hall and invited Priest Lake school children, offering them "plenty of good things, treats for all and presents." The commander reporting on the occasion commented, "The veterans enjoyed the entertainment as well as the children who will remember it as an event in their lives for many years to come."[23]

Remaking the Forest

After George Cannata and his company finished constructing their camp at Kalispell Bay, the men began their Forest Service assignments. Cannata helped build roads into a burned area to be cleared. He joined a three-man rock breaker crew to move boulders too big for the bulldozer. "We would make a hole with a hammer and chisel, put in dynamite, light it, and run like hell to hide." With safety always an issue for the unskilled young men, his foreman made sure Cannata passed his blaster's examination and carried his "card of competency." CCC crews, by agreements with unions, could build roads providing access to timber but not ones solely for public travel. Projects opened up access to much of the region, including roads

at Squaw Valley, up Lamb Creek, on the south fork of Granite Creek, and at Hughes Meadows. On the east side, crews built a road from Cavanaugh Bay to Indian Creek over the mountains, along with another to Horton Ridge and Chimney Rock.[24]

Ranger Henry Peterson could hire twelve Local Experienced Men (LEM) to help him supervise projects at the Kalispell Bay camp. The men, mostly seasonal rangers and unemployed loggers, served as foremen over specific operations such as road building and tree planting or with skilled labor such as carpentry. Bonner County's Democratic chairman Bob Dow approved the employment of all the local men. The Priest River insurance man and former Forest Service ranger "cleared all requests regardless of political party affiliation," according to Peterson.[25]

At Priest Lake like other northwest forests, "there were no 'made jobs' to give the boys work. And many a ranger, to his delighted surprise, found jobs being done this year that he had not hoped to get done for many years, if ever."[26] The huge CCC workforce allowed the Forest Service to focus on fire hazard reduction and timber stand improvement in areas devastated by the 1926 fires. The agency located all three west-side Priest Lake camps in the largest burns. Chief forester F. A. Silcox believed with CCC manpower the Forest Service could launch "the final assault on fire." The majority of men, whether on federal or state land, worked toward the agency's policy of all-out fire suppression by creating infrastructure and supporting new growth in burn areas.[27]

Projects often took the men miles away from their camps. They sometimes spent only four hours of actual work out of their eight-hour day because of truck travel. The army closely regulated the enrollees' hours of work and living conditions, so the Forest Service established "spike" camps to overcome issues of distances. "Smaller crews are the best, but with CCCs there is not sufficient adequate overhead to supervise these small crews." Forester Ernie Grambo supervised a spike camp building a trail

grandchildren of those who did this fine piece of work, it will be a heritage of millions of dollars of good commercial timber, streams well stocked with trout, and game in abundance."[44]

The CCC program stabilized the economies of Priest Lake and Priest River in a region reeling from the Great Depression. In the program's third year, Forest Supervisor Jim Ryan emphasized the tremendous local benefits of the camps. He reminded residents, "The CCC has helped relieve the local unemployment problem. More local men were employed as experienced enrollees, skilled workers and foremen than could have been employed had the CCC not been with us."[45] He mentioned the wages enrollees spent on their weekends in Priest River, Sandpoint, and Newport and listed the huge orders for food and supplies placed with regional merchants. The camps bought more than half of their food, along with "postal service, hardware items, blasting power, soaps and many sundry items" in Priest River alone.[46]

Ryan also promised long term economic gains with the new CCC recreational facilities, "rapidly increasing the number of people who are using the Kaniksu forest for vacations." He cited the economic benefits to the regional businesses as the tourists bought provisions and gear. Ryan concluded by calling attention to the vast number of conservation projects completed. "Timber has been saved to furnish future employment through the actions of CCC crews in fire suppression, hazard reduction and planting."[47] On a personal level, the CCC gave many of the men "a sense of being." George Cannata reflecting on his time at Kalispell Bay asserted, "The year I spent in the CCC was one of the best in my life."[48]

LUBY BAY GUARD STATION

The Forest Service Guard Station at Luby Bay remains one of the most visible legacies of the Civilian Conservation Corps at Priest Lake. The original guard station, inhabited in the 1930s by semi-retired ranger Jim Ward and his wife Helen, was a former houseboat pulled up on shore.[49]

The makeshift guard station was replaced with a large log cabin built by a CCC crew from the Kalispell Bay camp, led by LEM foreman Fulton Messmore. Clyde Fiscuss, a government architect, designed the house and garage in the rustic, nostalgic architecture style used by most CCC projects. Each week for a couple of summers, two truckloads

Ranger Jim Ward and his wife Helen lived in the original Luby Bay guard station in the 1930s. The former houseboat, pulled up on shore, listed on its cedar float logs. Helen found the slanted floor tiresome. When they moved into the new CCC cabin, she appreciated the new level floors, but found the cabin interior dark. *Priest Lake Museum*

of CCC enrollees, about thirty men, arrived to work on the Luby Bay cabin. They used native materials, covering the roof with cedar shakes and the front porch with slabs of slate. The crews cut and notched white pine logs, then planed and varnished them. They gathered rocks and with the help of another LEM built "an excellent fireplace."[50] Unlike most log cabins on the lake, the crews added modern conveniences like running water, a basement, and garage with a concrete floor.[51]

The Priest Lake Museum is housed in the Luby Bay Guard Station, completed by CCC workers in 1935. *Priest Lake Museum*

The cabin, finished in 1935, was deemed as "one of the best pieces of work to be found anywhere."[52] Rangers and their families lived in the cabin until 1989. The Forest Service agreed to lease the historic cabin to the Priest Lake Museum Association for exhibits on the region's heritage. Open during the summer, the museum includes information about the CCC companies who originally built the rustic log cabin on Luby Bay.

Chapter Thirteen

Extracting More or Less

The Diamond Match Company operated two camps in Priest Lake forests most years during World War II. War Production Board (WPB) rulings created equipment shortages that complicated efforts to cut increasingly remote patches of timber but Diamond managed to profit anyway. The industry lauded Diamond's efforts: "Here is evidence of desire of a pine operator to produce logs for the war effort under difficult conditions."[1]

Manager Jack Barron struggled to keep his crews full. He found "sawyers to be the scarcest item in woods manpower situation. Many of the younger men have been lost to the Army." Lumberjacks still cutting trees with cross-cut saws deserted the woods for less arduous and better paying jobs in the war plants. Barron also faced a shortage of gyppos, independent loggers, who either found better jobs outside of the woods or were getting into business for themselves. The War Production Board tried to get Diamond and other camps to reduce food consump-

tion. The timbermen fought back, arguing "this hardest of physical work calls for the intake of plenty of calories by the logger." The logging camps continued to provide eleven pounds of meat per man every week.[2]

Fred Forsythe managed Diamond Match's Camp One on Cougar Creek, drawing on old and new technologies. He used a bulldozer to blaze roads into the isolated white pine stands but still relied on teams of horses to skid the logs. His crew created a "jammer" to deck the logs using booms on the stripped-down chassis of old heavy trucks that accelerated the loading process. Better roads allowed Forsythe to use logging trucks for the six-mile haul to the booms on Cavanaugh Bay.[3]

A jammer on an old truck chassis.
U.S. Forest Service, Northern Region

155

Booms around the lake, shown here, held the logs securely until the spring drive. *Russ Bishop, Weber Album, Priest Lake Museum*

The Timberman magazine asserted, "No combined logging and sawmill enterprise in the West makes better use of water transportation than Diamond."[4] The company contracted with the Northern Navigation Company to move booms of logs down Priest Lake. Captain Ed Elliot, daughter Mona, and son-in-law Russ Bishop operated the steamboat *Tyee*. Each week the boat left the company dock in Coolin and went first to Diamond's Camp One in Cavanaugh Bay where they picked up the boom sticks and chains. Boom sticks were used to corral the logs. The sticks were forty feet long white pine logs with a hole in each end so they could be chained together with a toggle link to form a wooden lasso around the floating logs.

Elliot then headed to the Diamond camps on Squaw Bay or Indian Creek where he used the smaller steamboat, *The Ridley*,

"like a sheep dog rounding up logs for the bigger *Tyee*."[5] Elliot linked together sixty boom sticks to form a "big bag boom." It took three hundred feet of towline to move the million board feet of logs down lake.

The process took sixty hours and required a crew of three that often included Mona Elliot Bishop. She grew up working on her father's steamboats so she willingly took her turn on the six-foot wheel to pilot the *Tyee*. She performed the same jobs as the men including connecting the boom sticks. She bragged about being able to walk all the way around on the sixty floating boom sticks, jumping from one to another with her caulk boots. But for all her skills, she drew the line at taking on the job of engineer, which required greasing the steam engine regularly. She recalled, "I loaded lots of wood but when they started to teach me to grease, I said, 'That's where I quit.'"

The Idaho Bureau of Mines and Geology compiled a list of all the mines and prospects around Priest Lake.[21] It identified fifty-seven individual historic properties but only three mines ever shipped any ore. Only the Idaho Continental Mine ever produced enough revenue to cover its expenses. A geologist summed up sixty years of prospecting dreams around the lake when he declared, "There are literally thousands of recorded mineral claims in Bonner County and 99 percent of them are worthless."[22] The history of Priest Lake mining backs up his statement.

GOING NUCLEAR AT PRIEST LAKE

The nuclear age and the uranium "rush" of the 1950s brought a renewed interest in Priest Lake's mineral potential. Radioactive minerals were found in small placers at Two Mouth, Cougar, Hunt, and Indian Creeks, along the east side of Priest Lake and near Chipmunk Rapids on Priest River. None of these prospects ever had significant work done on them. In the early 1950s, the Fire Chief Mining Company staked new claims on Nickel Plate Mountain and boasted a tungsten discovery. A United States Geological Survey geologist and a Bureau of Mines engineer examined the property in 1952 and both concluded that while there were minor amounts of the tungsten mineral scheelite, no tungsten ore existed on the claims.[23]

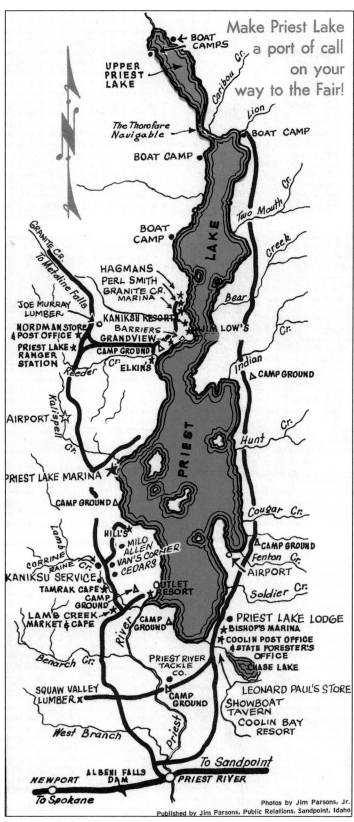

Priest Lake businesses and resorts came together to market tourism
after the war. In 1962, using promotional materials like this map, the
Chamber of Commerce hoped to get more tourists on their way to the
Seattle World's Fair. *Priest Lake Museum*

CHAPTER FOURTEEN

Tourism in the Atomic Age

In September of 1952 Priest Lake Chamber of Commerce president George Hill hosted a "Show-Me" trip, inviting the most influential men in Idaho to tour the lake by boat and pack train. Guests accepting the Chamber's invitation included Governor Len Jordan and future governors Don Samuelson and Robert Smylie. State land commissioner Edward Woozley joined them, along with Diamond Match officials, Forest Service representatives, and reporters from Spokane and Seattle. Camp boss John Sudnickovich rounded up enough mules for the tour even though "we find horses and pack strings scarce articles in the automobile age." In the evenings, the men dined on steak, fried chicken, baked ham, and fresh fish. Afterward around the bonfire Hill introduced a nightly series of discussions prefaced with a reminder of changing times: "ours is a small world in the atomic age."[1]

Hill and the Priest Lake Chamber of Commerce hoped the trip would "be the kick-off to closer cooperation between state and federal land agencies and the people in our area." Around campfires at Two Mouth Lake, atop Squawman Mountain, on Mosquito Bay, and up at American Falls, Priest Lake businessmen used time with their powerful audience to discuss pressing issues shaping the future of the lake. They focused on water quality, wildlife, fishing, timber, and especially recreation.

Resort owners and other businesses depending on tourism were caught in the middle of rapidly changing mindsets about the environment. They had grown frustrated as state policies governing the lake's eastern shoreline conflicted with federal policies developed for the western shoreline. They warned, "We no longer enjoy at our back door a vast unexplored domain of apparently unlimited resources." George Hill and the other men interested in the expanding tourism economy understood the devil's bargain with their plans. They admitted, "One of the greatest dangers to scenic beauty and natural surroundings of Priest Lake is recreational use itself. If not properly planned and managed the recreationists can and will destroy the wild primitive charm of the lake."

The Chamber hoped the high-profile trip would create more collaboration among the state and federal agencies that affected decisions at Priest Lake. Members pleaded, "We feel our public agencies should discuss and agree on a uniform policy for the lakeshore lands." The chamber also felt timber interests were progressively at odds with the growing recreational economy at Priest Lake. They cited as evidence the slow *Tyee* pulling logging booms down lake juxtaposed with the "gay zooming speedboat." Some argued that, "The incompatibility of timber production to certain aspects of recreation affects us all."[2]

Over the next decade some of those officials who sat around the campfires that September responded to the conversations. They acted on issues ranging from rural liquor laws to securing the Upper Priest River Scenic Area. More immediately, Priest Lake received national press for the "Show-Me" tour. Even though *Spokesman-Review* photographer Clint Watkins broke his leg during the trip, he still brought back pictures that filled an entire page of the newspaper

In its desire to promote recreational opportunities around the lake, the Priest Lake Chamber of Commerce cited the incompatibility of timber booms with the "gay zooming speedboat." *Priest Lake Museum*

highlighting the vast possibilities of Priest Lake for the Inland Empire.[3]

"A Cult with Many Vacationists"

Some northern Idaho leaders embraced tourism as their economic future after the war. Experts noted that tourism was the region's second largest economy and "recreation in the Priest Lake area is potentially nearly as great an economics factor as timber production." They predicted it would only grow in the coming years thanks to transportation advancements, a rising middle-class standard of living, more people receiving vacation time, and the Inland Empire's population increase from workers who migrated during the war.[4]

After the war, Idaho put more money into road systems and Priest Lake businessmen finally were able to boast a highway paved all the way to Nordman.[5] They estimated the completed road

"will in all probability increase the pressure of recreational use by 50 to 100 percent in the next few years." New roads or not, families flocked back to the lake after the war in record numbers. A Spokane paper observed, "Priest Lake has become a cult with many vacationists. They will drive past the larger Coeur d'Alene or Pend Oreille and fight for reservations months ahead at the two dozen lodges or groups of cabins."[6]

Priest Lake resorts welcomed the changes brought by the newly organized power cooperative Northern Lights, beginning in the late 1940s. As visitors came to expect more amenities, electricity transformed rustic cabin camps by offering lights at night, refrigerators instead of iceboxes, and indoor plumbing. *Northern Ruralite* magazine's Northern Lights Edition jested, "Today's outdoorsman is a man who wants to take it all with him, including the kitchen sink and the automatic dishwasher."[7]

Priest Lake resort owners fashioned an informal portrait as they cut the huge ribbon opening a paved Highway 57 from Priest River to Priest Lake in 1957. Many had lobbied for years to improve the route to the west side of the lake. Among those pictured here are Perl Smith, Don and Della Howell, Betty, Heidi, and Nikki Stephan, Addy Smith, Bryon "Steph" Stephan, Vern Howell, Kenneth Woods, Al Elkins, Walt Hunziker, and George Hill. *Priest Lake Museum*

"THE MOTHER LODE OF ANGLING"

When Frank Anselmo Jr. caught a fifty-one-pound mackinaw trolling off Kalispell Island in 1953, he snagged what was claimed to be the

Betty and "Steph" Stephan from Priest Lake Marine promoted the lake at the Spokane Sportsmen's Show in 1958. *Priest Lake Museum*

biggest lake trout ever caught in the West and changed Priest Lake fishing forever.[8] The press responded to his catch promising, "Large fish excite the sportsman and attract large numbers of fishermen. Resort owners have found large fish to be a major factor in stimulating business." Lake entrepreneurs argued, "Fish and wildlife are so interrelated with recreation that it is hard to tell where one begins and the other ends." During the 1950s the macks, bluebacks, and cutthroats satisfied "the trophy fisherman, the troller and the fly fishing enthusiast." They also provided economic survival for fishing resorts on Priest Lake.[9]

The macks first arrived at Priest Lake in 1925 in twenty-four milk cans. For years they remained modest in size and elusive until the kokanee or bluebacks, a land-locked salmon, were introduced in 1942.[10] The macks ballooned while dining on the bluebacks and

Frank Anselmo changed fishing at Priest Lake when he caught a fifty-one pound mackinaw in 1953. *Priest Lake Museum*

starting in the fall of 1952 "a rush to the new Mother Lode of angling was on."

Small resort owners Jim Low and Willard Stevens catered primarily to fishermen beginning in the 1930s on strips of private land near Granite Creek. After the war, other businessmen joined them. Perl Smith sold his motel and service station on Trent Avenue in Spokane to buy land north of Granite Creek in 1945. He built six rental cabins, a store, docks, and because he was "a good boat and motorman," Smith and his resort became indispensable for boat owners at the north end of the lake.

Jim and Betty Hagman began their resort in 1957. Hagman purchased the land years earlier from the Northern Pacific Railway, using funds he earned as a teenager delivering newspapers and working as a pole cutter in Priest River. The family moved to live year round at the lake and began by clearing an old logging landing. They built two lakeside homes and soon fol-

lowed with twelve modern units. They advertised Hagman's Resort as a "quiet family-type vacation spot" with lots of fishing. Other small neighboring resorts included Groop's Mountain View, Port Young's Camp, Corey Morgan's Fish Camp, and Barrier's Resort.[11]

Walt and Rose Hunziker started their Outlet Resort with fishing cabins in 1936. During World War II they purchased the neighboring resort, known as Pawnee Farms, which straddled both sides of the Priest River. Since the 1910s Fred Williamson offered cabins for rent but those staying on the south side of the river needed to honk their car horn, "a blast of two long and two shorts," to signal they wanted to be ferried across.[12]

Many older Priest Lake resorts smartened up after World War II, especially as electricity reached them. The newspaper noted, "Priest Lake, Idaho, for many years a haven for bristle-faced fishermen, is sprucing itself up and

Resorts like Grandview, shown here, welcomed the enthusiasm for Priest Lake fishing and took photographs of guests with their catches. *Priest Lake Museum*

providing more conveniences and soft living for the visitors it expects to follow the new road up the shore." Even the venerable Northern Inn at Coolin received a postwar facelift. Known then as the Hillcrest Lodge, the Staples family from Lake Chelan bought it from Fred Forsythe. They envisioned it "becoming a meeting place for many Inland Empire sportsmen and tourists." They promoted the lake's "only complete lodge with cocktail lounge." While a drink could be found at most resorts, Idaho liquor laws limited serving alcohol to establishments within incorporated municipalities. The Hillcrest owners convinced Priest River officials to extend their city limits more than twenty miles to qualify for a liquor permit. When someone broke into the lodge and stole all the liquor, their license was revoked.[13]

After Vern and Della Howell bought Grandview Resort near Ledgewood Bay in 1948 they joined other resort owners to promote Priest Lake not only to sportsmen but also to a growing number of vacationing families. They slowly renovated it from a fishing camp to a modern resort. They advertised "recreation for the entire family with a children's fenced-in playground."[14] In 1955, they were one of the first resorts to extend their season to stay open all year, instead of just Memorial Day to Labor Day.

While the Howells and other new owners worked to modernize their cabin resorts, a number of operations on the lake failed. Some owners found it more lucrative to sell as the demand for vacation homes on deeded land skyrocketed. Paul-Jones Beach in Coolin changed hands in 1946 and ran through four owners until 1961 when it was subdivided and sold. Further up the bay Ida Handy's son Harry ran his family's Camp Sherwood Resort while operating circuses in India. During World War II he sent his Australian bareback-riding wife Tiny to Priest Lake and Leonard Paul helped her get into the country through Canada. She managed the cabins until Handy retired. After his death in 1949, the cabins were sold and eventually became private.[15]

"A CONGENIAL GROUP WHO WISH TO ENJOY SIMPLE CAMPING LIFE"

On February 1, 1948, Washington State College president Wilson Compton and his wife Helen invited staff and faculty to their home to discuss sharing ownership in a retreat at the head of Priest Lake. Originally the Comptons hoped to acquire surplus land from the Farragut Training Base on Lake Pend Oreille. While they waited to hear about that land, Compton commented during a staff meeting about the "need for a retreat for overworked administrators." Bacteriology professor Victor Burke suggested a place he knew of where "members of the faculty could relax and enjoy."[16]

Burke vacationed at Elmer Berg's rustic resort Shady Rest at the head of Priest Lake, near the Beaver Creek Ranger Station. Swede Elmer Berg had bought land after the Clearwater Timber Company logged it in 1922 on Beaver Creek.[17] He started his resort by insulating his cabin so he could rent it to early fishermen and late hunters. As a host, Berg could be "temperamental as hell. He had a hard time getting along with his neighbors."[18] Eventually, Shady Rest included eight cabins, a gazebo, and a boathouse. The unexpected death of his neighbor Pete Chase prompted Berg to sell out in 1945 to Bill Muehle for $15,000. When Burke approached Muehle about selling to the college, he offered the fifty-four acres for $50,000. Compton said no. A couple of months later, in need of some quick cash, Muehle offered the property for $25,000. This time the Comptons said yes.[19]

The Comptons paid for the property and then leased it back to the newly formed Beaver Creek Camp Association (BCCA), or as they promoted it, "Washington State College on Vacation, Priest Lake, Idaho." Compton made it clear no state or college money was involved, but trusted the new association would secure funds to cover his cost in the next two years. He added, "It was the will of the group that it be developed as a congenial group who wish to enjoy simple camping life at low cost." The

Elmer Berg built this "homestead" in 1923 and expanded it in the 1930s, showing why he became the best known of the log builders at Priest Lake. Washington State College president Wilson Compton and his wife Helen bought Berg's homestead and resort in 1948, then leased the land to the Beaver Creek Camp Association. *Priest Lake Museum*

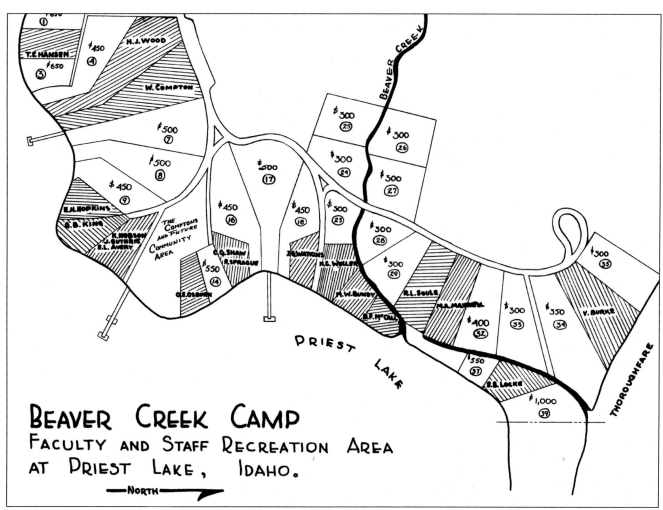

Washington State College (WSC) faculty and staff formed the Beaver Creek Camp Association to manage Elmer Berg's former resort. To attract more members, organizers created a promotional brochure that included this map. *Washington State University Libraries, Manuscripts, Archives, and Special Collections*

interested committee envisioned renting out the cabins while association members could secure options on lots which restricted some types of construction, "to preserve the natural beauty of the wilderness."[20] Helen Compton organized logistics so members could enjoy the isolated camp at the mouth of the Thorofare, which had no roads or electricity. She secured two surplus ship-to-shore landing crafts, dubbed "the launches," which met members and guests at the Granite Creek Marina at the end of the road and transported families north to Beaver Creek. By spring of 1948 twenty-two faculty members signed on. The family-oriented environment and communal aspects appealed to some. For others, they joined for the fishing or an opportunity to buy a cabin on a professor's salary.[21]

The first couple of years proved rocky for the BCCA. Compton mused, "I have been surprised at the small number of staff who seemed to have been genuinely interested."[22] The association argued over how communal the camp should be, whether membership should be restricted only to WSC staff, and how the lots should be laid out. Rumors flew about the faltering project. Association president Robert Hungate commented, "It is perhaps unduly optimistic to hope that the association can function in the spirit of the original intent but…it would be premature to abandon the idea of a cooperating group."[23] The BCCA survived and by the mid-1950s it sold all the available lots.

The spruce beetle challenged the BCCA communal experience in 1954. The Forest Service constructed a road over Blacktail Mountain that year to salvage timber affected by the destructive insect. Members could now drive all the way to Beaver Creek and the launches became obsolete. The arrival of phone lines and electricity once again prompted association members to redefine the camp experience.[24] In 2008, the BCCA celebrated its sixtieth anniversary, still debating changes as the membership transitioned through generations.

A SECOND SUN VALLEY

Rumors began spreading around the lake in 1940 that a California company was ready to lease land in Cavanaugh Bay to create a millionaire's resort patterned on the immense and elegant Sun Valley in southern Idaho.[25] Opened in 1936, the successful year-round destination resort redefined a modern tourist economy in the West that involved a considerable investment of outside capital.[26] After World War II several entrepreneurs tried to transform Priest Lake's rustic fishing camp accommodations into expansive contemporary resorts like Sun Valley.

Rex Sutton imagined a "big new resort" on the property in Cavanaugh Bay that was passed over by the California company. He bought and leased land beginning in 1940. After the war Sutton lobbied the Idaho State Land Board to sell him the lots he leased along with three additional ones. He constructed a lodge with a dance floor and a recreation hall with a dining room specializing in chicken and steak dinners. He opened a cocktail lounge in 1959 after suing the county liquor board to implement changes in the Idaho law in support of alcohol at resorts.[27]

Sutton hoped to entice wealthier guests by offering a dude ranch experience and providing a boathouse to "service and dry dock the largest cruisers." He envisioned the type of guests who could forego the dusty east side road and fly in with their private planes. Sutton transformed the homestead fields of the Fenton's into a landing strip. When he opened his new airstrip in 1950, fifty-four planes with the Inland Empire Aviation Association came for a breakfast fly-in fish fry. A month later the strip's first crash occurred when a plane overshot the runway while trying to land. It would not be the last plane to suffer that fate.[28]

LINGER LONGER

Bud Thompson, a Spokane businessman, first came to Priest Lake in 1910 and by 1928 he owned a cabin. A decade later he built The Cedars, a west side tavern near the road to Luby

Bay. After World War II, Thompson put his Priest Lake experience together to open Linger Longer on land he bought from homesteader Chester Helme at Kalispell Bay. He first offered a tent camp in 1947. Two years later he opened "The Timber Room" which included drinking and gambling.[29]

By 1958 Thompson envisioned Linger Longer as a year-round destination resort. He offered guests a modern motel with "sun decks for quiet relaxation." The resort boasted a driving range for the golfer, a stable of excellent horses for riding, and shuttle service for vacationers who preferred to fly into the Forest Service airfield at Hanna Flats.

Envisioning a year-round vacation destination rivaling Sun Valley, Bud Thompson installed a ski run at his Linger Longer Resort in 1960. *Priest Lake Museum*

Thompson expanded the dining room into the largest on the lake, seating 180 people along with a twenty-stool snack bar. On the weekends, he shut down the dining room at 10:00 p.m. to accommodate the popular summer dances with "excellent music of a five piece orchestra." Linger Longer's scale allowed Thompson to host regional conferences including Rural Electrification Administration managers, the Idaho Association of Commissioners and Clerks, the Northwest Society of Clinical Pathologists, and the Idaho Press Association. Thompson promised guests that Linger Longer in 1958 "will rival anything of its kind in the west."[30]

Linger Longer became an all-season destination resort in 1960 when Thompson added downhill skiing. Other resort owners had tried to expand their tourism season before the popularity of snowmobiles in the late 1960s, but Thompson made it a reality. He leased the hill behind the resort from the Forest Service and installed a 1500-foot rope tow. For skaters, he smoothed and scraped the ice in front of the dining room.[31]

Neither Bud Thompson nor Rex Sutton could finance their resorts at a scale that moved them beyond a regional resort to something comparable to Sun Valley. For all his plans,

political activities, and legal wrangling, Sutton's "big new resort," never became a destination spot. By 1961 he sold his airstrip to the state land board. Thompson quickly found he was not "totally satisfied with the response" to his ski run and modern resort.[32] "Tired of working so hard," he sold Linger Longer to the Jesuit Society in 1961.[33]

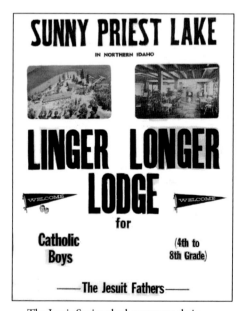

The Jesuit Society had outgrown their seminary facility at Twin Lakes so they bought Bud Thompson's Linger Longer in 1961. *Priest Lake Museum*

MODERN RESORTS FLOURISH

After World War II, an ad announced, "Ike Elkins is back and has made many improvements to make this [resort] the finest, best equipped in the Inland Empire. New docks, splendid beaches, beautiful lodge with dining room service." Elkins' plans were not as grandiose as some of his competitors but he constantly upgraded his resort. In 1953 he signed over his Forest Service special use permit to his son Al and wife Phyllis.[34]

On Luby Bay, the Farris Resort came up for sale and caught the interest of George Hill. He chose not to join his father in the family's Spokane shoe store after his discharge from the Navy following the war. He relished his Priest Lake summers growing up at the Hunt Creek cabins owned by his father and grandfather so he bought the Farris Resort. "When he heard this place was for sale, he convinced his folks to help him" buy it, recalled Lois Hill.[35]

Hill expanded his resort, building more cabins and cooking at his modest lunch counter with the menu hanging behind him on the wall. Both Hill and Elkins provided for the fishermen, but also appreciated a growing interest in other recreational activities, especially water sports. As early as the 1930s Elkins bought water skis from Carter Crafts "at a reasonable price because skiing was starting to become popular."[36]

As Hill succeeded in capturing a new generation seeking family-centered vacations, his next-door neighbors at the Luby Bay Resort decided to give up their Forest Service special use permit. The agency, impressed with Hill's operations, encouraged him to purchase the adjoining property and granted him an additional permit. The expansion allowed the Hills to transform the scale of their resort. They hoped to host the conventions that Linger Longer had started to attract, noting, "Many organizations are now holding meetings at lakes and recreational areas. We're sure that in the future many firms and other organizations will be holding their meetings at the lake."[37]

The Hill and Elkins resorts competed with each other, but the families also worked together to promote Priest Lake and expand tourism opportunities.[38] They both received good ratings from the American Automobile Association (AAA). They entertained travel writers and planned special events to attract more visitors. They promoted winter sports, fall retreats, and weekly special barbeques. They served as the local representatives with Spokane investors to establish a golf course at Priest Lake in 1965.[39] They balanced a respect for the undeveloped nature of the shoreline with accommodations desired by affluent vacationers. They created models for successful resorts on Priest Lake. Ike Elkins commented on the transformation, over nearly half a century, of his rustic fishing cabin into a modern resort, "I didn't figure on the thing turning out how commercial like it is."[40]

Ike Elkins built this resort dining room in 1932, but in the 1950s the family renovated the room around a double fireplace. Forest Service policies now allowed alcohol but the 1958 permit stipulated they needed a separate room for a cocktail lounge only. The new lounge featured a large dance floor. *Priest Lake Museum*

Luby Bay on beautiful Priest Lake, where cares are easily forgotten

Your hosts, George and Lois Hill

While other resorts advertised fishing boats, George Hill's resort on Luby Bay gained a reputation with water sport enthusiasts. By 1960, with the help of his wife Lois, whom he met at a Linger Longer Resort dance, Hill modernized his lodge, opened a new marina with covered slips, and offered ski docks, which were advertised in the brochure pictured here. *Priest Lake Museum*

The Hills expanded their resort when they moved the 1934 Luby Bay Lodge down closer to their own and joined the two buildings with a contemporary dining room in between. The old resort building became a modern cocktail lounge. *Jim Parsons, Priest Lake Museum*

Jan Elkins grew up working at her family's resort. After she married in 1960, Jan opened the Drift Inn on the Thorofare. For seven years she served breakfast and lunch with no electricity or telephone. Supplies came in by boat. *Priest Lake Museum*

CHAPTER FIFTEEN

Our People's Lives:
Postwar Priest Lake Community

The modern world caught up with Priest Lake after World War II. New timber production equipment allowed families instead of corporations to run the local mills and logging operations. The Forest Service and other agencies expanded year-round personnel. Resort owners catering to summer people stretched their season longer and longer until some stayed open all winter. A new highway and increased economic opportunities almost doubled year-round residents in just a decade. Business and community services expanded with the increased population. At the same time however, the "deep snows and long seasonal layoffs have a tendency to produce a lethargic influence on our area."[1] Local poverty challenged a new generation of leaders who recognized that "if we are to prosper and grow we must work toward nullifying this influence. We are rich in things, it is up to us to provide the enrichment of our people's lives." Community life at Coolin, Lamb Creek, and Nordman altered with the changes in modernity, growth, and the shifts in populations.

"The Dams Would Not be Feasible"

When electricity arrived at Priest Lake, Nell Carey White rejoiced, "Oh, the advent of washing machines, indoor plumbing, refrigeration. That was the big thing, refrigeration."[2] White came to her family's Outlet homestead as a baby in 1908, when there were no roads and no electricity. Thirty-five years later she and her husband Bill owned the Lamb Creek Inn, a tavern along the west side road. Each winter the Whites put up forty tons of ice from Chase Lake and in the summer crushed up the blocks to keep bottles of beer cold and food fresh.

Franklin Roosevelt's 1930s New Deal created government-aided cooperatives for regions no commercial power companies would serve. The arrival of the North Idaho Rural Electrification

Electricity changed the way Priest Lake did business and brought improvements to accommodations like the Elkins Resort cabin shown here. Electric stoves replaced wood burning ones and lights replaced gas lanterns. *Priest Lake Museum*

175

Rehabilitation Association (REA) power lines in the late 1940s brought lights and electricity to run refrigerators, ice machines, and water pumps for flush toilets. By 1960, the co-op—renamed Northern Lights in 1941—serviced six hundred houses and businesses.[3] Thanks to the REA, Nell White now cooked on an electric stove instead of a wood stove and she could make ice all summer long. Electricity allowed modern equipment on ranches like the Warren Dairy in Coolin Bay. They no longer needed to milk by hand or use a little gasoline engine milker.[4]

As electricity began reaching the lake, a dam was finally constructed at the Outlet. The Forest Service had long anticipated a dam and had warned for years of the pending three-foot rise in the summer water levels with notices on the summer residence permits. Cabin owners lobbied annually for a dam since the lake got so low by August. Many sportsmen argued it would improve fishing. After the last log drive in 1949 an emergency change to the Idaho State Codes allowed a "water control structure" to be built the following year at the Outlet.[5] Most welcomed the state dam in 1950 control lake levels. It required that the dam maintain the level of the lake after spring runoff until the close of the recreational season when "lake waters may be released and the surface level permitted to recede below said elevation." Originally, it took six men and a wrecker truck to raise the boards that regulated the flow of the water over the dam. It created a cumbersome, inexact system that meant required water levels were not always maintained.[6] Washington Water Power operated it even though the dam generated no power.

Interest in hydroelectricity from the Priest River dated back to 1909 with Andy Coolin's failed Priest Lake Electric Railway and Power Company. In 1928 the Federal Power Commission gave permission to the City of Sandpoint to construct a hydroelectric dam on the river but it never happened.[7] The Bonneville Power Administration next considered a dam two miles below the Outlet but built one at Albeni

Falls instead. Northern Lights first got permission to dam Priest River at the Outlet in 1941, but it needed to provide a spillway for the log drives each spring. Arthur Hooper headed up the effort but the War Production Board ended the construction, ruling that the necessary steel was needed for the war effort.[8] A few years later Northern Lights applied to build two dams on either side of the Dickensheet Bridge. The State Reclamation Engineer dismissed protests lodged by Priest Lake citizens and granted permission in 1957.[9]

Arthur Hooper, shown here on the left, oversaw an ill-fated attempted to build a dam at the mouth of the Priest River during WWII. *Priest Lake Museum*

These dams threatened to raise Priest Lake another three feet above summer levels, flooding out cabins in low-lying areas like Beaver Creek and turning stretches of the river into slack water ponds. The Northern Lights plan incensed Wilbour "Shorty" Broun, who lived on the river, so he formed the Priest Lake Association. He challenged the argument that the need for power was more important than the environmental effects it would have on the lake. He contended, "The dams would not be feasible, they would damage wildlife and they would diminish property values."[10] Broun and other groups successfully argued before the Federal Power Commission against the Northern Lights dams, much to the surprise of state officials.

At Priest Lake, and across the country, more Americans questioned the use of public lands and waterways for private gains. Organizations like Broun's formed to protest other government management decisions. Some groups like the Priest Lake Sportsmen's Association focused on orchestrating environmental changes that supported fishing and hunting. They grew politically savvy about lobbying state and national agencies that controlled much of Priest Lake.

HIGHWAY 57

When Nell and Bill White bought the Lamb Creek Inn in 1945, they had only a handful of neighbors living on the west side road heading to Nordman. Soon new businesses sprang up on surrounding private land, a legacy of the homesteaders twenty years earlier. The transformation of the west side road into Highway 57 during the 1950s by the state of Idaho spurred more development. Unlike the resorts on the lake, these businesses remained open year-round and served both residents and summer tourists. They played a critical role in expanding the regional economy and encouraging community development.

Charles and Martha Van Dervort moved to Priest Lake in 1941 and the next year established Van's Corner on the west side road at the Luby Bay road cutoff. They inherited two cabins to rent, but "one we had to reserve for a teacher each year."[11] Down the road from the Van Dervort's, Spokane businessman Bud Thompson sold the tavern he opened in 1937 to Ada Mae Martin and her husband. The Martins operated The Cedars for a year before Millie and Ward Adams took over in 1946 and expanded it into a memorable lake institution. "Millie would either like you immediately or not like you just as quick. Her language was something terrible." Millie Adams's generosity was also legendary, "If she had a dirty shirt on her back, she would give it to you if you needed it."[12]

Ward and Millie Adams took over The Cedars tavern in 1946. *Priest Lake Museum*

Most at Priest Lake celebrated the state road improvements in 1948 but not Dottie and Deke Bruno, who ran the Buckhorn Inn in Nordman. The relocated road bypassed them and several other buildings that made up Nordman. The Forest Service agreed to trade land with the Brunos so they could access the road. The new Nordman Club and Store, constructed by Tom Jarrett, a "wonderful log builder," quickly "became the gathering place for social events, Thanksgiving, and community meetings for the fifteen families who lived in the area year round."[13]

Making a go of a Priest Lake business was not for the faint-hearted. Nell White remembered in the summer time "we didn't go to bed or get our clothes off from Friday night until Monday morning." But in the winter "the whole thing kind of gets narrow. You have a limited clientele, when the tourists are gone. And you have the feeling when you see them coming through the door that you know the exact words they're going to say before they even get the door closed behind them." Some days during the winter months the Whites only took in thirty-five or forty cents. Business owners came together for support and entertainment to mark events like the ice harvest. They cooperated putting up ice and afterward celebrated with the Iceman's Ball. White recalled, "They'd all get together and have a big dinner and a dance and everybody would get gloriously drunk."[14]

The Nordman Club and Store, along with the post office, became an important community gathering place. The "Nordman Gang," gathered here c. 1955, included from the left, John Sudnickovich, Archie Brunner, Perry McNiece, Ray Boehm, and Art Harris. *Priest Lake Museum*

Dancing at Van's Corner

When the Whites bought the Lamb Creek Inn it featured a dance hall. On Saturday nights in the summer, three hundred people "came from all over—out of the woodwork more or less." Musicians from Blue Lake including pianist Mary Ellen Black entertained the crowd. Coolin teenager Charlotte Jones enjoyed the dances on the west side, "One of my favorite places was Van's Corner where we could dance to the music of Mert and Ernie Trefern. Mert was the best drummer in the business and Ernie could play anything if you could just sing it first."[15] In 1952 Chet Burns bought Van's Corner and his family band continued offering lively dances. Chet played the mandolin and horn with his brother Jim on guitar. Little brother Roy joined them when he learned to play the drums. He asserted, "The Burns Brother Band was so popular on the lake because Chet and Ray had such a personality that they always had something good to say."[16]

The Priest Lake Community Sportsman Club sponsored Friday and Saturday summer dances in the early 1960s at the former Nordman School. While popular, "it seemed the Priest River crowd and the Spokane 'Lake' crowds were frequently at odds and fights became more and more frequent. Some morally corrupt sneak in the community made a unilateral decision that the school was more of a nuisance than a community asset and decided to burn the building down."[17] Dance spots moved around the lake with new bands and the latest dances.

"An Innate Closeness to the Land and the Rhythms of its Seasons Stabilized Us"

When Lois Jansson's husband Bob became ranger at Priest Lake in 1950, she found to her dismay "thirteen bars and no churches or Sunday schools."[18] Jansson and other newcomers with children found the lack of community institutions disheartening and the poverty disquieting. One of her first experiences moved her to action. Since the ranger's house hosted one of the few phones in Nordman Jansson received a call from the Priest River doctor about the death of a migrant timber worker. The worker's family lived fifteen miles north of Nordman in a clearing. When she went to break the news, she finally located the family at the Forest Service garbage pit hunting bear to keep from starving. She discovered what others at Priest Lake knew too well. "Hidden behind the scenery are situations and social problems."[19]

More families arrived with new sensibilities and expectations, especially for enriching

Priest Lake forests isolated families. Mike Sudnickovich, shown here, remembered growing up "bored, lonely and poor." In fact, he elaborated, "This was the grand lake of my youth—boring as hell, poor as hell—not a grand vacation on the lake! Winters were the worst." *Priest Lake Museum*

Della Brennan and Betty Hagman." For a generation of Priest Lake children, "all those volunteers played such an important part of raising up the community." Living year-round at Priest Lake challenged families but Hagman explained, "An innate closeness to the land and the rhythms of its seasons stabilized us."[21]

"A Few Punches Among Drunken Loggers Who Messed Up His Prayer Meeting"

Missionary Dick Ferral preached occasionally at the Nordman School during the 1940s.[22] Known as the Lumberjack Preacher, he had cauliflower ears from his days as a prizefighter and had "thrown a few punches among drunken loggers who messed up his prayer meeting." In 1950 he called on Lois Jansson, the new ranger's wife, when he heard she "thought her children needed to go to Sunday school."[23] Together they invited locals to join them and sixteen people came out to organize a formal Sunday school with teachers, a superintendent, and a board of the directors.

the lives of their own children and the others around the lake. Local leaders resolved, "Let us not overlook the health, welfare, education and spiritual guidance of our children."[20] They organized Boy Scouts, Camp Fire Girls and swimming lessons in the summer. At the 4-H meetings, Arley Sue Hagman said, "I still recall the forestry lessons by Betty Kedish and Katherine Joyce, and the sewing and cooking lessons of

Ranger Bob Jansson organized the Boy Scout Troop camping and hiking trips. The newly formed Camp Fire girls joined them to plant trees in front of the new Nordman store after the road was moved. *Priest Lake Museum*

Resort owners donated old sheets for choir robes at the first Christmas program for the formally organized Sunday school in 1950. The power was out for eleven days so mothers fussed about not being able to press the robes, but then again, Lois Jansson recalled, "without electricity that didn't matter as we had to hang up lanterns at the schoolhouse and the wrinkles didn't show in the dim lights." They lined the Nordman School windows with cellophane and strips of wrapping paper to create their own stained glass. The power came back on Christmas Eve. *Priest Lake Museum*

The Sunday school began as a community effort. Timms Resort put a collection jar on their counter to "help buy Sunday School papers for the children attending Sunday School classes."[24] After a year, enough adults attended Sunday school so they formed the Priest Lake Community Church. The next summer youth minister Herb Long approached people about supporting a church building. Lulah Schneider, wife of the Kalispell homesteader, recalled, "He came by and introduced himself and then explained his reason for visiting, a building site was needed." Though the Schneiders were not regular church-goers, they decided to donate lots above Kalispell Bay. While appreciative of the offer, many in the group preferred a site closer to Nordman. Location proved just one of many issues that vexed the congregation. "Before the church was built we found out all the things Protestants can manage to divide over," bemoaned Lois Jansson.[25]

The small congregation looked to the Spokane Council of Churches to support their mis-sion. The council provided a rotation of ministers from a range of denominations and some financial assistance. The group found themselves homeless for a season when the school district decided to renovate the Nordman School. They gamely improvised with the Church in the Woods, an outdoor chapel in a beautiful clearing south of Nordman created by a youth work camp from Whitworth College. "They built a rustic pulpit, altar and baptismal font and set of log benches out under the open sky in a forest setting."[26]

The congregation broke ground in 1955 for a permanent church building, but a lack of consistent leadership plagued the project. Twenty members made up the congregation, but summer brought attendance up to one hundred. The seasonal changes meant the weight of direction fell back to a handful of the faithful each fall. The Priest River Congregational Church minister James Estes began conducting regular services at the Lamb Creek School in 1957 for the Priest Lake Community Church. The relationship seemed to work. The Sunday school attendance grew to eighty children and "drew us out with many of the retired or older leaders picking up carloads of kids along the way."[27] The non-denominational group decided

Spokane architect and Luby Bay cabin owner Victor Wulff designed a modern A-frame church building with windows that overlooked the lake. Construction began slowly, as shown here, often lacking both funds and volunteer labor. Eventually, resort owner Perl Smith "sort of picked up the pieces and took over the direction." *Priest Lake Museum*

for its future stability to join Congregational Christian Churches and to share a pastor with Priest River. This allowed the building project to advance and services were held in the new church by 1958.

OUR LADY OF THE LAKE

During the 1930s priests and ministers offered religious services for the men in the Civil Conservation Corps camps. When an officer at the Kalispell Bay camp told the priest that mass interfered with mess hall, the McWilliams family offered their Luby Bay cabin for services. When the congregation grew too large, the group moved again to the old Lamb Creek Inn. People brought boat cushions to sit on the floor in the empty building. An ordinary summer Sunday brought sixty cars of "tourists and the people of the lake," so Reverend J. B. Kunkel from Priest River wrote to the Bishop in 1955 asking for a building. Like the Community Church, attendance expanded rapidly during the 1950s and Kunkel warned, "Next year and thereafter when the roads are in good condition we can logically expect many more people at the lake."

Kunkel found a site on the main highway that "Mr. Walter Kettleson, not even a Catholic, has promised to donate for our purpose." Members added their support. It took three years before the congregation received permission to raise funds for the church. The Catholic Church Extension Society donated about a third of the construction monies and insisted on naming the new parish St. Blanche instead of the congregation's preferred "Our Lady of the Lake." The Catholics decided on a prefabricated building from the Timberib company instead of facing a long, drawn-out building project like the Community Church. The building went up in a couple of weeks and the congregation celebrated mass under its own roof August 23, 1959. It lacked running water or electricity, but offered two outhouses out behind.[28]

The evolution of Priest Lake churches demonstrated the community's response to a rapidly expanding residential population with diverse expectations and a stronger connection to the conventions of the outside world. The churches balanced the mixed blessing of congregations made up of "tourists and the people of the lake." Unlike most churches, attendance peaked in the summer. That lead to frustrations since it limited seasonal support from the bulk of the congregations. Both groups received donated land from nonmembers in the community, acknowledging the roles churches filled in the growing, shifting region.

"A LITTLE LOG CABIN WHICH MIGHT HAVE DELIGHTED ABRAHAM LINCOLN"

In 1956 Jean Anglin groused, "Lamb Creek School is a little log cabin which might have delighted Abraham Lincoln but this is 1957." She had "become fed up with lack of facilities for school children living around the Priest Lake."[29] As postwar Americans placed more emphasis on education, the conditions of the schools became unacceptable, especially to the new families. Anglin joined a growing number of Priest Lake parents lobbying for a new consolidated school. Summer people rarely supported the one-room schools at Coolin, Lamb Creek, Squaw Valley, and Nordman, unlike other regional institutions that depended on both year-round residents and vacationers. It took voters like Anglin to transform education at Priest Lake.

Recruiting teachers proved to be an annual challenge in part because of the dismal conditions. A student recalled in her one room school, "We had a new teacher every year, up through the eighth grade."[30] At the Nordman School in 1957 the teacher's quarters consisted of a small room located behind the furnace in the basement. A trip to the bathroom required a walk up a rickety flight of stairs and out the front door to the outhouse.[31] In an effort to provide a hot lunch on cold days, one teacher brought an electric fry pan so students could heat their sandwiches.

A month after Alyce Allen moved to Priest Lake for her husband's work in 1949, two school board members offered her a teaching job at Lamb Creek. An experienced teacher from California, Allen was shocked at the conditions of Priest Lake schools.[32] She found textbooks so outdated they no longer met Idaho requirements. Lamb Creek school lacked running water and the two outhouses out back were "mighty cold sitting in winter when 20 below."[33] A double-barreled wood stove heated the room.

Allen found the lack of consistent teaching more threatening than the physical conditions. The year before she arrived, the children endured three different teachers all in one school year. "Some students were three or four years below their grade level... However they had been promoted." She challenged a couple of boys who chose not to do their schoolwork. "We always get promoted," they replied to her warning and declined to change their habits. At the end of the school year Allen refused to promote the boys to the next grade. They looked

During Lamb Creek School teacher Alyce Allen's first winter in 1956, her husband Milo hooked a trailer to his tractor to get his wife and the students to school, shown here. In one late 1940s winter, Corrine Raine brought her children to school with a team of horses and a bobsled.
Priest Lake Museum

at their report cards in amazement exclaiming, "She did it."[34] Allen reported the next year they grew to be more disciplined "and became fine young men."

Allen established the Priest Lake Parent Teacher Association in 1952. They voted first to sponsor Camp Fire Girls and Boy Scouts. They added a Ladies Study Club that met monthly to give "the hard-working mothers some intellectual and social life as they planned school projects and fundraisers." They held card parties to raise money for new school equipment like a movie projector. They applied to join the state milk program, convinced local people to donate refrigerators, and covered the cost for families unable to pay.

"Driving Away Good Teachers, Conscientious Parents...and New Businesses"

Priest Lake parents began working for a new consolidated school in 1953. They donated gas money for a representative to attend every Bonner County school board meeting in Sandpoint to advocate for a new facility at the lake.[35] In the meantime, they secured running water and indoor plumbing for the four area schools and rearranged the grades between buildings to help ease overcrowding. Countywide bond levies failed again and again, revealing tensions that came from the earlier consolidation of smaller school districts in the county, and from a growing resentment towards raising educational expectations in the postwar era. After one defeat a member of the Mother's Committee for Education remarked in frustration, "Our responsibility is great, for we are not only handicapping our children now but the world in which they will live as citizens, and we are driving away good teachers, conscientious parents...and new businesses." On Election Day in 1959, Priest Lake voters overwhelmingly supported a new school 159 to 9, but the levy failed in the rest of the county.[36]

The levy failed the next year too but it forced the Bonner County School Board to address the

Priest Lake Elementary school opened in 1961 with 103 students and four teachers.
National Archives, College Park

conditions at Priest Lake by finding funds to construct a new, modern elementary school.[37] Communities on both sides of the lake rallied to help build the consolidated Priest Lake Elementary School in the spring of 1960. Local people brought their trucks and dozers to the donated land near Lamb Creek. "Many men and a great deal of equipment worked nearly every weekend." As the men cleared the land for the new school, they also cut and sold the timber. The money they raised went to a hot lunch program.[38]

The men fitted the new school with playground equipment from the old schools. When the school finally opened in fall 1961, 103 students and four teachers enjoyed running water, a kitchen, electric heat, and modern desks. Recalled one student, "None of us really knew what differences that it would make in our lives. School movies and dances, disorganized social recesses, and other extracurricular activities at the new Priest Lake Elementary became part of our once simple school lives as modern society raced in."[39] In just a generation, Priest Lake residents created or transformed local institutions like the schools to "provide the enrichment of our people's lives."

Meanwhile, the one-room school houses continued to provide community anchors. The Coolin Civic Club took over their school building "where we vote, where we started our fire district. We've had planning and zoning meetings here and the Priest Lake Grange uses the center. Without it there wouldn't be a hub for anyone on this side of the lake."[40] The Lamb Creek School became a teacherage until 1973. It was remodeled and opened as the Priest Lake Library in 1974.

The log WPA-era Lamb Creek School become the Priest Lake Library in 1974. Students shown here in spring 1961 are Wayne Pettit, Dezri Dean, Helen Kedish, Mitchell Jayo, and Julie Turnball.
Priest Lake Museum

After World War II vacationers overwhelmed Priest Lake facilities. Boat ownership soared and many people took to water sports like waterskiing. *Jim Parsons, Priest Lake Museum*

CHAPTER SIXTEEN

Recreation and the Greatest Good

Ours is a small world in the atomic age. We are living in a world grown small by virtue of our modern transportation, increased population and increased standards of living. We no longer enjoy at our back door a vast unexplored domain of apparently unlimited resources.

—Priest Lake "Show-Me" trip brochure, September 1952

Thanks to the paving of Highway 57 in 1957, people could visit Priest Lake for just the weekend. They stayed fewer days, but came more frequently, and more of them wanted their own cabins. Visitors overwhelmed the lake's campgrounds, and "no vacancy" signs were posted most summer days by 1958. Recreational demands on the lake increased a dramatic 500 percent after World War II.[1]

Technological improvements and greater disposable income made boat ownership appealing, and vacationers hauled their new motorboats to the lake in droves. Priest Lake saw an overwhelming increase in boat usage.[2] Some boaters fished, but many now enjoyed water sports and explored the bays and islands in ways they could not earlier. A resident complained, "On a weekend it is virtually impossible to fish thanks to the boats and waterskiers."[3] Water sports became so popular George Hill proposed water skiing rules for Luby Bay to handle the chaotic boat traffic in 1959. Local leaders marveled at the escalating lake visitation, but cautioned, "One of the greatest dangers to scenic beauty and natural surroundings of Priest Lake is recreational use itself."[4]

"THE KEY TO KEEPING PRIEST LAKE A NATURAL GEM"

The Chamber of Commerce hoped the 1952 "Show-Me" tour could offer thoughtful responses to the rapid, profound, and vexing post-war changes. They voiced concerns that Priest Lake would evolve like Lake Tahoe, where commercialism overwhelmed the natural environment that drew people there in the first place.[5] Leaders asserted, "The key to keeping Priest Lake a natural gem is our public lands surrounding the lake. Public lands are and must be retained as buffer zones between private development and other uses."[6]

Federal and state land made up 77 percent of the shoreline at Priest Lake. Businessmen like George Hill and Vern Howell asserted, "Here the public can control and police itself for public benefit. We feel our public agencies should discuss and agree on a uniform policy for the lakeshore land."[7] The Chamber of Commerce hoped to get the agencies to cooperate to make that possible. They also wanted to convince residents and summer people to support land policies that served the "greatest good for the greatest number." They had their work cut out for them.

The demand for cabins, camping, and boat access overwhelmed the Forest Service and the state of Idaho. Vacationers, and the growing number of Priest Lake business owners who served them, began to challenge the traditional uses of public land. The Forest Service managed 43 percent of the shoreline, mostly on the west side, along with the islands. The agency started to focus more on recreation especially after federal resources become available through the 1956 "Operation Outdoor" project. The five-year program allowed planning and implementation of recreational changes the Priest Lake district had considered for years. It could "provide more space now for future generations to enjoy the lake area."[8]

Priest Lake's "deeded" land made up only 23 percent of the shoreline, including 6 percent acquired by the Diamond Match Corporation.[9] In 1955, there were only 155 vacation cabins on private lake land.[10] These small parcels signified the earlier movement of public lands into private hands through homesteading, government railroad grants, mining claims, and sales of state land. The lack of control on private land concerned regional leaders since "shorelines can be cluttered with human occupancy structures or urbanized if care is not exercised to prevent this."[11] Their concerns were valid especially since by 1984 more than 779 cabins now occupied deeded lots.[12]

The State Board of Land Commissioners, known as the Land Board, managed the school endowment lands on the east side that included 34 percent of the lake shoreline. The Idaho constitution mandated a "maximized economic return to the state school endowment fund from timber production." The directive became increasingly complicated as more vacationers camped at Indian Creek and hundreds of families demanded more leased cabin sites. Public pressure forced the state to change land designations to address the recreational realities at Priest Lake.[13]

"Private Enrichment instead of Public Gain"

Indian Creek beach and other popular east shore spots presented a conundrum for the state. Idaho's constitution prevented the designation of a park on school endowment land "unless it provided the best long term gain for the state." As early as 1927 officials acknowledged the

Shown here touring with the Priest Lake Timber Protective Association in 1962 are members of the Land Board, which included state representatives and senators, forest products officials, Forest Service rangers, timber land owners, state forester Roger Guernsey, and Governor Robert E. Smylie. *Priest Lake Museum*

shoreline held appeal for recreational use, but it provided little income and in fact required more state spending. The legislature amended the Idaho code. It allowed land adjacent to Priest Lake to "be devoted to public use in connection with the preservation" of the lake "as a health resort and recreation place" but remain under state ownership. A decade later, the State Board of Land Commissioners responded to growing public demand and developed plans for more roads and cottage sites. The land commissioner promised the developments will be "in such a manner that the natural beauty of the lake will not be destroyed."[14]

When the Priest Lake Timber Protective Association (PLTPA) started construction on an east shore road in 1952, it predicted, "When this road is finished hundreds of lots suitable for summer homes, resorts and public campgrounds will be accessible for development."[15] The state responded by adding another 150 leased cabin lots to the 205 they already administered. This brought substantial changes to the east side of the lake where for decades the road ended at Cavanaugh Bay.

The new road prompted the Land Board in 1958 to open up thirty-six new cottage sites at Pinto Point, a narrow spit of land just west of Indian Creek. Republican governor Robert Smylie accused the Democrat-dominated land board of doling out the coveted leases to their politically connected friends. He charged the lots were "let without publicity and without a competitive offering of any kind." Smylie surmised, "It is now obvious that there were more than thirty-six people interested in acquiring these valuable leases." State land commissioner John Walters responded that Washington state residents held 276 of the state's cottage leases and only eight Idahoans enjoyed permits. He argued the boards' actions made sure "Idahoans were taken care of first."[16] Since 1912, Forest Service summer residential permits restricted elected officials from benefiting, but eastside state leases contained no such language.[17]

Smylie asserted in 1961 that after only two years the original well-connected leaseholders at Pinto Point transferred 75 percent of the lots at a profit. He demanded the Land Board explain why "prominent North Idaho Democrats or their relatives" claimed the leases and now enjoyed "private enrichment instead of public gain," especially since most of the cabin sites went to Washington residents. The governor pushed for an investigation, but the Land Board dismissed the move as politically motivated. However, Walters declined to explain why the North Idaho Park superintendent abruptly resigned before testifying at the Land Board meeting. He also agreed to Smylie's proposals for competitive bidding at a public auction and stricter leasing rules. The governor responded, "I applaud the board's actions, but in a sense it is like locking the barn door after the horse is gone."[18]

"Bears Rummage Around for Tasty Stuff"

The Forest Service transferred control of the big, beautiful beach at Indian Creek in 1917, along with the other state's school endowment lands. The agency reserved the beach for public use and forbade cottage sites. The state of Idaho continued to respect public access to the beach until the late 1940s when Diamond Match Corporation operated a logging camp at Indian Creek. A decade later the company floated its camp buildings from Indian Creek to Lion Creek at the same time the PLTPA opened the new road up along the east side. Indian Creek campground's popularity increased and by July 4, 1961, more than two thousand vacationers set up camp on six acres of ground, competing over the two-pit toilet facilities and a hundred tables.[19]

Arguing that it would generate tourist dollars for northern Idaho, Governor Smylie secured state funds to make improvements to the beach in 1958.[20] Funds covered pit toilets and a campground supervisor, but not site planning or improvements. The state also granted a private concession for a camp store and bar

Evening entertainment for a generation of campers included a trip to see bears pick through piles of trash at public and resort dumps, like this one at Elkins. At the Indian Creek camp dump, a visitor remembered watching the bears "rummage around for tasty stuff. It was kind of a Priest Lake Drive-in Movie." Demands to improve environmental conditions at the lake, especially water sanitation, prompted dump closings beginning in the late 1960s and brought an end to the popular summer ritual. *Priest Lake Museum*

Indian Creek campground, shown here c. 1960, received a much-needed facelift after the state created the Idaho Department of Parks and Recreation in 1966. They designated campsites and added running water, flush toilets, and limits on the number of campers. *Jim Parsons, Priest Lake Museum*

that contributed to some lively Saturday nights. In 1972 the state used federal land and Water Conservation Fund monies to purchase Indian Creek, along with the Lionhead and Dickensheet campgrounds, from the school endowment funds and established the Priest Lake State Park.[21]

"A Form of Public Subsidy"

The Forest Service believed the state of Idaho mistreated Priest Lake's east shore by subdividing it "with very little thought to zoning and public recreation needs." As a result, the agency felt that the weight of managing the overwhelming post-war demand for recreation facilities fell on its west side public lands. The Forest Service's own negligence exacerbated problems since at Priest Lake, "recreation management has, until recent years, been on a hit or miss basis. All too often it was miss."[22] Resolved, the ranger district sponsored studies, developed recreation plans,

and began to implement changes that promised to produce the greatest good in the national forest. The United States Congress passed the Multiple Use-Sustained Yield Act in 1961, mandating the Forest Service respond to public pressure to make recreation a priority of the national forests.[23] At Priest Lake, as the agency increased recreational opportunities to meet the congressional mandate, it collided with its own expansive summer residence program.

Ranger Hank Peterson struggled in 1934 to create interest in the Forest Service summer residence lots south of Luby Bay in the Osprey and Neopit tracts created by the Civilian Conservation Corps. "Applications slowed down and some pressure was exerted for me to obtain more summer home permittees." Fifteen years later, the agency received sixty-three applications for just four lots and implemented a lottery as new sites became available.[24]

Bob Marshall proposed an Upper Priest River Primitive Area in 1935 and conservationists had long expressed interest in preserving the area that remained undeveloped even after World War II.[45] The state of Idaho and the Forest Service controlled most of the upper lake and the Thorofare. Earlier in the century three homesteaders received patents for about four hundred acres, which in 1960 represented five small parcels of private land left undeveloped by the owners.[46] This changed in 1961 when two doctors from Spokane, Kermit Petersen and Don Babcock, acquired most of the Geisinger homestead at the south end of the lake and along the Thorofare. They subdivided the shoreline and made plans to sell the lots.

Vernon Kidd, president of the Priest Lake Sportsmen's Association, shuddered at the idea of cabins along the Thorofare and the upper lake. He joined forces with Art Manley, president of the Wildlife Federation, District 1. Together the men rallied support to keep Upper Priest Lake undeveloped. They explored ways that the private land could be acquired and then added to the more protected public land.

The debate about preserving Upper Priest Lake mirrored growing conversations across the country. Forest Service conservationists began in the 1920s advocating for the country's need to set aside its wildest forest lands. After the war, "The implications of living in a nuclear age" spurred even more Americans to express concerns about the diminishing wilderness. Even as debates about Upper Priest Lake progressed in Idaho, Congress was considering a Wilderness Act.[47]

Idaho State Forester Roger Guernsey also "got all fired up" hoping to save the upper lake by exchanging state land for the doctors' private property.[48] He and PLTPA president Lee White explored the possibility of getting special Idaho legislation to permit the exchange. They found the state constitution barred such action. White admitted, "The situation certainly doesn't look encouraging from here as we feel that time is fast running out." The men next considered

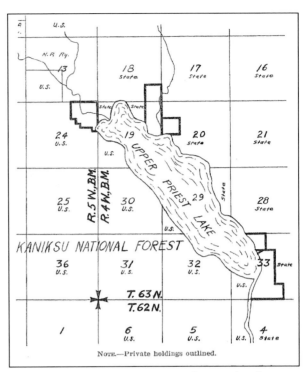

Three homesteads on Upper Priest Lake created pockets of private land. When developers threatened to line the Thorofare with cabins, preservationists worked to insure the area remain a wild place. *Priest Lake Museum*

"looking around for some rich public spirited citizen who would buy the property and donate it to the state."[49]

In the meantime, the doctors applied for a road right-of-way from the state to bring in equipment to clear the land. Guernsey felt there might be a slim chance the doctors would relent if the state denied their request while also prohibiting the development of docks. Governor Smylie supported Guernsey's decision. Dr. Petersen responded by suing the state of Idaho. Then he "walked a dozer across state land anyway and started grading off cabin sites. Skuttlebutt is that the dozer man was just sent up to scratch around and force the issue with the state," according to Guernsey. The Idaho Attorney General began pursuing trespassing charges against Petersen.[50]

Art Manly called a meeting on November 8, 1963, hoping to work out a compromise. He invited "representatives of every Federal and State agency we could think of that might be interested" along with Priest Lake businessmen, the owners, and their lawyer. They considered possible state actions such as land swaps and purchasing funds. The realities of Idaho politics meant any solution would take a long time, involve legislation, and perhaps even require amending the constitution. The doctors set a deadline of May 15, 1964, for a solution or they would begin selling lots in order to raise money for their mortgage.[51]

Manley and others worked diligently to find support and funds before the deadline. They attended conservation meetings throughout Idaho, Washington, and Montana. *Outdoor Life Magazine* featured their plight and gained national attention. Vernon Kidd's Priest Lake group organized parties to support the effort. But as the May deadline ticked closer, Manly declared, "in spite of our very best efforts, we have failed to solve the problem on a local or state level. The owners cannot give us another four years. We believe there is no further hope except through Federal help."[52]

Priest Lake supporters turned to Senator Frank Church. Guernsey explained to him, "The big problem is somehow to secure 160 critical acres now in private ownership. I don't know what can be done about it but this is one

area which I would be happy to have the federal government acquire it if we can't figure out a way for the state to get it."[53] Church embraced the challenge.

The senator worked with the Forest Service and ascertained the agency could legally purchase the land under the 1911 Weeks Act, which provided funds to buy lands that supported navigable waterways. However, the Weeks Act's annual allocation came to only $500,000 for the entire country and Upper Priest Lake alone required $400,000. Church tried other strategies to get separate funds appropriated before the deadline. His efforts got tangled up in a filibuster over the Civil Rights Act of 1964 and he failed.

Three days before the deadline Manley and others met with the doctors. They agreed to extend the deadline fifteen days and offered to give the effort another year if the group provided $30,000 to pay off the doctors' mortgage.[54] Manley recalled, "When it looked as if all was lost, a national organization, Nature Conservancy, came to the rescue."[55] The organization lent the money interest free, granting Upper Priest Lake a year of grace.

Back in Washington, D.C., Church introduced Senate Bill 3067 "to promote protection

Grandview Resort ownder Vern Howell (left) entertained Attorney General Robert E. Smiley (center) and Governor Len Jordan in the early 1950s. *Priest Lake Museum*

and conservation of the outstanding scenic values and natural environment of Upper Priest Lake in Idaho and lands adjacent thereto for public use and enjoyment." It authorized the Secretary of Agriculture to acquire at fair market value the five private holdings, making up the 417 acres. It also extended the boundaries of the Kaniksu National Forest to encompass the lands once they were purchased. Congress had already resolved the issue of funds to buy the private land with the creation of a Land and Water Conservation Fund. Idaho Senators Church and Jordan along with Washington's "Scoop" Jackson amended the fund's legislation before it passed to include money for the upper lake.[56]

"Upper Priest Lake is Good Medicine for Everyone"

Nevada Senator Alan Bible headed up the Subcommittee on Public Lands that first considered Bill 3067. He held a hearing at Priest Lake on a cold, rainy day in October 1964. Senators Church and Jordan attended, along with district Congressman Compton White. Twenty people testified and another 89 sent letters to be included. Much of the testimony became a love fest. For example Spokane doctor Thatcher Hubbard formed the Inland Empire Committee for the Preservation of Upper Priest Lake. Out of his 87 members, 75 were physicians. In his eloquent testimony he stated, "We just think being on the Upper Priest Lake is good medicine for everyone."[57] The editor of *Field and Stream* magazine wrote, "I am sure that if Upper Priest Lake is preserved in its natural state, its recreational and aesthetic value will increase steadily far into the future." The four hundred members of the Priest Lake Sportsmen's Association headed by Vern Kidd offered support for the government action. The Priest Lake Chamber of Commerce had explored options for years and understood that federal intervention "is the only way it can be saved."[58]

Two land owners, Sylvia Gumaer Burwell and Fern Geisinger, also responded to the hearing. The women struggled together in the

1920s trying to make a living on Upper Priest Lake. In 1923 Gumaer and her husband, "had $10 to our names besides two teams of horses" for logging, until the severe winters killed the horses. She declared, "In the past twenty years I have had numerous opportunities to sell this place however I have refused these offers because I wanted the places for my son and grandchildren." Burwell's daughter-in-law argued the upper lake would not be accessible for the "good of all of the people," because you had to own a boat. Her husband added that the area was not primitive because, to get there, boaters passed all these cabins that "at night it looks like the main streets of Los Angeles." Geisinger, who sold most of her land to the doctors, simply wrote, "I want to keep this land." The doctors, whose actions spurred the legislation, did not attend the hearing nor send any statements.[59]

Several Idahoans expressed concern about more land under government control and less in private hands to contribute to the Bonner County tax base. A group of summer cottage permittees suggested that federal land should be a net gain and offered to buy the land under their own cabins. Roy Leland promised, "Many of these present leaseholders including myself would be desirous in purchasing these lots." The Taxpayers League of Sandpoint gathered ninety-five signatures supporting the preservation of Upper Priest Lake. They stipulated the federal government needed to "make available for private ownership an equal value of similar land in this same general area."

Congressman Compton White introduced the elephant in the room that morning concerning the landowners on Upper Priest Lake. "I think it would be only fair that I should say at this time that purchase at fair market value means condemnation in the exercise of eminent domain." Art Manley assured him that "the owners of almost all the property have already indicated not only their willingness, but their desire to sell." The reality of the government condemning the land stirred several in the audience. Nordman's Bernard Staum demanded,

"What is to prevent our omnipotent Government from sometime seizing my home and land on the same pretext?"[60] J. R. McFarland of the Taxpayer League conceded that, "if the right to condemn is precluded, there would be no protection against lifting prices beyond the point of value and if prices are hijacked out of reach, then I couldn't justify the spending of tax money." Many people pressed for assurances the land would be acquired through negotiations and exchange and not condemnation.[61]

Frank Church's bill passed and President Lyndon Johnson signed it on June 15, 1965, creating the Upper Priest Lake Scenic Area. As predicted, the Forest Service had to resort to condemnation. After an appraisal, the agency offered the five landowners a total of $354,034. Aware the government had allocated more money, several parties held out for more, in spite of the assessed value of their land. The *Priest River Times* editor sarcastically summed up the situation, "Smokey the Bear's dilemma is one of no choice—either the property owners accept the independent appraisal or Congress directs him to haul them into court."[62] After two years, the two largest landowners settled out of court, with a final payout of $400,600 for all the acres.[63]

Frank Church expressed little concern for the inevitable condemnation process. The government had systems to manage that process. What it lacked, however, was a model for the Forest Service to jointly manage the Upper Priest Lake Scenic Area with the state of Idaho. Since the creation of the Forest Reserve in 1897, the state and the federal government sparred about how to manage public land at Priest Lake. Supporters worried that after all the efforts to secure the private land to preserve the upper lake the state of Idaho might destroy it by leasing lakeshore land for timber or mining operations.[64] They suggested that either the Forest Service or the state might develop a road into the little lake or agree to clear cutting on the Thorofare. The Senate Subcommittee of Public Lands sought written assurances from the state of Idaho to agree "to manage its lands on the Upper Priest Lake so as to keep them in a natu-

Forest Service representatives and Idaho state officials at Navigation Campground on the Upper Priest Lake Scenic Area in the early 1960s. *Priest Lake Museum*

ral condition, free of homes, business or industrial facilities. Management would be principally for recreation and aesthetic purposes." Idaho State Forester Roger Guernsey responded, "We are most happy about the way this partnership operation is developing.[65]

Governor Smylie and Neal Rahm of the U.S. Forest Service signed a Memorandum of Understanding with a joint management defining both the formal boundaries and what a scenic area and a primitive environment meant to each agency. Together, they needed to figure out how to administer and monitor the region, deciding who had authority to mandate changes and who was going to enforce them.[66] They both predicted, "Conflicts between fishing and water-skiing and between motorboats and canoes will become more pronounced as use increases."[67] Three years later in 1968 the Forest Service and Idaho Governor Don Samuelson officially introduced the six thousand acre Upper Priest Lake Scenic Area, "a scenic gem in an attractive and unspoiled forest setting."[68]

USHERING IN A NEW ERA AT PRIEST LAKE

The Upper Priest Lake Scenic Area offered a hopeful model for the region. The 1952 "Show-Me" tour leaders managed to get the public agencies to cooperate about shoreline policies. People debated over rights of private land ownership and public land expectations. It generated conversations about how public land should be used and the role of government. The process challenged considerations about who can have access to the lake and where. It made people consider the aesthetics of the Priest Lake shoreline. It contrasted economic development with the value of preserving the natural environment. Residents voiced their concerns along with the desires of the summer population. These issues continue to be debated. But with the Upper Priest Lake Scenic Area, the Forest Service and the State of Idaho became good stewards together, private land owners made a profit, and each year thousands of people still enjoy the beauty of the little lake.

THE END OF THIS STORY

Development and challenges to public land use continued to transform Priest Lake after the 1960s. Even with the changes, the historical roots of the lake remain visible. In 2006, one hundred years after the Leonard Paul Store opened, the annual Memorial Day parade passed by the review stand set up on the porch. Logging trucks, the Forest Service's Smokey the Bear, the Idaho Department of Lands, a float with Priest Lake Elementary School students, and marching cabin owners all paraded down the Coolin hill. This eclectic mixture represented historical legacies that still provide form and function to the region into the twenty-first century.

Notes

Abbreviations

IDL—Idaho Department of Lands

IMIR—Idaho Mine Inspector Report

KNF—Kaniksu National Forest

MASC—Washington State University Libraries Manuscripts, Archives, and Special Collections

MJA—Midwest Jesuit Archives, De Smetiana Collection

PLM—Priest Lake Museum Archives

PLRS—Priest Lake Ranger Station

PRT—*Priest River Times*

USFS—U.S. Forest Service

Chapter One: Putting Priest Lake on the Map

1. Geographical references throughout this book will usually be the current U.S. Geographical Survey name; Kevin J. Lyons, "Kalispel Ethnohistoric Uses of the Priest Lake Basin," Kalispel Natural Resources Department, Kalispel Tribe of Indians, Usk, WA (February 2009), 4, 10; John Fahey, *The Kalispel Indians* (Norman: University of Oklahoma Press, 1986), 27-28; "Lake Roothaan," Map IX C8-36, MJA, St. Louis, Missouri.

2. "Victor's Map," Map IX C8-35, MJA.

3. Richard P. Erwin, "Indian Rock Writing in Idaho," Idaho State Historical Society (1922), 47.

4. The missionary's name and spelling varies, but his order, the Missouri Province of the Society of Jesus, uses Peter John De Smet. Robert C. Carriker, *The Kalispel People* (Phoenix, AZ: Indian Tribal Series, 1973), 21. The finding aid for De Smet maps in the De Smetiana Collection at the Midwest Jesuit Archives reads "De Smet baptized Victor in 1841 and the chief died shortly thereafter. This map therefore is dated to 1841." However, Victor did not die in the 1840s and it could be that this is confused with the Flathead chief Victor instead of the Kalispel Victor Alamiken. Jacqueline Peterson identifies the mapmaker as Victor Alamiken in *Sacred Encounters: Father De Smet and the Indians of the Rocky Mountain West* (Norman: University of Oklahoma Press, 1993).

5. James Ronda, "'A Chart in His Way': Indian Cartography and the Lewis and Clark Expedition," in G. Malcolm Lewis, ed., *Cartographic Encounters: Perspectives on Native American Mapmaking and Map Use* (Chicago: University of Chicago Press, 1998), 141; Map 1X-C8-35 (translated from French), MJA.

6. Lewis, *Cartographic Encounters*, 62; "Map Showing the Relative Positions of the Different Tribes and Missions in the Territory of the United States," Prepared by Captain A. Pleasanton, 2nd Dragoons, from the Maps of the Reverend Father P. J. De Smet, S. of J. (Washington, D.C.: Office of Chief Engineers, 1861). Photocopy from the National Archives in the collection of the Bonner County Historical Society, Sandpoint, Idaho; Map IX C8-36.

7. Ronda, "A Chart in His Way,'" 144; On Victor's map, the Pend Oreille River is labeled "Salmon" and Lake Pend Oreille is "Kootenay"; Map IX C8-36, MJA.

8. A.M.D.G., St. Ignatius, July 25, 1846, Madam [S. Parmentier] from P. J. De Smet, S. J.; Pierre-Jean De Smet, S. J., *Oregon Missions and Travels over the Rocky Mountains in 1845-46* (Fairfield, WA: Ye Galleon Press, 1978), 252.

9. Robert C. Carriker, *Father Peter John De Smet: Jesuit in the West* (Norman: University of Oklahoma Press, 1998), 81, 217.

10. De Smet redrew the Priest Lake map a second time, a modified version of Map IX C8-36, with the same notations in a block print instead of cursive. On map IX C8-36, the Upper Lake is labeled in pencil with "De Smet," and on the second map, the description reads "the Upper Lake" instead of "De Smet's Lake."

11. De Smet to Col. Mitchell, July 1, 1857, in H. M. Chittenden and A. T. Richardson, eds., *Life, Letters and Travels of Father Pierre-Jean De Smet, S. J., 1801-1873* (New York: Francis Harper, 1905), 4:1497.

12. Gilbert J. Garraghan, "The Oregon Missions, II," *The Jesuits of the Middle United States*, vol. II (New York: America Press, 1938), 347.

13. Garraghan, "Oregon Missions," 218; Elers Koch, "Derivation of Geographic Names in Montana and Idaho," Kaniksu National Forest Collection, GN-USFS, Museum of North Idaho, Coeur d'Alene.

14. Map IXC8-13.

15. Hoecken to De Smet, October 18, 1855, Rev. P. J. De Smet, *Western Missions and Missionaries* (New York: James B. Kirker, 1863), 284; Chittenden and Richardson, *Life, Letters and Travels*, 766.

16. Dr. George Suckley, "Voyage in a Canoe From Fort Owen to Vancouver," Olympia, Washington Territory, December 19, 1853, reprinted in *Reports of explorations and surveys, to ascertain the most practicable and economical route for a railroad from the Mississippi River to the Pacific Ocean* (Washington, D.C.: United States War Department), XI: 296.

17. Suckley, "Voyage in a Canoe," 296; De Smet, *Western Missions*, 284.

18. De Smet, *Western Missions*, 290. Also see Garraghan, "Oregon Missions," 422; Hoecken to Roothaan, March 25, 1849.

19. Garraghan, "Oregon Missions," 468; Carriker, *Father Peter John De Smet*, 108.

20. Hoecken to De Smet, October 18, 1855, in De Smet, *Western Missions*, 284; Joseph Joset (Joset Roll 4), 324.

21. Carriker, *Father Peter John De Smet*, 82, 152, 157.

22. John J. Killorne, *Come, Blackrobe: De Smet and the Indian Tragedy* (Norman: University of Oklahoma Press, 1994), 231.

23. "Map Showing the Relative Positions of the Different Tribes of Indians and Missions in the Territory of the United States between the Cascades and Rocky Mountains," prepared by Captain A. Pleasonton.

24. Jack Nisbet, *Mapmaker's Eye: David Thompson on the Columbia Plateau* (Pullman: Washington State University Press, 2005).

25. William E. Cox, "Finding Aids to George Suckley Papers," 1849-1861, Record Unit 7191, Smithsonian Institution Archives. See also Suckley, "Voyage in a Canoe," 293.

26. Suckley, "Voyage in a Canoe," 293.

27. Edwin F. Johnson, "Map of the Proposed Northern Route for a Railroad to the Pacific," 1853.

28. Custer relied on Native Americans for his "first information on topographical features" and recorded their place names. See Linda Nash, "The Changing Experience of Nature: Historical Encounters with a Northwest River," *Journal of American History* 86, no. 4 (March 2000): 1606.

29. Marcus Baker, *Survey of the Northwestern Boundary of the United States*, 1857-1861. (Washington: United States Geological Survey, Department of Interior, 1900), 12.

30. Ibid., 75.

31. Henry Custer, "Report of Henry Custer, Assistant of Reconnaissances Made in 1859 over the Routes in the Cascade Mounts in the Vicinity of the 49th Parallel," Northwest Boundary Records, RG 76, NARA (College Park).

32. Baker, *Survey*, 71; H. Custer to Lt. J. G. Parke, N.W.B.C., Rec'd August 10, Camp Near Mission, July 25, 1860, Northwest Boundary Records, RG 76, NARA (College Park).

33. Henry Custer to Lt. J. G. Parke, July 25, 1860. Custer writes, "This confirms the statement of an Indian who was with me on the Lake the first time." Also, in the corner of a map of his Priest Lake trip in different script is written "Arrived at Lake June 17th 1860 H. Custer." However according to his report to Parke, Custer would not have arrived until the first of August. It could be that the Indians took him up to the Kalispel trail but he did not think he could get the mules through. On his map, he showed a trail coming down to Kalispell Bay.

34. Custer to Lt. J. G. Parke, July 25, 1860. Custer drew the Kalispel trail from the Pend Oreille River to Priest Lake on the map entitled "U.S. North West Boundary Survey: Map of Eastern Section," John G. Parke, U.S. Eng., Chief Astronomer and Surveyor, Washington, 1866. NARA Rg 76, Series 66 and discussed by David H. Chance in "An Ethnographic Review of Sylvis Trail," commissioned by the Plum Creek Timber Company, Moscow, Idaho, 1993.

35. Joseph Smith Harris papers, MSS S-1293, February 20, 1860, Yale Collection of Western Americana, Beinecke Rare Book and Manuscript Library.

36. Kaniksu National Forest report, n.d., Victor negotiated with Dr. R. H. Lansdale, Priest Lake Ranger Station archives, 75.

37. Custer to Lt. J. G. Parke, Chief Ast. & Survr. U.S.B.C. Recd. September 8, Chelemten the 29th of August 1860. RG 76, Series 66, NARA (College Park).

38. Custer Map of Priest Lake, RG 76, Series 66, NARA (College Park).

39. Custer to Lt. J. G. Parke, August 29.

40. Ibid.

41. Ibid.

42. Ibid.

43. Ibid.

44. Baker, *Survey*, 18.

45. Ibid.

46. Richard U. Goode, "The Northwestern Boundary Between the United States and Canada," *Journal of the American Geographical Society of New York* 32, no. 5 (1900): 468.

47. Robert Marshall, *Retracement of the Boundary Line Between Idaho and Washington*, Bulletin 466, United States Geological Survey (Washington, D.C.: GPO, 1911), 14.

48. Ibid.

49. Ibid., 15.

Chapter Two: Intrepid Adventurers

1. *New York Times*, July 25, 1886; Kaniksu National Forest Report, undated, Priest Lake Ranger Station archives, 75.

2. *Spokane Daily Chronicle*, September 29, 1891.

3. *Spokesman-Review*, September 30, 1891.

4. "Colonel William R. Abercrombie," *Spokane and the Spokane Country, Pictorial and Biographical* (Spokane, WA: S. J. Clarke Publishing Company, 1912), 1:117. Fort Coeur d'Alene was renamed Fort Sherman in 1887.

5. Special meeting minutes from the Society of Amateur Photographers of New York, September 20, 1887, page 633, published in *Anthony's Photographic Bulletin*.

6. "Adirondack Vandals: Mr. Holberton Describes the Ravages of Lumbermen and Others," *New York Times*, October 28, 1889; "The Protection of Game," *New York Times*, February 14, 1882.

7. Wakeman Holberton, *The Diary of Our Trip to E-Soc Quet By One of the Party*, September 3, 1887, Beinecke Rare Book and Manuscript Library, Yale University.

8. Ibid.

9. Ibid., September 4.

10. "In All Their Splendor: Hosts of Speckled Trout on View," *New York Times*, April 1, 1888.

11. Holberton, *Diary of Our Trip*, September 4 and 22.

12. Ibid., September 8 and 26.

13. Ibid., September 4 and Preface.

14. Ibid.

15. *New York Times*, June 15, 1895.

16. "A Curious Book That Can't Be Bought," *Spokane Falls Review*, March 16, 1890.

17. *New York Times*, "In All Their Splendor."

18. "The Gold of St. Kaniksu," *Spokane Daily Chronicle*, September 4, 1891.

19. "Indians of the Pend Oreille Country," In Marylyn Cork, *Beautiful Bonner: The History of Bonner County, Idaho* (Dallas, TX: Curtis Media Corporation, 1991), 9; "Priest Lake Country," *Spokane Daily Chronicle*, July 17, 1891.

20. *Spokane Daily Chronicle*, September 4, 1891.

21. "Hunters Paradise at Priest Lake," *Spokane Daily Chronicle*, August 30, 1898; *Bonners Ferry Herald*, August 3, 1895.

22. "Opens a Rich New Land," *Spokane Daily Chronicle*, May 1, 1894; *Spokane Daily Chronicle*, "Hunters Paradise."

23. *Spokane Daily Chronicle*, September 4, 1891; Inventory, 4th Class Post Office records for Coolin, Kootenai County, 1893-1907, PLM.

24. *Spokane Daily Chronicle*, "Hunters' Paradise"; "Original Survey, Meanders of the Little Lake, the Right and Left Bank Priest River, and Priest Lake," Twp 59N-4W, Id, Boise 1897, General Land Office Records, Bureau of Land Management.

Chapter Three: Speculating on Priest Lake Mining

1. Quotes from longtime Priest Lake merchant Leonard Paul appearing as epigraphs throughout this chapter are from James F. Estes, *Tales of Priest Lake* (Spokane, WA: self-published, 1964).

2. Bonner County deed records 1800-1910; *Spokane Daily Chronicle*, September 4, 1881 and March 23, 1888; *Spokane Falls Weekly Review*, September 10, 1891.

3. John B. Leiberg, *The Priest River Forest Reserve, Extract from the 19th Annual Report of the Survey, Part V, Forest Reserves* (Washington, D.C.: United States Government Printing Office, 1899), 233.

4. A. K. Klockmann, "A. K. Klockmann Diary," 1940 manuscript, typed in July 1959, Priest Lake Ranger Station archives, 4, 14.

5. *Spokane Daily Chronicle*, July 17, 1891; *Spokane Falls Weekly Review*, September 30, 1891; *Kootenai Herald*, January 16, 1892.

6. Klockmann Diary, 5, 9.

7. Henry Steidler recorded the Continental, Blue Joe, and Jasper claims on November 19, 1891, the same day that Colon S. Spencer Smith filed proof of labor for the mines. From Samuel K. Garrett, *Albert Klockmann: The Man and His Memoir* (Fairfield, WA: Ye Galleon Press, 1991), 11.

8. Besides the contemporary newspaper accounts from the 1890s, the first extensive telling of Klockmann's tale shows up in the *Northwest Mining Truth*, "Romance of Idaho-Continental," 1917, PLM. He modified his tale for the USFS in 1931 while defending his construction of the road in A. K. Klockmann, "Data on the Private Road from Porthill to the Continental Mine used by the Forest Reserve, 1931," Historical Collection, 1905-1990, Box 29, 2400, Region 1, RG 95, National Archives (Seattle).

9. For examples of the Continental Mine partnership lawsuits see the *Kootenai Herald*, April 21, 1894, and January 5, 1895.

10. *Spokane Daily Chronicle*, September 4, 1891.

11. Virgil R. D. Kirkham and Ernest W. Ellis, *Geology and Ore Deposits of Boundary County, Idaho*, Idaho Bureau of Mines and Geology Bulletin No. 10 (1926): 52; Robert N. Bell, Idaho Inspector of Mines Annual Report (IMIR), 1906, 92.

12. Klockmann Diary, 19, 36, 37.

13. Bell, IMIR, 1905, 77.

14. Klockmann Diary, 3; Estes, *Tales of Priest Lake*, 59.

15. *Spokane Daily Chronicle*, August 9, June 8, 1904; *Spokesman-Review*, July 9, 1904.

16. William Burke correspondence, September 21, 1904–December 15, 1904, PLM.

17. Klockmann Diary.

18. Burke.

19. Ibid.

20. Ibid.

21. Klockmann Diary, 36.

22. Klockmann, "Data on the Private Road."

23. Klockmann Diary, 39; Bell, IMIR 1913, 109.

24. John Kaufman, Earl H. Bennett, Victoria E. Mitchell, "Site Investigation Report for the Abandoned and Inactive Mines in Idaho on U.S. Forest Service Lands (Region 1), Idaho Panhandle National Forests," vol. 7, Priest Lake Ranger District, Bonner and Boundary Counties, Idaho, Idaho Geological Survey (2000): 149.

25. Klockmann Diary, 42, 44, 45.

26. G. N. Green, *Report on the Idaho Continental Mine, Boundary County, Idaho*, unpublished report (1974): 23, Appendix A, U.S. Bureau of Mines, Production Data for the Idaho Continental Mine, Boundary County, Idaho, 1914-1955. This was the value of the smelter returns at the time of the sales. In 2013 the equivalent metal production would be worth approximately $100,000,000.

27. *PRT*, September 18, 1919; "Ellen Baker," Cork, *Beautiful Bonner*, 215.

28. *PRT*, April 24, 1919, September 20, 1915.

29. *Northern Idaho News*, July 15, 1904; Bell, IMIR, 1906, 94.

30. Harry M. Booth, Mineral Examiner's Report of the Woodrat Lode Mining Claim, 1908, USFS, United States Department of Agriculture, PLM.

31. William Warren oral interview, PLM.

32. *PRT*, September 30, 1915.

33. Estes, *Tales of Priest Lake*, 63.

34. Kaniksu National Forest Mining Claims, 1906-1908, MIN-KNF, Museum of Northern Idaho.

35. Stewart Campbell, Idaho Inspection of Mines Annual Report (IMIR), 1929, 110; Kaufman et al., "Site Investigation Report," 149.

36. Arthur L. Hooper, Kaniksu Mining Company report, November 4, 1944, Kaniksu Mining Company Collection, PLM.

37. "Mining Equipment Arrives," *PRT*, September 30, 1915; January 24, 1918; and November 14, 1915.

38. Campbell, IMIR, 1922, 35, 55; *PRT*, March 12, 1917, June 13, 1918, and November 14, 1918.

39. Campbell, IMIR, 1922, 33.

40. David D. Alt and Donald W. Hyndman, *Roadside Geology of Idaho* (Missoula, MT: Mountain Press Publishing Co., 1989), 10.

41. Kaufman et al., "Site Investigation Report," 19.

Chapter Four: Locking Up Priest Lake

1. Gifford Pinchot Diary, July 18, 1897, Gifford Pinchot Papers, Reel 1, Manuscript Division, Library of Congress; "Forests Tied Up," *Spokesman-Review*, February 25, 1897; "Into the Forests," *Spokesman-Review*, July 24, 1897.

2. *Spokesman-Review*, "Forests Tied Up."

3. Samuel P. Hays, *The American People and the National Forests: The First Century of the U.S. Forest Service* (Pittsburgh: University of Pittsburgh Press, 2009), 20; William S. Shiach, John M. Henderson, and Harry B. Averill, *An Illustrated History of North Idaho* (Spokane, WA: Western Historical Publishing Company, 1903), 773.

4. *Spokesman-Review*, "Into the Forests."

5. Harold K. Steen, *The U.S. Forest Service: A History* (Seattle: University of Washington Press, 1976), 50.

6. Char Miller, *Gifford Pinchot and the Making of Modern Environmentalism* (Washington, D.C.: Island Press, 2001), 120.

7. *PRT*, March 6, 1932; "Big Cedar Trees," *Spokane Daily Chronicle*, November 13, 1884.

8. Gifford Pinchot, *Breaking New Ground* (New York: Harcourt, Brace and Co., 1947), 124, 125.

9. *Kootenai Herald*, March 17, 1900.

10. Pinchot, *Breaking New Ground*, 125.

11. "Ending the Forest Survey," *Spokesman-Review*, September 12, 1897.

12. Pinchot Diary, July 21, 1897.

13. Leiberg, *Priest River Forest Reserve*, 217; U.S. Congress, Senate, Surveys of the Forest Reserves, Sen. Doc. 189, 55 Cong. 2, March 15, 1898, 35-39, 43.

14. Leiberg, *Priest River Forest Reserve*, 219.

15. Ibid., 241, 243.

16. Ibid., 242.

17. USFS, *Western White Pine*, October 1945 (Washington, D.C.: Government Printing Office), 6.

18. Steen, *U.S. Forest Service*, 51.

19. Cort Sims, *A Land Office Business: Homesteading in Northern Idaho* (Coeur d'Alene, ID: USFS, 2003), 11.

20. "Idaho Forest Reserves," *The Deseret News*, February 22, 1901.

21. *North Idaho News*, September 16, 1904; Leonard Paul oral interview, 1963, PLM.

22. Rudo Fromme memoir, 1956, included in the Leonard Paul interview, PLM. Other versions of Fromme's memoir are at the Forest History Society and RG 95, NARA (Seattle).

23. Fromme memoir.

24. Pinchot, *Breaking New Ground*, 264.

25. Everett Dick, *The Lure of the Land: A Social History of the Public Lands from the Articles of Confederation to the New Deal* (Lincoln: University of Nebraska Press, 1970), 334.

26. Paul Redington, Inspection Report, October 17, 1907, Inspection Reports, 1905-1944, Kaniksu Box 9, Idaho Panhandle NF Records, RG 95, NARA (Seattle).

27. Fromme memoir; Redington, Inspection Report, October 17, 1907.

28. Paul interview.

29. Fromme monthly reports, Box 8, Olympic NF, RG 95, NARA (Seattle).

30. Fromme memoir.

31. Redington, Inspection Report, October 10, 1907.

32. Redington, Inspection Report, October 17, 1907.

33. Cort Sims, *Ranger Stations on the Idaho Panhandle National Forests* (Coeur d'Alene, ID: USFS, 1986), 4.

34. Fromme memoir.

35. Ryle Teed, "Reminiscences of Early Days in the Forest Service," October 1955. In USFS, *Early Days in the Forest Service*, vol. 2 (Missoula, MT: USFS Northern Region), 50.

36. Harold K. Steen, ed., *The Conservation Diaries of Gifford Pinchot* (Durham, NC: Forest History Society, 2001); Jay O'Laughlin, *Idaho's Endowment Lands: A Matter of Sacred Trust*, Report No. 1, March 5, 1990 (Moscow: University of Idaho), 3.

37. Albert Potter, "Hearing Before the U.S. Congress House Committee," Land for Educational Purposes, Committee on the Public Land, House of Representatives, 64th Congress, April 1, 1916 (Washington, D.C.: GPO), 176.

38. "About the State Lands," *PRT*, February 11, 1915. The east side of the lake was selected for transfer to the state because on the west side the headwaters of the streams were in Washington, which would have made administration difficult.

39. Silcox to Chief Forester Henry Graves, Confidential Memo, State Land Exchange, Spokane, WA, February 15, 1913, Land Boundaries Box 2, Idaho Panhandle NF Records, RG 95, NARA (Seattle).

40. Carl G. Krueger, "First Year in the Forest Service," *Early Days in the Forest Service*, vol. 4, 210.

41. Francis G. Caffey to The Forester [Henry S. Graves, successor to Gifford Pinchot], Department of Agriculture, Office of the Solicitor, Washington, D.C., October 27, 1915, Land Boundaries Box 2, Idaho Panhandle NF Records, RG 95, NARA (Seattle); *PRT*, 1914-1916; "Committee on Public Land," April 1, 1916. See also Report of Land Committee, 39.

42. Krueger, "First Year," 210.

43. Ibid.

44. Robert Rutledge, Assistant District Forester, Memorandum of Conference, Idaho Cooperative Agreement, April 28, 1915, Land Boundaries Box 2, Idaho Panhandle NF Records, RG 95, NARA (Seattle).

45. Silcox to Graves, February 15, 1913.

46. Caffey to The Forester, 1915.

47. Silcox to Graves, February 15, 1913.

48. Caffey to The Forester, 1915.

49. "Committee on the Public Lands," 176.

50. Silcox to Graves, February 15, 1913.

51. Ibid.

52. William H. Taft, "National Forest in the State of Idaho by the President of the United States of America, A Proclamation," March 3, 1913, Land Boundaries Box 2, Idaho Panhandle NF Records, RG 95, NARA (Seattle).

53. District Forester to Lee Berry, Priest River Town Council, April 7, 1913, D-1 S Kaniksu, Sales, Idaho Panhandle NF Records, RG 95, NARA (Seattle).

54. *PRT*, February 11, 1915.

55. "Committee for Public Lands," 126.

Chapter Five: Homesteading

1. John Ise, *The United States Forest Policy* (New Haven, CT: Yale University Press, 1920), 141.

2. *Spokesman-Review*, July 29, 1895; C. H. Bartoo oral interview, Archives, Northwest Museum of Arts and Culture, Spokane, Washington.

3. Ise, *United States Forest Policy*, 139; *Kootenai Herald*, March 17, 1900.

4. Commissioner, General Land Office to Forest Supervisor Robert Bragaw, May 5, 1902, Kaniksu–Claims, Lewis Chace H.E. 1452, Series IPOI: Alpha Files: L-Claims, Box 6, Idaho Panhandle NF, RG 95, NARA (Seattle).

5. F. McConnell to R. N. Dunn, Register Coeur d'Alene General Land Office, March 24, 1906, Kaniksu–Claims, Box 6.

6. Sims, *Land Office Business*, 33.

7. Ibid., 33, 11.

8. "Forest Reserves in Idaho," U.S. Department of Agriculture, Forest Service-Bulletin, No. 67, Gifford Pinchot, Forester (Washington, D.C.: GPO, 1905).

9. Henry Graves, Report of the Forester, September 23, 1914, "Claims and Alienations (Washington, D.C.: GPO, 1914); Nancy Langston, *Forest Dreams, Forest Nightmares: The Paradox of Old Growth in the Inland West* (Seattle: University of Washington Press, 1996), 19.

10. *Spokesman-Review*, August 20, 1907; *Missoula Herald*, October 23, 1907.

11. Fromme memoir.

12. Paul interview; Dorothy R. Powers, "Homesteader, 93, Finds Life Great," *Spokesman-Review*, June 28, 1970; Sims, *Ranger Stations*, 9.

13. Nell Carey White oral interview, 1983, PLM.

14. Powers, "Homesteader."

15. White interview; *Spokesman-Review*, June 28, 1970.

16. John Nordman, H.E. 02039, Kaniksu–Claims, Box 13.

17. Nordman, H.E. 02039; *PRT*, January 13, 1938; F. Forsythe, "Abstracts from Intensive Land Classification Report," Kaniksu National Forest, 1916.

18. Leiberg, *Priest River Forest Reserve*, 222.

19. Ibid., 223, 241.

20. Stanford J. Layton, *To No Privileged Class: The Rationalization of Homesteading and Rural Life in the Early Twentieth-Century American West* (Provo, UT: Brigham Young University, 1988), 7; White interview.

21. *Missoula Herald*, October 23, 1907; *North Idaho News*, December 30, 1904; Paul interview.

22. Sims, *Land Office Business*, 11.

23. James Hawley, *History of Idaho: The Gem of the Mountains* (Chicago: S .J. Clarke Publishing Company, 1920), 2:801; Alvin C. Vinther, "The Kerr Sister," *Kaniksu and Tales of Priest Lake and Priest River* (self-published, 1976), 113; "Pettit, Marshall and Family," F682, Cork, *Beautiful Bonner*, 572; "Tangle of Idaho Woods Slows Search," *North Idaho News*, July 14, 1985; "Johnson, Jess and Lillian," F422, Cork, *Beautiful Bonner*, 434.

24. Layton, *To No Privileged Class*, 7.

25. Forsythe, "Abstracts," 1916.

26. Sims, *Land Office Business*, 29.

27. *PRT*, February 19, 1915, June 23, 1914, September 23, 1915. *PRT*, March 11, 1915, September 10, 1914, and October 21, 1915.

28. *PRT*, September 2, 1915, October 21, 1915; Cork, "Johnson, Jess and Lillian," 434.

29. *PRT*, August 25, 1915, July 11, 1918; Homestead Entry Survey No. 683. U.S. Department of Agriculture, Forest Service, Field Notes, Historic Files, USFS Priest Lake Ranger Station.

30. *PRT*, September 2, 23, 30, 1915; March 21, 1918.

31. Forsythe, "Abstracts," 1916; *PRT*, June 1915, February 17, 1916, and September 1918.

32. *PRT*, May 1 and October 3, 1918; Cork, "Johnson, Jess and Lillian," 434; Cork, "Pettit, Marshall and Family," 572; *North Idaho News*, July 14, 1985.

33. Harry G. Ade, "Abstracts from Intensive Land Classification Report," Kaniksu National Forest, 1922.

34. *PRT*, August 25, 1915.

35. Forsythe, "Abstracts," 1916; Ade, "Abstracts," 1922.

36. Ade, "Abstracts," 1922; *PRT*, February 7, 1918.

37. *PRT*, January 13, 1938.

Chapter Six: Andy Coolin's Schemes

1. "Coolin is Acquitted," *Spokesman-Review*, March 3, 1892; *PRT*, January 16, 1936. *Spokane Daily Chronicle*, January 17, 1907, October 4, 1909. Andy Coolin hired a Spokane surveyor to lay out a town site on his homestead. His village plat featured long neat blocks paralleling the waterfront that often ignored topographical realities. He reclaimed the original village name, Coolin, that he used to establish the post office in 1893. When Northern Inn owner Walter Williams took over the post office in 1900, the town briefly took on his name.

2. *Spokane Daily Chronicle*, January 17, 1907, June 3, 1907; *Spokesman-Review*, May 5, 1907.

3. *Spokesman-Review*, February 5, 1907, May 11, 1907.

4. *Pend Oreille Review*, January 7, 1908.

5. *Spokane Daily Chronicle*, March 30, 1906, March 18, 1908; "Priest Lake Idaho for Your Midsummer Outing," brochure, c. 1910, PLM.

6. Paul interview; *Spokesman-Review*, February 5, 1907, May 5, 1907.

7. *Spokane Daily Chronicle*, August 30, 1898, March 30, 1906; Harriett Allen oral interview, PLM.

8. "The Idaho Panhandle," booklet published by News' Publishing Company, Sandpoint, Idaho, c. 1907, PLM; *Pend Oreille Review*, January 7, 1907; "Survey a Railway to Pass Priest Lake," *Spokane Daily Chronicle*, August 9, 1904. Also mentioned in *Northern Idaho News*, May 17, 1907.

9. Paul Leake, "Thomas Payne," *History of Detroit* (Chicago: Lewis Publishing Co., 1912), 3:1088; *Northern Idaho News*, May 17, 1907; *Pend Oreille Review*, May 23, 1907.

10. *Northern Idaho News*, May 17, 1907; Panhandle Electric Railway and Power Company Articles of Incorporation, Coolin Abstract, PLM; District Forester W. B. Greeley to Commissioner of the General Land Office, Kaniksu-Boundaries, Outlet Administrative Site, February 20, 1909, filed under S-Sales, Kaniksu, 1905-1912, Idaho Panhandle NF, RG 95, NARA (Seattle).

11. Redington, Inspection Report.

12. Ibid.

13. District Engineer's Report on the Cost of Constructing and Operating a Railroad from Priest River to Priest Lake, by E. W. Kramer, June 30, 1912, filed under S-Sales, Kaniksu, 1905-1912, Idaho Panhandle NF, RG 95, NARA (Seattle); W. B. Greeley to Commissioner of the General Land Office, February 20, 1909 and *Lewiston Morning Tribune*, January 20, 1909.

14. *Northern Idaho News*, October 28, 1910.

15. "Midsummer Outing" brochure.

16. *Pend Oreille Review*, May 23, 1907; *Spokesman-Review*, October 25, 1909; *Northern Idaho News*, May 24, 1910.

17. *Spokane Daily Chronicle*, October 4, 1909; *Inland Herald*, May 15, 1910.

18. "Millions Spent in Panhandle," *Northern Idaho News*, May 24, 1910.

19. *Spokane Daily Chronicle*, March 31, 1910.

20. "The Idaho Panhandle," *Spokane Daily Chronicle*, March 31, 1910; *Northern Idaho News*, May 24, 1910; Paul interview.

21. "The Idaho Panhandle," *Spokane Daily Chronicle*.

22. *Inland Herald*, May 15, 1910.

23. Robert E. Wolf, "National Forest Timber Sales and the Legacy of Gifford Pinchot: Managing a Forest and Making it Pay," in *American Forests: Nature, Culture, and Politics*, ed. Char Miller (Lawrence: University Press of Kansas, 1997), 91.

24. Forest Supervisor, Coolin Idaho to District Forester F. A. Silcox, July 12, 1912, filed under S-Sales, Kaniksu, 1905-1912, Idaho Panhandle NF, RG 95, NARA (Seattle).

25. Assistant Forester W. B. Greeley to District Forester F. A. Silcox, December 10, 1912, filed under S-Sales, Kaniksu, 1905-1912, Idaho Panhandle NF, RG 95, NARA (Seattle).

26. District Forester F. A. Silcox to L. C. Gilman, Great Northern Railroad, December 6, 1912, filed under S-Sales, Kaniksu, 1905-1912, Idaho Panhandle NF, RG 95, NARA (Seattle).

27. Assistant Forester W. B. Graves to District Forester F. A. Silcox, December 10, 1912.

28. Silcox to The Forester Henry S. Graves, December 14, 1912; C. R. Grey, Great Northern Railway Company president, to F. A. Silcox, February 22, 1913, filed under S-Sales, Kaniksu, 1905-1912, Idaho Panhandle NF, RG 95, NARA (Seattle)

29. Correspondence between Andy Coolin and C. W. Beardmore, 1913-14, PLM.; *William Vane, Plaintiff v. Priest Lake Transportation Co.*, Judgment, District

Court of the Eighth Judicial District of the State of Idaho, in and for the County of Bonner, May, 1914, PLM and *Spokesman-Review*, January 28, 1915.

30. *PRT*, June 11, 1914; *Spokane Daily Chronicle*, October 2, 1928 and July 25, 1931.

31. Andrew Coolin, Alpha Files: L-Claims: Mineral 1908-40, Box 3, Idaho Panhandle NF, RG 95, NARA (Seattle), and *Spokane Daily Chronicle*, 1936.

Chapter Seven: Forest Service Transformations

1. Fromme memoir; Redington, Inspection Report.

2. J. A. Larsen, "Natural Reproduction after Forest Fires in Northern Idaho," *Journal of Agricultural Research* 31, no. 12 (1925): 1180.

3. Redington, Inspection Report, October 17.

4. Forest Supervisor Mallory N. Stickney to District Forester, Big Creek Fire District 4 Report, December 30, 1914, Historical Collection, Box 50, Idaho Panhandle NF Records, RG 95 NARA (Seattle); Redington, Inspection Report, October 17.

5. Clarence B. Swim, February 23, 1944, *Early Days in the Forest Service*, vol. 1.

6. Stickney to District Forester.

7. *North Idaho News*, January 4, 1908; Teed, "Reminiscences," 51.

8. Stickney to District Forester; Hays, *American People and the National Forests*, 20.

9. Gary Weber, "The Evolution of the Present Priest Lake Ranger District," Priest Lake Ranger Station Archives.

10. Kaniksu National Forest brochure, c. 1930, Historical Collection, Box 50, Idaho Panhandle NF Records, RG 95, NARA (Seattle).

11. Ernie Grambo oral interview, PLM; Teed, "Reminiscences."

12. Hank Diener interview, Claude and Katherine Simpson papers (MG115), Special Collections and Archives, University of Idaho Library.

13. Warren interview.

14. Elers Koch Inspection Report, 1920, Inspection Reports, 1905-1944, Kaniksu, Box 9, Idaho Panhandle NF, RG 95, NARA (Seattle).

15. Barney Stone interview, PLM.

16. Thomas F. Lacy, *Kaniksu Two: Masselow, Fabled Waters, She Who Sees, and Other Stories* (Self-published, 2003), 52.

17. Stone interview.

18. Beth Rhodenbaugh and Dorine Goertzen, *The History of State Forestry in Idaho, State of Idaho Department of Forestry*, (Boise, ID: Idaho Department of Forestry, 1961), 13.

19. Ibid.

20. William G. Robbins, *American Forestry: A History of National, State, and Private Cooperation* (Lincoln: University of Nebraska, 1985), 52; *Deseret News*, May 21, 1921.

21. PTLA Biennial Reports, Idaho State Historical Society. In 1926, the state of Idaho was assessed for 188,637.31 acres; Diamond Match Corporation at 25,409.71; Dalkena Lumber Company at 1,960; Humbird Company at 2,196; Kaniksu Cedar (eventually Schaefer-Hitchcock) at 246; Clearwater Timber Company at 1,351.2; and the Northern Pacific Railway Company at 3,316.5. From the PTLA voucher ledger 1921-1930.

22. Hays, *American People and the National Forests*, 60; Robbins, *American Forestry*, 63; PLTPA journal.

23. Inspector Report, August 1923; James Ward Retirement Letters, September 1938, PLM.

24. PLTPA voucher ledger.

25. Ibid.

26. *PRT*, April 6, 1926; Clarence C. Strong, "Some Highlights of My Forestry Career," *Early Days in the Forest Service*, vol. 3.

27. Strong, "Some Highlights."

28. Henry Peterson, "Recollections and Memoirs of an Early Day Forest Ranger in the Priest Lake Country," January 12, 1968, *Early Days in the Forest Service*, vol. 4.

29. Howard Flint, District Forest Inspector, "The Fire Season of 1926 in Idaho," Historical Collection, Box 50, RG 95, NARA (Seattle); *PRT*, July 26, 1926.

30. Betty James memoirs, edited by Ann James Paden and Beth James Nicholson, PLM.

31. Thomas F. Lacy, *Kaniksu: Stories of the Northwest* (Sandpoint, ID: Keokee Co. Publishing, 1994), 25; Betty James memoirs.

32. Strong, "Some Highlights"; Weber, "The Evolution of the Present Priest Lake Ranger District."

33. Sam Billings, "Timber Cruising on the Kaniksu Following the Big Fires of 1926," *Early Days in the Forest Service*, vol. 4.

34. District Forester Fred Mottell to Pete Chase, January 13, 1927, Personnel, Kaniksu, Idaho Panhandle NF, RG 95, NARA (Seattle).

35. Weber, "The Evolution of the Present Priest Lake Ranger District."

36. PLTPA Biennial Report, 1926; Priest Lake Timber Protective Association, "Special 49-Year Analysis of Fires," Idaho Department of the Lands; Inspector reports, May 11, 1926.

37. Krueger, "First Year."

38. Cameron Ward interview, PLM.

39. Hays, *American People and the National Forests*, 39; Krueger, "First Year."

40. "Bismark Ranger Station withdrawn October 26, 1906," 1913 report, Museum of Northern Idaho; Sims, *Ranger Stations*, 42; Inspection Report, October 1939.

41. Peterson, "Recollections and Memoirs."

42. James G. Lewis, *The Forest Service and the Greatest Good: A Centennial History* (Durham, NC: Forest History Society, 2005), 80.

43. Ray Kresek, *Fire Lookouts of the Northwest* (Spokane, WA: Historic Lookout Project, 1998), 10.

44. Weber, "The Evolution of the Present Priest Lake Ranger District."

45. Ward interview.

46. Bob Marshall, "Recreation Inspection Report for the Northern Region," November 10, 1939, E4 Records of the Chief of the Forest Service, Box 60, RG 95, NARA (College Park).

47. Clark, Forest Examiner, "Roosevelt Grove of Ancient Cedars," 1919, PLRS archives and *Spokesman-Review*.

48. William C. Tweed, *A History of Outdoor Recreation Development in the National Forests, 1891-1942* (Clemson, SC: Clemson University Department of Parks, Recreation and Tourism Management, n.d.), 12, PLRS archives.

49. "Forest Service, Using CCC, Opens Up Reeder Bay," *Spokesman-Review*, September 22, 1935.

50. Marshall, "Recreation Inspection Report," November 10, 1939.

51. Clark, "Roosevelt Grove."

52. Peterson, "Recollections and Memoirs"; Inspector's Report, February 12, 1929. Inspections 1904-1940, Kaniksu Box 9, Idaho Panhandle NF Records, RG 95, NARA (Seattle).

53. William R. Matney correspondence, PLRS archives; George Grossman, "Blister Rust Years," PLM.

54. Inspection Report, February 12, 1929, Inspection Reports, 1905-1944, Kaniksu Box 9, Idaho Panhandle NF Records, RG 95, NARA (Seattle).

55. Anne Marie Moore and Dennis Baird, eds., *Wild Places Preserved: The Story of Bob Marshall in Idaho* (Moscow: University of Idaho Library, 2009), 155.

56. Wurth M. Coble Jr., "The Blister Rust Days Memoirs," PLM.

57. David Asleson, "Former German POW goes back in time," *PRT*, January 24, 2001.

58. Coble.

59. Kirsten Cornelis, "Prisoners of War," *Progress 2007, Sandpoint Daily Bee*; Asleson.

60. *PRT*, September 15, 1914; *PRT*, June 2, 1914.

61. Moore and Baird, *Wild Places Preserved*, 12.

62. Diener interview.

Chapter Eight: White Pine and Water

1. "The Idaho Panhandle," *Northern Idaho News*, Sandpoint, ID, c. 1910.

2. S. Blair Hutchinson, "A Century of Lumbering in Northern Idaho," *The Timberman* 39 (November 1938) reprint: 4; N. C. Brown, Deputy Forest Supervisor, "Timber Sales," read before Annual Ranger Meeting Coolin, Idaho, May 29-June 2, 1911, S-Sales, Kaniksu, Box 105, Idaho Panhandle NF Records, RG 95, NARA (Seattle).

3. Brown, "Timber Sales"; "Memorandum for Franklin H. Smith," F. A. Silcox, District Forester, October 1912, Idaho Panhandle NF Records, RG 95, NARA (Seattle); Langston, *Forest Dreams*, 103; Hays, *American People and the National Forests*, 39.

4. Thomas R. Cox, *The Lumberman's Frontier: Three Centuries of Land Use, Society and Change in America's Forests* (Corvallis: Oregon State University Press, 2010), 358.

5. Leon F. Neuenschwander, et al., "White Pine in the American West: A Vanishing Species—Can We Save It?" University of Idaho and the Rocky Mountain Research Station, General Technical Report RMRS-GTR-35 (August 1999), 5; Leiberg, *Priest River Forest Reserve*, 231.

6. Forest Supervisor W. N. Millar to District Forester, Missoula, MT, December 4, 1911, S-Sales, Idaho Panhandle NF Records, RG 95, NARA (Seattle); Hays, *American People and the National Forests*, 41.

7. "Solving Forest Problems," *Newport Miner*, December 21, 1911; District Forester Fred Forsythe to Forest Supervisor, DE-Reports, Kaniksu-Log, Idaho Panhandle NF Records, RG 95, NARA (Seattle); "Log Driving & Fluming," District Forester Fred Forsythe to Forest Supervisor W. N. Millar, July 12, 1912.

8. Millar to District Forester, December 4, 1911.

9. Cox, *Lumberman's Frontier*, 317.

10. Wolf, "National Forest Timber Sales," 91; Hays, *American People and the National Forests*, 40.

11. Greeley to Earle H. Clapp, October 14, 1912, S-Sales, Kaniksu, 1905-1912, S-Sales, Idaho Panhandle NF Records, RG 95, NARA (Seattle).

12. Prospectus: Timber Offered For Sale on Kaniksu National Forest In Idaho, 1913.

13. Forester Henry S. Graves to Secretary of Agriculture James Wilson, December 28, 1912, S-Sales, Idaho Panhandle NF Records, RG 95, NARA (Seattle);

F. A. Silcox, District Forester to C. R. Gray, President, Great Northern Railway, St. Paul, MN, February 19, 1913, S-Sales, Idaho Panhandle NF Records, RG 95, NARA (Seattle).

14. David Chance, "The Lumber Industry of Washington's Pend Oreille Valley, 1888-1941," Prepared for the Colville National Forest (June 1991), 106.

15. Cort Sims, "Dalkena Logging Railroad," December 2002, Coeur d'Alene, Idaho. Report No. R2001010401207, USFS.

16. F. A. Silcox to Forest Supervisor, Coolin, ID, July 12, 1912; C. W. Beardmore, "With the Lumber Men," c. 1925, PLM; F. A. Wilcox to Gilman, Great Northern Railroad.

17. Nancy Foster Renk, *A Glorious Field for Sawmills: Humbird Lumber Company 1900-1948* (Boise, ID: Idaho Transportation Department, 2014), 64.

18. *PRT*, June 29, 1972, April 23, 1914, June 13, 1916; Interview with Mr. Gillespie in Reverend James F. Estes, "The Early Days of Priest River," 1961, PLM.

19. "Dalkena buys 50,000,000," *PRT*, December 1915.

20. "New from the Camps," *PRT*, October 12, 1917.

21. C. S. Webb, "Some Incidents Occurring During My Employment with the U.S. Forest Service, 1913-1949" in *Early Days in the Forest Service*, vol. 2; Mrs. E. M. Butler oral interview, Idaho State Historical Society.

22. Claude and Catherine Simpson, *Panhandle Personalities* (Moscow: University of Idaho Press, 1984), 320.

23. Webb, "Some Incidents."

24. *Salt Lake Tribune*, March 22, 1914.

25. Silcox, "Memorandum for Franklin H. Smith."

26. *PRT*, November 9, 1916.

27. Clarence C. Strong and Clyde S. Webb, *White Pine: King of Many Waters* (Missoula, MT: Mountain Press Publishing Co, 1970), 115.

28. *PRT*, June 13, 1918.

29. Peterson, "Recollections and Memoirs," 44; Chance, "The Lumber Industry," 137.

30. Bill Whetsler interview in James F. Estes, "The Early Days of Priest River"; Elers Koch, *Forty Years a Forester* (Missoula, MT: Mountain Press, 1998), 163.

31. Estes, "The Early Days."

32. Peterson, "Recollections and Memoirs," 44; Koch, *Forty Years a Forester*, 164.

33. Robert Marshall, "Contribution to the Life History of the North-Western Lumberjack," *Social Force* VIII, no. 2 (December 1929): 173.

34. Estes, "The Early Days."

35. Butler interview.

36. Marshall, "Contribution to the Life History," 173.

37. "The Diamond Match Experience," Cork, *Beautiful Bonner*, 108.

38. *PRT*, January 30, 1922, June 30, 1930.

39. *PRT*, May 24, 1923.

40. *PRT*, April 3, 1917; Estes, "The Early Days."

41. James Rowan, *The I.W.W. in the Lumber Industry* (Seattle, WA: Lumber Workers' Industrial Union No. 500, 1918), 25; *Newport Miner*, June 28, 1917.

42. Marshall, "Contribution to the Life History," 172.

43. *PRT*, April 3, 1917.

44. Robert C. Sims, "Idaho's Criminal Syndicalism Act: One State's Response to Radical Labor," *Labor History* 14, no. 4 (1974): 512.

45. Peterson, "Recollections and Memoirs," 44; David R. Berman, *Radicalism in the Mountain West, 1890-1920: Socialists, Populists, Miners, and Wobblies* (Boulder: University Press of Colorado, 2007), 270; Robert L. Tyler, *Rebels in the Woods: The IWW in the Pacific Northwest* (Eugene: University of Oregon Press), 92; Strong and Webb, *White Pine*, 46.

46. Peterson, "Recollections and Memoirs," 44.

47. *PRT*, November 28, 1917; Peterson, "Recollections and Memoirs," 44; Whetsler interview, 329.

48. *PRT*, February 21 and May 7, 1918; see Hugh T. Lovin, "The Red Scare in Idaho, 1916-1918," *Idaho Yesterdays* 17, no. 3 (Fall 1973): 8.

49. John Fahey, "Big Lumber in the Inland Empire: The Early Years, 1900-1930," *Pacific Northwest Quarterly* (July 1985), 100; *PRT*, May 7, 1918.

50. *PRT*, August 1, 1918, October 2 and 16, 1919, November 20, 1919; Estes; *Bonners Ferry Herald*, May 15, 1919.

51. E. B. Mittelman, "The Gyppo System," *Journal of Political Economy* 31, no. 6 (December 1923): 840; Ike Elkins oral interview, PLM; Chance, "The Lumber Industry," 160.

52. *Industrial Worker*, October 7, 1922.

53. Peterson, "Recollections and Memoirs," 142.

54. Sims, "Dalkena Railroad," 8; *Northern Idaho News*, May 1, 1923 and *PRT*, July 19, 1923.

55. *PRT*, October 20, 1921.

56. "Billings, Roger and Nola," Cork, *Beautiful Bonner*, 234.

57. David H. Williamson, "Some Effects of Social and Economic Changes on Gyppo Loggers," *Anthropological Quarterly* 50, no. 1 (January 1977): 31.

58. Logging Costs Memorandum, Newport, Washington, March 11, 1925, S-Sales Kaniksu, Box 104, Idaho Panhandle NF Records, RG 95, NARA (Seattle); Simpson, *Panhandle Personalities*, 61; Joe T. Zigler, "Fifty Years of Logging," *Big Smoke* (Newport: WA: Pend Oreille Historical Society, 1974), 26; Cort

Sims, "Cultural Resources: The Log Chutes of North Idaho," Report No. 8 (Missoula, MT: United States Department of Agriculture, Forest Service Northern Region, 1983), 10.

59. Sims, "Cultural Resources," 10; K. D. Swan, *Splendid was the Trail* (Missoula, MT: Mountain Press, 1968), 163; James F. Estes, "The Early Days of Priest River," 1961, PLM.

60. Sims, "Dalkena Logging Railroad," 8.

61. Fuller Joyce, "Hanna Flats Information," Priest Lake Ranger Station.

62. Sims, "Dalkena Logging Railroad," 8; Langston, *Forest Dreams*, 82; *PRT*, April 17, 1919; *Spokesman-Review*, November 13, 1923.

63. *Northern Idaho News*, November 13, 1923; Sims, "Dalkena Logging Railroad," 21; Insurance map filed March 29, 1924, Dalkena Collection, MASC.

64. Sims, "Dalkena Logging Railroad," 15; *PRT*, April 13, 1925.

65. Sims, "Dalkena Logging Railroad," 8; A. Richard Guth and Stan B. Cohen, *A Pictorial History of the U.S. Forest Service 1891-1945: Northern Region* (Missoula, MT: Pictorial Histories Publishing Company, 1991), 10.

66. Herbert Manchester, *The Diamond Match Company: A Century of Service, of Progress, and of Growth* (Chicago: Diamond Match Company, 1935), 95.

67. Fahey, "Big Lumber," 101; Chance, "The Lumber Industry," 196.

68. Cox, *Lumberman's Frontier*, 342.

69. Roger W. Billings, "Diamond City," *Big Smoke*, (Newport: WA: Pend Oreille Historical Society, 1974), 4; *PRT*, January 1, 1924; Peterson, "Recollections and Memoirs," 37; Herbert Manchester, *The Romance of the Match* (Chicago: The Diamond Match Co., 1926), 37.

70. Fahey, "Big Lumber," 99.

71. "Diamond Match Company—The West's Newest and Most Modern Narrow Gauge Logging Railroad," Appendix II, 120, PLM; Peterson, "Recollections and Memoirs," 27.

72. Peterson, "Recollections and Memoirs," 27, 30, 61.

73. *Spokane Daily Chronicle*, July 29, 1933; Lewis, *Forest Service and the Greatest Good*, 95; Wolf, "National Forest Timber Sales," 93; Fahey, "Big Lumber, 103.

74. Chance, "The Lumber Industry."

75. Manchester, *The Diamond Match Company*, 80.

76. Ibid.; Chance, "The Lumber Industry," 258; Clarence C. Strong, "Notes made during interview with Jack Barron at Scottsdale, Arizona on April 29, 1965," PEO-Barron, MNI.

77. Simpson, *Panhandle Personalities*, 349.

Chapter Nine: Living by the Seasons

1. Fahey, *The Kalispel Indians*, 31; Stewart H. Chalfant, "Aboriginal Territory of the Kalispell Indians" in *Interior Salish and Eastern Washington Indians III*, ed. David Horr (New York: Garland Press, 1974), 225.

2. Cort Sims, "Archaeological Excavations at Priest Lake, Idaho, 1993-1996" (Coeur d'Alene, ID: USFS), 5; Fahey, *The Kalispel Indians*, 33; Chalfant, "Aboriginal Territory," 219.

3. Claude and Catherine Simpson, *North of the Narrows* (Moscow: University Press of Idaho, 1981), 98, 120.

4. Charlotte Jones correspondence, PLM; Warren interview.

5. Milton DeWitz, *Priest Lake and Kaniksu Forest: The Early Years* (Spokane, WA: National Color Graphics, 1981), 50.

6. *PRT*, September 6, 1917, April 17, 1919.

7. Hilma Sherman diaries, 1927, PLM.

8. Regional assistant forester R. F. Hammatt quoted in Rebecca T. Richards and Susan J. Alexander, "A Social History of Wild Huckleberry Harvesting in the Pacific Northwest" (Corvallis, OR: Pacific Northwest Research Station, 2006), 28.

9. Bernadine Stevens McDonald memoirs, PLM.

10. DeWitz, *Priest Lake and Kaniksu Forest*, 51; Sherman diaries, 1935; Simpson, *North of the Narrows*, 119, 135.

11. Marjorie Paul Roberts oral interview, PLM; Simpson, *North of the Narrows*, 99.

12. Rose Chermak Meyers oral interview, PLM.

13. Simpson, *Panhandle Personalities*, 13.

14. Roberts interview; *PRT*, September 23, 1915.

15. *PRT*, January 15, 1919.

16. Allen interview, PLM; *PRT*, January 17, 1942.

17. *PRT*, May 1, 1919.

18. Simpson, *North of the Narrows*, 16.

19. Ward interview.

20. Sherman diaries, January 22, 1931.

21. Madlyn Byars Gills interview, Simpson papers.

22. Warren interview.

23. Simpson, *North of the Narrows*, 96.

24. Ibid., 134, 98; *Panhandle Personalities*, 51.

25. Warren interview.

26. *PRT*, December 31, 1914, December 30, 1915.

27. *PRT*, January 17, 1917, January 31, 1918, January 2, 1919; Simpson, *North of the Narrows*, 96.

28. Paul interview.

29. *PRT*, February 24, 1916.

30. *PRT*, February 3, 1915, January 20, 1916; March 11, 1924.

31. *Loon Lake Times*, February 22, 1913.

32. Vinther, *Kaniksu*, 117; Gloria Chevraux interview, PLM; DeWitz, *Priest Lake and Kaniksu Forest*, 83.

33. John Nunemaker correspondence, June 2, 2010, PLM.

34. "Win Desperate Struggle for Life in Snow and Cold of Northern Idaho," *Spokane Daily Chronicle*, January 19, 1924; "Nell Shipman Makes Heroic Effort to Save Husband," *Spokane Daily Chronicle*, January 7, 1924; "Wife Fights Snow," *Rochester Evening Journal*, January 9, 1924; and others.

35. Roberts interview; Harold Branyan correspondence, PLM; *Northern Idaho News*, May 25, 1910.

36. Paul interview; Roberts interview; Ralph Salesky, *Barefoot Renegade* (Fairfield, WA: Ye Galleon Press, 1992),12.

37. Roberts interview.

38. McFatride, Special Agent, Memorandum, Treasury Department Bureau of Prohibition, Sand Point, Idaho, June 7, 1930; Don B. Rogers, Special Agent, to Captain R. A. Beman, Special Agent In Charge, Treasury Department, Bureau of Prohibition, Spokane, WA June 22, 1930. RG 56, Record of the Treasury, Box 19, NARA (Seattle); Vinther, *Kaniksu*, 118; *PRT*, October 25, 1926.

39. Kate Batey interview, Simpson papers; Roberts interview; McFatride memorandum.

40. "Stills in the Hills," *Big Smoke* (Newport: WA: Pend Oreille Historical Society, 1983); *PRT*; Vinther, *Kaniksu*, 118.

41. McDonald memoirs.

42. Simpson, *North of the Narrows*, 111; "Pete Chace [sic] Funeral," account of donations and possession, PLM.

43. *PRT*, February 26, 1917, February 7, 1918.

44. *PRT*, December 24, 1914.

45. *PRT*, June 8, 1915; Simpson, *North of the Narrows*, 98.

46. Vinther, *Kaniksu*, 116.

47. *PRT*, September 15, 1914, August 12, 1917.

48. Simpson, *Panhandle Personalities*, 226.

49. Ibid., 239.

50. Estes, *Tales of Priest Lake*; Vinther, *Kaniksu*, 119.

51. Paul interview.

52. "Johnson, Jess and Lillian," Cork, *Beautiful Bonner*, 434; *PRT*, August 12, 1915, May 1, 1917.

Chapter 10: Campers to Cabin Owners

1. *PRT*, June 11, 1914.

2. *Recreation Residence Historical Contexts for Eight National Forests in USDA-Region One-Idaho*

Panhandle National Forest, prepared by HHM INC., July 2006, USDA Forest Service Contract AG-03KP-C-05-0010. P 5-2.

3. Ibid., P 5-16.

4. Fromme monthly reports, February 1909.

5. Fromme monthly reports, July 1, 1907.

6. Stephan E. Matz, "Summary of Recreation Residence, National Register of Historic Places Eligibility and Management Recommendations for the Idaho Panhandle National Forest, ID," March 10, 2009, P 6-4.

7. Ibid.

8. "Instructions for the Survey of Cottage Sites on Priest Lake," October 15, 1910, L-Kaniksu-Uses-Supervision, IPO4-Alpha Files: U-Adjustment to Trespassing 1910-1958, Box 1, RG 95, NARA (Seattle); "Cottage Sites on Priest Lake, Priest Lake Survey," December 1910, J.B. Surveyor, Idaho Panhandle National Forests Headquarters, Coeur d'Alene, Idaho.

9. Superintendent W. R. Miller, May 12, 1911. From notes in the historical files at the Priest Lake Ranger Station; "Suggestions to Those Desiring to Occupy Lots for Cottage and Summer Resort Purposes within the Kaniksu National Forest at Priest Lake, Idaho and Other Lakes within the Forest," (Newport, WA: Newport Miner Print, c. 1910), MASC.

10. *Northern Idaho News*, May 1910 and "Suggestions to Those Desiring to Occupy Lots," 5.

11. Denny Jones, "Priest Lake History, Lots 11 and 12 Diamond Park," unpublished memoir, PLM; Heatfield File, SPE-KNF, Museum of Northern Idaho, Coeur d'Alene.

12. About $250 in 2010 dollars.

13. *Recreation Residence*, 5-3.

14. Ibid., 3-4.

15. Inspection–Priest River National Forest, Section VI, Uses, Redington, November 1, 1907, Inspection Reports 1905-1944, Kaniksu Box 9, RG 95, NARA (Seattle).

16. "Spokane College Plans Lake Camp," *The Spokesman-Review*, July 24, 1910.

17. "Build Priest Lake Lodge," *The Spokesman-Review*, July 6, 1910.

18. *PRT*, May 28, 1914, June 4, 1914.

19. Harriet Allen, MS 137, Archives, Northwest Museum of Arts and Culture, Spokane, WA.

20. Roberts interview.

21. Richard Stejer interview, PLM; Simpson, *Panhandle Personalities*, 21.

22. *PRT*, July 30, 2008; *Pullman Herald*, May 30 and September 3, 1915; Robert Hungate, "Priest Lake and the Hungates," PLM.

23. Brian Shute, "Rum Running During the Prohibition Era," *Nostalgia Magazine*, January-February 2011, 20.

24. Melanie Shellenbarger, *High Country Summers: The Early Second Homes of Colorado, 1880-1940* (Tucson: University of Arizona Press, 2012), 6; "Region One Construction Standards for Summer Homes under National Forest Permit," 1934, copied in *Recreation Residence*, 5-23.

25. *Recreation Residence*, 5-23.

26. "Region One Construction Standards for Summer Homes."

27. Ibid.

28. Richard Hungate interview, PLM.

29. Allen interview, PLM; Betty James memoirs, PLM; Rose Hendrickson oral interview, PLM.

30. "Cottage Sites on Priest Lake, Priest Lake Survey" and "History of Vinther and Nelson and Eight Mile Island," IPNF, December 1980, Historical Files, Priest Lake Ranger District Office.

31. Vinther, *Kaniksu* and "History of Vinther and Nelson."

32. Warren interview; Hendrickson interview.

33. Vinther, *Kaniksu*; Betty James memoirs.

34. Betty James memoirs.

35. Hendrickson interview.

36. Diener interview, Simpson papers.

37. Betty James memoirs.

38. Ibid.

39. Hendrickson interview.

40. Shellenbarger, *High Country Summers*, 14.

41. Luby Bay Fellowship Club archives, PLM.

42. Ibid.

43. *Recreation Residence Historical Contexts*.

44. Shellenbarger, *High Country Summers*, 33.

45. Luby Bay Fellowship Club.

46. "Forest Service, Using CCC."

47. *Recreation Residence*, 5-30.

48. Hendrickson interview.

Chapter Eleven: Fishing Camps to Resorts

1. Inspection Report of 1930, 1905-1944, Kaniksu Box 8, Idaho Panhandle NF Records, RG 95, NARA (Seattle).

2. Ibid.

3. *Spokesman-Review*, June 26, 1931; Elkins interview; *Spokane Chronicle*, August 20, 1932.

4. *Spokesman-Review*, June 26, 1931, June 27, 1930.

5. *Spokane Chronicle*, August 11, 1933.

6. *Spokesman-Review*, May 24, 1934; Elkins interview.

7. Elkins interview; Kenneth Carter, "Carter Craft Boats," *Big Smoke* (Newport, WA: Pend Oreille Historical Society, 1991); Simpson, *North of the Narrows*, 180.

8. Simpson, *North of the Narrows*, 16, 19; Justice Docket Byars vs. Lloyd, PLM; Madlyn Byars Gillis interview, Simpson papers.

9. *PRT*, February 8, 1926; Gillis interview; Simpson, *Panhandle Personalities*, 125; Simpson, *North of the Narrows*, 22.

10. Inspection Report, 1930; *Spokane Chronicle*, April 14, 1938; Luby Bay Fellowship Club archive, PLM.

11. Lacy, *Kaniksu Two*, 47; Inspection report, 1930; *Spokesman-Review*, June 26, 1931.

12. *PRT*, June 2, 1921; Roberts interview.

13. *PRT*, April 18, 1935.

14. "Paul-Jones Beach, Priest Lake, Idaho," Pamphlet, c. 1925, Archives, Northwest Museum of Arts and Culture, Spokane, WA.

15. Roberts interview.

16. *PRT*, June 18, 1914; McDonald Memoirs; Harriet Allen, 1983 Museum Survey, PLM; *Spokane Chronicle*, June 29, 1923.

17. *Spokane Chronicle*, May 25, 1927; *PRT*, May 27, 1927.

18. Paul Croy, 1983 Museum Survey, PLM; Warren interview.

19. *PRT*, May 26, 192; Gillis interview.

20. Charlotte Jones to Lee Daniels correspondence, PLM; Salesky, *Barefoot Renegade*.

21. Salesky, *Barefoot Renegade*; *PRT*, June 9, 1932.

22. Russ and Mona Jane Bishop oral interview, PLM.

23. *Spokesman-Review*, May 26, 1944.

24. Edward W. Nolan, *Frank Palmer, Scenic Photographer* (Spokane, WA: Eastern Washington State Historical Society, 1987).

Chapter Twelve: Civilian Conservation Corps

1. Peterson, "Recollections and Memoirs," 76.

2. Kalispell Bay camp was first labeled F-31 but renumbered F-142. Forest Service camp designations began with F and the state camps on the lake's east side began with S. The camp designations remained stable but the companies that occupied them usually changed every six months or a year.

3. Hays, *American People and the National Forests*, 60; Robbins, *American Forestry*, 141; Bishop interview; "C.C.C. Camp Moved In Day," *Spokesman-Review* June 30, 1933; "Eighth Anniversary Civilian Conservation Corps, 1933-1941" booklet, Company 2358, S-263, Camp Priest Lake, Coolin, Idaho, PLM.

4. "Biography of George Cannata," James F. Justin Civilian Conservation Corps Museum, justin-museum.com/oralbio/cannatagbio.html. Giorgio Giuseppe "George" Cannata enlisted on June 6, 1933. He used the name Bertani to get into the CCC.

5. Ibid.

6. Cecil Wylie oral interview, PLM.

7. Ibid.

8. Lewis, *Forest Service and the Greatest Good*, 99. Other military branches supervised CCC camps, but the army coordinated efforts at Priest Lake.

9. *Times Square Journal*, October 1937, Co. 1235, Camp F-127 Experiment Station camp, Priest River, Idaho; F-142 Inspection, April 8, 1938, Kaniksu Camp Inspections 1935-43, Box 21, Record of Emergency Programs, 1933-1941, RG 95, NARA (Seattle).

10. *Kalispell Breeze*, December 20, 1935, Co. 1994, F-142, Kalispell Bay, Idaho; *The Times Square Journal*, October 1937; *Cavanaugh Breeze*, June 17, 1935, Co. S-263, Co. 572, Cavanaugh Bay, Idaho.

11. Cannata biography.

12. *Fort George Wright C.C.C. District Annual*, 1938.

13. Inspection December 18, 1938; *Fort George Wright C.C.C. District Annual*, 1937, 74; F-102 Inspection Report, June 10, 1940.

14. Joseph Speakman, "Into the Woods," *Prologue* 38, no. 3 (Fall 2006); *The Times Square Journal*, October 1937.

15. *The Times Square Journal*, October 1937.

16. Simpson, *North of the Narrows*, 298.

17. "Priest River Racial War Merely Hazing," *Spokane Press*, July 20, 1934. Kenneth D. Swan, *Splendid was the Trail*, 150; Koch, *Forty Years Forester*, 183.

18. Cannata biography.

19. "Company 1994," *Fort George Wright C.C.C. Annual*, 1935.

20. Elers Koch Inspection, May 28, 1934, Supervision Emergency Program, Kaniksu NF, Box 12, Record of Emergency Programs, 1933-1941, RG 95, NARA (Seattle); "CCC Trains Move Out," *Spokesman-Review*, September 23, 1934.

21. Peterson, "Recollections and Memoirs," 82; *The Time Journal*, October 1937; "History of Company 1924," *Fort George Wright C.C.C. District Annual*, 1936.

22. "CCC Party for Ladies," *Spokesman-Review*, November 9, 1934.

23. "History of Company 1924."

24. Cannata biography; CCC inspection, December 18, 1936; Camp Priest Lake, 1941 brochure, PLM.

25. Peterson, "Recollections and Memoirs," 24.

26. Gerald W. Williams, *The U.S. Forest Service in the Pacific Northwest* (Corvallis: Oregon State University Press, 2009), 118.

27. Mark Hudson, *Fire Management in the American West* (Boulder: University Press of Colorado, 2011), 26.

28. Inspection Report, June 10, 1940; Grambo interview.

29. *Fort George Wright C.C.C. District Annual*, 1938; Bishop interview.

30. "Kalispell Creek," *Fort George Wright C.C.C. District Annual*, 94.

31. "Forestry Busy Fight Fires," *Metaline Falls News*, August 13, 1936.

32. Peterson, "Recollections and Memoirs," 113.

33. James E. Ryan, "The Kaniksu National Forest," *Fort George Wright C.C.C. District Annual*, 1938.

34. *Dunkirk Evening Observer*, Wednesday, October 17, 1934.

35. William C. Tweed, *Recreation Site Planning and Improvement in National Forests 1891-1942* (Washington, D.C.: Forest Service FS-345, November 1980), 16, 21.

36. "Forest Service, Using CCC."

37. *Spokane Chronicle*, August 11, 1933; "Forest Service, Using CCC"; and Master Plan of Work for 10th enrollment period.

38. *Fort George Wright C.C.C. District Annual*, 1938.

39. *Kalispell Breeze*, December 1935; Luby Bay Fellowship Club, PLM.

40. Peterson, "Recollections and Memoirs," 144.

41. Luby Bay Fellowship Club.

42. *Fort George Wright C.C.C. District Annual*, 1938; Ryan letter, 1938; Inspectors Report, December 2, 1940.

43. Charlotte Jones, 1983 Museum Survey, PLM.

44. "Kalispell Creek," *Fort George Wright C.C.C. District Annual*, 94.

45. "Ryan Praises CCC Workers," *Sandpoint Daily Bulletin*, April 15, 1936.

46. Jack Quinn, "Idaho and the Civilian Conservation Corps," in Cork, *Beautiful Bonner*, 106.

47. "Ryan Praises CCC Workers."

48. Cannata biography.

49. Ward interview.

50. Fulton Messmore oral interview, PLM.

51. Wylie interview.

52. "New Priest Lake Areas Are Opened by Busy CCC Camps," *Spokesman-Review*, January 16, 1938.

Chapter Thirteen: Extracting More or Less

1. Chance, "The Lumber Industry," 277.

2. Intermountain Logging Conference, *The Timberman*, May 1943; "Eager to Set New Record," *West Coast Lumberman*, May 1943, 31.

3. "Diamond Match Company's Winter Fill-Camp," *West Coast Lumberman*, January 1943, 12 and "Diamond Match Logging Operations," *The Timberman*, July 1943, 12.

4. *Timberman*, July 1943.

5. *Spokesman-Review*, November 15, 1959.

6. Bishop interview.

7. *PRT*, December 5, 1951.

8. "Elliott and Nesbitt, Bridge Builders" and "Markham, Melvin Clarence (Cap)," Cork, *Beautiful Bonner*, 339, 478; *Spokesman-Review*, November 15, 1959.

9. *Spokane Daily Chronicle*, February 4, 1954.

10. Priest Lake District Budge Fiscal Year 1955, Nordman, Idaho, April 25, 1955; Wolf, "National Forest Timber Sales," 94; Arnold W. Bolle, "The Bitterroot Revisited: 'A University [Re]View of the Forest Service,'" in *American Forests*, 163.

11. *Spokane Daily Chronicle*, December 11, 1952, March 24, 1953; Richard Rutter, "A Diamond Jubilee of Progress," *New York Times*, March 11, 1956.

12. *Men of Timber: The Presidents of the Pacific Logging Congress* (Peoria, IL: Caterpillar Tractor Company, 1954), 76; *Spokane Daily Chronicle*, June 24, 1946; "The Diamond Match Experience," Cork, *Beautiful Bonner*, 109.

13. Simpson, *Panhandle Personalities*, 347, 351.

14. *Spokane Daily Chronicle*, August 29, 1947; *Spokane Daily Chronicle*, May 2, 1951.

15. "Raine, Owen and Corrine," Cork, *Beautiful Bonner*, 587.

16. Eugene Murphy oral interview, PLM.

17. Peterson, "Recollections and Memoirs," 45; Cork, *Beautiful Bonner*, 108; Robbins, *American Forestry*, 199.

18. *Spokane Daily Chronicle*, June 17, 1929, November 17, 1931; Kaniksu Mining Company letter to The Honorable Henry Dworshak, October 11, 1958, Kaniksu Mining Company files, PLM.

19. Campbell, Arthur, IMIR, 1939, 174-175. The dump is still visible today.

20. Campbell, IMIR, 1932, 94; Campbell, IMIR, 1931, 100; Milwaukee Mines, Inc. Company records, IGS Archives, Moscow, Idaho; Richard Green oral interview, PLM.

21. Gale S. Hustedde, William B. Strowd, Victoria E. Mitchell, and Earl H. Bennett, *Mines and Prospects of the Sandpoint Quadrangle, Idaho*, Bureau of Mines

and Geology, Mines and Prospect Map Series (1981): 14.

22. Pauline Battien, *The Gold Seekers: A 200 Year History of Mining in Washington, Idaho, Montana and Lower British Columbia* (Colville, WA: Statesman-Examiner Inc., 1989), 106.

23. C. N. Savage, "Geology and Mineral Resources of Bonner County." Idaho Bureau of Mines and Geology, County Report No. 6, 1967, 104; Idaho Geological Survey (formerly Idaho Bureau of Mines and Geology [IBMG]), Mineral Property files, Moscow, Idaho.

Chapter Fourteen: Tourism in the Atomic Age

1. "Priest Lake and Priest River Chambers of Commerce Present A 'Show-Me' Trip in the Priest Lake Area," September 10-14, 1952, booklet, PLM.

2. "'Show-Me' Trip"; *Spokesman-Review*, June 14, 1953.

3. *Spokesman-Review*, September 18, 1952. See also September 17, 1951.

4. *Spokane Chronicle*, June 4, 1948.

5. State Highway record book, Idaho State Historical Society, Boise.

6. "'Show-Me' Trip"; *Spokesman-Review*, May 11, 1947.

7. *Northwest Ruralite*, Northern Lights Edition, Vol. 8, No. 8, August 1961.

8. *Spokesman-Review*, June 2, 1953.

9. Mike Ball, "Go Deep for Top-Prize Lake Trout," *Field and Stream Annual Fishing Contest*, 1954; "'Show-Me' Trip."

10. Ted C. Bjornn, "A Survey of the Fishery Resources of Priest and Upper Priest Lakes and their Tributaries," A Federal Aid to Fish Restoration Project, State of Idaho Department of Fish and Game with the Cooperative Wildlife Research Unit, University of Idaho, Moscow, 1957.

11. "Hagman's Resort," Brochure; Arley Sue Hagman interview, August 2012, PLM.

12. Ron Walker, "Outlet Bay History," Self-published, 2000.

13. *Spokesman-Review*, May 22, 1949 and May 24, 1958; City of Priest River Ordnance, 116.

14. *Spokesman Review*, May 22, 1949.

15. Roberts interview; *PRT*, December 4, 1952.

16. Simpson, *North of the Narrows*, 289; *Spokesman-Review*, January 15, 1948.

17. *PRT*, April 1947.

18. Diener interview.

19. Minutes from February 1, 1948, Priest Lake Camp meeting, BCCA Records, MS.2010.40, MASC.

20. *Spokesman-Review*, March 29, 1948.

21. Simpson, *North of the Narrows*, 292.

22. Wilson Compton to the BCCA, July 27, 1949, BCCA Records, MS.2010.40, MASC.

23. Victor Burke to Wilson Compton, September 1949, BCCA Records; Letter to attorney from Association President Robert Hungate, November 4, 1949, BCCA Records.

24. Simpson, *North of the Narrows*, 304.

25. *PRT*, May 2, 1940.

26. Hal K. Rothman, *Devil's Bargains: Tourism in the Twentieth-Century American West* (Lawrence: University Press of Kansas, 1998), 201.

27. *Spokesman-Review*, June 12, 1948; *Spokane Daily Chronicle*, June 23, 1959.

28. *Spokesman-Review*, May 31, 1953; *Spokane Daily Chronicle*, June 14, July 28, 1950.

29. Tracee Anderson, "The History of Linger Longer and Cougar Run," unpublished manuscript, 2008, PLM.

30. White interview; "Linger Longer" Brochure, c. 1960, PLM; Anderson, "History of Linger Longer"; *Spokesman-Review*, May 24, 1958.

31. *PRT*, June 11, 1958; *Spokane Daily Chronicle*, March 15, 1960.

32. *Lewiston Morning Tribune*, June 21, 1961; *Northwest Ruralite*, vol. 8, February 1961.

33. Anderson, "History of Linger Longer."

34. *Spokesman-Review*, May 11, 1947; Term Special Use Permit, 1953, Elkin's Resort Improvement Plan, 1955, and Special Use Permit Amendment No. 2, USES, Kaniksu NF, SPE-KNF, Museum of Northern Idaho, Coeur d'Alene.

35. *Spokane Daily Chronicle*, February 13, 1946; Luby Bay Fellowship Club archive, PLM; Lois Hill oral interview, PLM.

36. Kenneth Carter, "Carter Craft Boats," *Big Smoke* (Newport: WA: Pend Oreille Historical Society, 1991).

37. Hill interview; *Spokane Chronicle*, April 15, 1963.

38. Hill interview.

39. *Spokane Chronicle*, January 11, 1965.

40. Elkins interview.

Chapter Fifteen: Our People's Lives

1. "'Show-Me' Trip."

2. White interview.

3. *Northwest Ruralite*, Northern Lights Edition, Vol. 7, No. 8, August 1960.

4. Warren interview.

5. Idaho State codes. Approved March 7, 1950.

6. Walt Hunziker oral interview, PLM.

7. Federal Power Commission permit to the City of Sandpoint, October 17, 1928, PLM.

8. *Daily Inner Lake*, July 27, 1945.

9. *Spokesman-Review*, May 10, 1957; *PRT*, January 15, 1957.

10. *Spokane Daily Chronicle*, October 11, 1956.

11. *Spokane Daily Chronicle*, June 20, 1973; Martha W. Van Dervort, 1983 Museum Survey, PLM.

12. Ada Mae Martin oral interview, PLM; *PRT*, February 13, 1968.

13. Martin interview; Pam Martin "History of Nordman," PLM; "Nordman Club and Store," Cork, *Beautiful Bonner*, 198.

14. White interview.

15. Charlotte Jones, 1983 Museum Survey, PLM.

16. Roy and Ray Burns oral interview, PLM.

17. Don Howell, "Memories of Nordman School, 1950s," PLM.

18. Lois Jansson memoirs, self-published, PLM.

19. "'Show-Me' Trip."

20. Ibid.

21. Arley Sue Hagman, "Roundheads and Squareheads: The Pioneering Generations," PLM.

22. Gayle Raine, "The History of the Priest Lake Community Church," May 1999, PLM.

23. Jansson memoirs.

24. Harold Nelson, "Background Information on the Priest Lake Community Church," PLM.

25. Jansson memoirs.

26. Lois Jansson to Pam Martin, August 23, 1995, PLM; Lois Jansson to Corrine Raine, May 1999, Priest Lake Community Church archives.

27. *Spokesman-Review*, August 24, 1957; Nelson, "Background Information."

28. Nate Pace, compiler, *The Faith Journey of St. Blanche Catholic Church*, 2009, PLM.

29. *Spokesman-Review*, February 20, 1957.

30. Sandra Brunner Magers, "Lamb Creek School 1954-1955," PLM.

31. "Teacherage in Cellar," *Spokesman-Review*, February 20, 1957.

32. Alyce Allen, "Memories of Lamb Creek School," PLM.

33. Wynona Raine Warren interview, PLM.

34. Allen, "Memories."

35. Alyce Allen, "A Short Resume of the Priest Lake PTA," PLM.

36. "School Board Authorizes 6-Room School for Priest Lake District," *Bonner County Bee*, April 28, 1960,

and "Turned Down School Bond Proposal, Read 'em and Weep," *PRT*, May 5, 1959.

37. "New School Building for Priest Lake Area," *PRT*, October 21, 1960.

38. Alyce Allen, "Memories."

39. Hagman interview.

40. "Save a piece of history," *Coeur D'Alene Press*, March 4, 1990.

Chapter Sixteen: Recreation and the Greatest Good

1. Russell Dahl, "Recreation Management Plan for Kaniksu National Forest, 1963," PLRS; correspondence between the Kaniksu National Forest and A. S. Heatfield, 1929-1959, MNE-SPE-KNF, Museum of Northern Idaho archives.

2. Dahl, "Recreation Management Plan."

3. Mona Bishop in *Northwest Ruralite*, Northern Lights Edition, February 1961.

4. Luby Bay Fellowship Club minutes, 1959, PLM; "'Show-Me' Trip."

5. Wolf, "National Forest Timber Sales," 91.

6. "'Show-Me' Trip."

7. Ibid.

8. Luby Bay Fellowship Club minutes, January 1956, PLM.

9. John R. Knorr, "Supply of Developed Recreation Facilities," December 1981, PLRS.

10. USNF Priest Lake District, "Priest Lake Summer Home Rates, 1955," in Luby Bay Fellowship Club archives, PLM.

11. "'Show-Me' Trip."

12. Cort Sims, "Cultural Resource Inventory of the Summer Home Special Use Permit Terminations," July 25, 1986, PLRS.

13. Knorr, "Supply of Developed Recreation Facilities."

14. Rick Just, *100 Years: Idaho and its Parks* (Boise, Idaho: Idaho Department of Parks and Recreation, 2008), 129; Larry Townsend, "History of Priest Lake State Park," IDL, Idaho State Code Section 67-4306, 1927; *Lewiston Morning Tribune*, June 20, 1937.

15. "'Show-Me' Trip."

16. *Spokesman-Review*, December 3, 1959; *Spokane Daily Chronicle*, November 5, 1959; January 28, 1960.

17. Vinther Nelson Special Use Permit, December 16, 1912, PLRS.

18. *Spokane Daily Chronicle*, November 5, 1959, December 16, 1960, March 23, 1961; *Lewiston Morning Tribune* and the *Spokane Daily Chronicle*, December 16, 1960.

19. *Northwest Ruralite*, Northern Lights Edition, August 1961.

20. *Lewiston Morning Tribune*, October 1, 1958.

21. Townsend, "History of Priest Lake State Park."

22. Keith K. Knutson, "Priest Lake Recreation Residence Termination Study," c. 1964 and KNF recreation management plan, 1963.

23. Lewis, *Forest Service and the Greatest Good*, 126.

24. Peterson, "Recollections and Memoirs," 144; and Luby Bay Fellowship Club archives, PLM.

25. Shellenbarger, *High Country Summers*, 120; Robert Marshall, Remarks on Priest Lake Inspection Report, 1939; "'Show-Me' Trip."

26. USFS, "Guide for Establishing Summer Home Rates, 1955," in the Luby Bay Fellowship Club archives, PLM; Luby Bay Fellowship Club.

27. Stephan E. Matz, "Summary of Recreation Residence," Historical Context, 6-7.

28. Marshall, Priest Lake Inspection Report, 1939.

29. Knutson, "Priest Lake Recreation Residence Termination Study."

30. Denny Jones, "Priest Lake History."

31. Knorr, "Supply of Developed Recreation Facilities."

32. Jones, "Priest Lake History."

33. Heatfield, February 11, 1959, MNE-SPE-KNF, Museum of Northern Idaho archives.

34. Heatfield correspondence, September 8, 1959.

35. Ibid.

36. Vinther-Nelson correspondence, PLRS.

37. Mining Within the Priest Lake Recreation Withdrawal Area, KNF Recreation Plan, c. 1971; Richard Greene interview, 2010 and Milwaukee Mines Archives, PLM.

38. Knutson, "Priest Lake Recreation Residence Termination Study"; and "Recreation: A Developing Dimension of Forest Management," in *National Forests of the Northern Region*: www.foresthistory.org/ASPNET/ Publications/region/1/history/chap10.htm.

39. Uses-Kaniksu, K. A. Klem to Wm. E. Hennessey, November 10, 1958, MNE-SPE-KNF, Museum of Northern Idaho archives.

40. *PRT*, February 2, 1962 and KNF Recreation Plan 1963.

41. Sims, "Cultural Resource Inventory."

42. Ibid.

43. Knutson, "Priest Lake Recreation Residence Termination Study."

44. Statement of Hon. Len B. Jordan, Hearings before the Subcommittee on Public Lands, S. 3067, October 8, 1964.

45. Marshall, November 26, 1935.

46. Statement of Art Manley, Vice President, Idaho Wildlife Federation, October 8, 1964.

47. Dennis Roth, "The National Forests and the Campaign for Wilderness Legislation," in Miller, *American Forests*, 243.

48. Roger Guernsey to Lee White, February 27, 1963, Upper Priest Lake Scenic Area correspondence, State of Idaho Department of Lands, Priest Lake Supervisory Area (Coolin).

49. Guernsey to White, February 27, 1963, IDL.

50. Roger Guernsey to Smylie, August 16, 1963, IDL and November 8, 1963 memo attention State Forester and Jack Gillette, IDL; Manley testimony, Public Lands Hearing.

51. Guernsey to Smylie; Manley testimony, Public Lands Hearing.

52. Senator Frank Church, Letter to Mr. President, "Last Chance to Save Upper Priest Lake," Public Lands Hearing.

53. Guernsey to Church, March 13, 1964, IDL.

54. Manley testimony, Public Lands Hearing.

55. Church, "Letter to Mr. President."

56. Hon. Frank Church statement, Public Lands Hearing.

57. Thatcher Hubbard statement, Public Lands Hearing.

58. Communications, Public Lands Hearing.

59. Eileen Gumaer statement, communications from Fern Geisinger, Sylvia Burwell, and Don Gumaer, Public Lands Hearing.

60. Hon. Compton I. White Jr. statement and Bernard Staum communications, Public Lands Hearing.

61. *Spokesman-Review*, October 8, 1964; J. R. McFarland statement, Public Lands Hearing.

62. Regional Forester Neil Rahm to Governor Robert Smylie, June 7, 1965, IDL and *PRT*, June 24, 1965.

63. "Beautiful Lake, Waterway Now Part of Public Domain," *Spokesman-Review*, July 17, 1966.

64. "Upper Priest Lake—Draft of Bill," Area Forester Wylie to State Forester Roger Guernsey, February 12, 1965, IDL.

65. "Memorandum of Understanding Between U.S. Forest Service and the state of Idaho," Roger Guernsey to Land Board Members, June 14, 1965; Regional Forester Neal Rahm to Governor Robert Smylie, June 7, 1965, IDL and State Forester Roger Guernsey to Regional Forester Neal Rahm, June 30, 1965, IDL.

66. Memorandum of Understanding, June 15, 1965, IDL and Chief Timber Management to Commissioner, May 14, 1968, IDL.

67. Interim Management Plan, Upper Priest Lake Scenic Area, IDL.

68. Forest Supervisor Harold E. Andersen to State Land Commissioner Gordon Trembley, August 12, 1968, IDL.

Additional Reading

Following are additional sources of interest not found in the endnotes. Full citations for sources in the notes are provided on first reference. Shortened citations will appear thereafter.

General Sources

Allen, Edward T. "Men, Trees, and an Idea: The Genesis of a Great Fire Protective Plan." *American Forests and Forest Life* 32 (1926): 529-532.

Arrington, Leonard. *The Changing Economic Structure of the Mountain West, 1850-1950.* Logan: Utah State University Press, 1963.

Austin, Judith. "The CCC in Idaho." *Idaho Yesterdays* 27 (Fall 1983); 13-17.

Ayers, Gary, Bob Betts, Erich Obermayr, Dennis Roubicek. "Cultural Inventory Survey of Indian Trail, Volume I." Colville National Forest. Cultural Resource Consultants, Inc., Sandpoint, Idaho, 1979.

Bancroft, Hubert Howe. *History of Washington, Idaho, and Montana.* San Francisco: The History Company, 1890.

Barton, David, ed. *Idaho Panhandle National Forests Oral History Study.* Contract Number 53-0281-9-110. U.S. Department of Agriculture, Forest Service, Coeur d'Alene, Idaho, 1980.

Beal, Merrill D. and Merle W. Wells. *History of Idaho.* New York: Lewis Historical Publishing Co., 1959.

Benedict, Warren V. *History of White Pine Blister Rust Control-A Personal Account.* United States Department of Agriculture Forest Service FS-355. Washington, D.C.: U.S. Government Printing Office, 1981.

Bryant, Ralph. *Logging: The Principles and General Methods of Operations in the U.S.* New York: John Wiley, 1913.

Boswell, Sharon, Margo Knight, Mary Reed, and Michael A. Stamper. "A Cultural Resource Overview for the Colville National Forests and the Bureau of Land Management, Volume II, Oral Traditions Overview." Cultural Resource Consultants, Inc., Sandpoint, Idaho, 1981.

Chalfont, Stuart. *Aboriginal Territory of Kalispell Indians, Interior Salish and Eastern Washington Indians.* New York: Garland Publishing, 1974.

Clary, David A. *Timber and Forest Service.* Lawrence: University Press of Kansas, 1986.

Cohen, Stan. *The Tree Army: A Pictorial History of the Civilian Conservation Corps, 1933-1942.* Missoula, MT: Pictorial Histories Publishing Co., 1980.

Cook, R.G. "Senator Heyburn's War against the Forest Service." *Idaho Yesterdays* 14:4 (1971): 12-15.

Cox, Thomas, et al. *This Well Wooded Land: Americans and Their Forests Colonial Times to the Present.* Lincoln: University of Nebraska Press, 1985.

Cronon, William. "A Place for Stories: Nature, History, and Narrative." *Journal of American History* 78:4 (March 1992): 1347-76.

Dick, Everett. *The Lure of the Land: A Social History of the Public Lands from the Articles of Confederation to the New Deal.* Lincoln: University of Nebraska Press, 1970.

Fahey, John. *The Kalispel Indians.* Norman: University of Oklahoma Press, 1986.

Felt, Margaret E. *Gyppo Logger.* Caldwell, Idaho: Caxton Printers, 1963.

Francaviglia, Richard V. *Hard Places: Reading the Landscape of America's Historic Mining Districts.* Iowa City: University of Iowa Press, 1984.

French, Hiram T. *History of Idaho.* Chicago: The Lewis Publishing Co., 1914.

Gates, Paul Wallace. *History of Public Land Law Development.* Washington, D.C: U.S. Government Printing Office, 1968.

_____. "The Homestead Law in an Incongruous Land System." *American Historical Review* 41, (1937): 652-81.

Guth, A. Richard and Stan B. Cohen, *A Pictorial History of the U.S. Forest Service 1891-1945: Northern Region.* Missoula, MT: Pictorial Histories Publishing Company, 1991.

Hays, Samuel P. *Conservation and Gospel of Efficiency: The Progressive Conservation Movement, 1890-1920.* New York. Athenaeum, 1979.

Henderson, John, et al. eds. *An Illustrated History of Northern Idaho Embracing Nez Perce, Idaho, Latah, Kootenai, and Shoshone Counties.* Spokane, WA: Western Historical Publishing Co., 1903.

Hidy, Ralph, Hill, Frank Ernest, and Nevins, Allan, *Timber and Men: The Weyerhaeuser Story.* New York: Macmillan, 1963.

Hidy, Ralph W. "Lumbermen in Idaho: A Study in Adaptation to Change in Environment." *Idaho Yesterdays* 6 (Winter 1962): 2-17.

Hirt, Paul. *A Conspiracy of Optimism: Management of the National Forests since World War Two.* Lincoln, NE: University of Nebraska, 1994.

Hudson, Lorelea, Sharon Boswell, et al. "A Cultural Resource Overview for the Colville and Idaho Panhandle National Forests and the Bureau of Land Management-Spokane and Coeur d'Alene Districts: Northeastern Washington/Northern Idaho. Volume I, Cultural Resource Narrative." Cultural Resource Consultants, Inc., Sandpoint ID, 1981.

Hyde, Anne Farrar. *An American Vision: Far Western Landscape and National Culture, 1820-1920.* New York: New York University Press, 1990.

Ise, John. *The United States Forest Policy.* New Haven, CT: Yale University Press, 1920.

Jackson, John Brinckerhoff. *Discovering the Vernacular Landscape.* New Haven, CT: Yale University Press, 1994.

Kensel, William H., "The Early Spokane Lumber Industry, 1871-1910." *Idaho Yesterdays* 12 (1968): 25-31.

Koch, Elers. "Geographic Names of Western Montana, Northern Idaho." *Oregon Historical Quarterly* (March 1948): 50-62.

Kohlmeyer, Frederick. "Northern Pine Lumbermen: A Study in Origins and Migrations." *Journal of Economic History* 16, no. 4 (Dec. 1956): 529-538.

Livingston-Little, D.E. *An Economic History of North Idaho, 1800-1900.* Los Angles: Lorrin L. Morrison Printing and Publishing, 1965.

Malone, Michael P. "The New Deal in Idaho." *Pacific Historical Review* 38 (August 1969): 293-310.

Mason, David T. *Timber Ownership and Lumber Production in the Inland Empire.* Portland: Western Pine Manufacturers Assn., 1920.

Merrill, Perry H. *Roosevelt's Forest Army: A History of the Civilian Conservation Corps, 1933-1942.* Montpelier, VT: P. H. Merrill, 1981.

Miller, Char. *Seeking the Greatest Good: The Conservation Legacy of Gifford Pinchot.* Pittsburgh: University of Pittsburgh Press, 2013.

_____. "Gallery: Char Miller on Gifford Pinchot, Photographer." *History Cooperative* 8, no. 2. (April 2003).

Meinig, D.W. *The Great Columbia Plain: A Historical Geography, 1805-1910.* Seattle, WA: University of Washington Press, 1995.

Pinchot, Gifford. *The Fight for Conservation.* New York: Doubleday, 1910.

_____. "The Frontier and the Lumberman" *American Forest* 9 (April, 1903): 176-77.

_____. "The Use of the National Forests," U.S. Department of Agriculture, 1907.

Otis, Allison T., William D. Honey. Thomas C. Hogg and Kimberly K. Lakin. *Forest Service and the Civilian Conservation Corps: 1933-42.* United States Department of Agriculture, Forest Service FS-395, 1986.

Pyne, Stephen J. *Fire in America: A Cultural History of Wild Land and Rural Fire.* Princeton, N.J.: Princeton University Press, 1982.

Rakestraw, Lawrence, *A History of Forest Conservation in the Pacific Northwest, 1891-1913.* New York: Arno Press, 1979.

Robbins, Roy M. *Our Landed Heritage: The Public Domain, 1776-1936.* Princeton, NJ: Princeton University Press, 1942.

Robbins, William G. *Land in the American West: Private Claims and the Common Good.* Seattle, WA: University of Washington Press, 2000.

_____. *Lumberjacks and Legislators: Political Economy of the U.S. Lumber Industry, 1890-1941.* College Station: Texas A&M University Press, 1982.

_____. "The Cultural in Natural Landscapes: North America and the Pacific Northwest." *Journal of the West* 38 (Oct. 1999): 8-14.

Rothman, Hal K., ed. *"I'll Never Fight Fire with my Bare Hands Again": Recollections of the First Forest Rangers of the Inland Northwest.* Lawrence: University Press of Kansas, 1994.

Sims, Cort. *An Agenda for the Preservation and Interpretation of Historic Sites on the Idaho Panhandle National Forest,* U.S. Department of Agriculture, Forest Service, June 1988.

_____. *Albert Klockmann, the Continental Mine and the Boundary Creek Road: A Chronology.* File No. 1220. Idaho Panhandle National Forests. Coeur d'Alene, Idaho, 2002.

Schwantes, Carlos. *The Pacific Northwest: An Interpretive History.* Lincoln, University of Nebraska Press, 1989.

White, Richard, "The Nationalization of Nature." *Journal of American History* 86, 3 (1999): 976-986.

_____. *"It's Your Misfortune and None of My Own": A New History of the American West.* Oklahoma, OK: University of Oklahoma Press, 1993.

Williams, Michael. *Americans and Their Forest: A Historical Geography.* New York: University of Oxford, 1989.

Priest Lake Sources

Dahl, James. *Bonner County Place Names*. Boise, ID: Idaho State Historical Society, 1969.

Deaver, Sherri, and James E. Lieb. *A Kalispel Cultural Geography*. Compiled by Ethnoscience, Inc. for the Kalispel Tribe of Indians Natural Resource Department. 2000.

Marti, Duane. *An Archaeological Reconnaissance of the Priest Wild and Scenic River Study Area Idaho Panhandle National Forests*. University of Idaho Anthropological Research Manuscript Series, No. 24. Laboratory of Anthropology, University of Idaho, Moscow, 1976.

Peters, Lloyd. *Lionhead Lodge, How the Movies Came to Spokane, Washington, The Friendly City and to Beautiful Priest Lake*. Fairfield, WA: Fairfield Press, 1967.

Renk, Nancy. *Driving Past: Tours of Historical Sites in Bonner County, Idaho*. Sandpoint, ID: Bonner County Historical Society, 2014.

_____. "Off to the Lakes: Vacationing in North Idaho During the Railroad Era, 1885-1917." *Idaho Yesterdays* 34 (1990): 2-15.

Sanders, Paul H., William Andrefsky Jr., and Stephan R. Samuels, eds. *The Calispell Valley Archaeological Project*. Vol. 1, Project Report Number 16. Center for Northwest Anthropology, Department of Anthropology, Washington State University, Pullman, WA, 1991.

Shipman, Nell. *The Silent Screen Star and My Talking Heart*. Boise, ID: Boise State University, 1987.

Smith, Allan H. *An Ethnographic-Ethnohistorical Guide to Archaeological Sites in the Kalispel Territory: Part III Albeni Falls, Washington, to Heron, Montana, Sector*. Unpublished draft, 1985.

Spoerry, G. W. "Camping Out on Priest Lake, Idaho." *Wilhelm's Magazine, The Coast*, (November 1906): 245-248.

Upper Priest Lake, Idaho. Hearing before the Subcommittee on Public Lands of the Committee on Interior and Insular Affairs United States Senate, S. 3067 A Bill to Extend the Boundaries of the Kaniksu National Forest, October 8, 1964, Priest Lake, ID. Washington, D.C.: U.S. Government Printing Office, 1965.

Index

About the Authors

Kris Runberg Smith is professor of history at Lindenwood University in St. Charles, Missouri. She holds a doctorate in American studies from Saint Louis University, a master's degree in American history from Washington State University, and a bachelor's degree in museum science from the University of Idaho. She has worked in museums including the Kansas, Ohio, and Missouri Historical Societies. She edited *Pioneer Voices of Priest Lake* for the Priest Lake Museum in 2007, and has written for both academic and popular audiences. Her family's connections to Priest Lake date back to 1897.

Tom Weitz is a retired geologist and mining manager. He earned a master's degree in geosciences from the University of Arizona, and a bachelor's degree in geology from Washington State University. He has been vacationing at Priest Lake since the late 1950s, first staying at Hill's Resort and later at his family's cabin on Kalispell Bay. He has served as president of the Priest Lake Museum Association since 2011.